GIBBON'S
THE DECLINE
AND
FALL OF THE
ROMAN EMPIRE

Gibbon's The Decline and Fall of the Roman Empire

A Modern Abridgment
By
Moses Hadas

FAWCETT PREMIER • NEW YORK

Copyright © 1962 by Moses Hadas

Published by Fawcett Crest Books, a unit of CBS Publications, the Education and Professional Publishing Division of CBS, Inc. by arrangement with G.P. Putnam's Sons, a division of The Putnam Publishing Group, Inc.

ISBN 0-449-30056-0

Printed in Canada

First Fawcett Premier Edition: June 1964
First Ballantine Books Edition: May 1987
Eighth Printing: December 1992

FOREWORD

No list of essential books can be so abbreviated, no curious literate can be so preoccupied, as to ignore the *Decline and Fall*. Its theme is the most overwhelming phenomenon in recorded history—the disintegration not of a nation but of an old and rich and apparently indestructible civilization. Its majestic architecture and the stateliness of its language are appropriate to the grandeur of its theme; our literature possesses no nobler monument of spacious prose. And even if we are indifferent to the significant experience of the past and deaf to the magic of magnificent utterance, Gibbon remains continuously relevant for his insights into the permanent patterns of human response to recurrent military and political challenges. He is a classic because he is concerned with the universal as well as the particular, because he is philosopher as well as chronicler.

Because the *Decline and Fall* is a work of art, with philosophy and chronicle and memorable language fused into a single mighty and balanced structure, presenting it in abridgment is like presenting the Parthenon by a column and a relief or *Paradise Lost* by a summary. Gibbon should be read as a whole, and there will always be unhurried people who will so read him—hopefully some who may be induced to do so by the present abridgment. But the spaciousness of earlier centuries is gone. Today a work of such scope would be written by a panel of professional scholars, and read only by other professional scholars. To make Gibbon accessible to the larger public which is entitled to know him, abridgment is as justifiable as it is necessary.

The aim of this abridgment is to present the essential Gibbon and his central theme, not to reduce him to a textbook of later Roman history. Accordingly, significant passages of considerable length are reproduced unaltered. When, in detailed narratives of events, telescoping has seemed advisable, disparate sentences of the text have been pieced together, where such a procedure seemed possible; in other cases the editor has supplied brief summaries to provide transitions. Omissions have been most drastic where Gibbon's detail is excessive or antiquated, and where the matter is peripheral to the central theme. In the first group are details of battles or of political negotiations, characterizations of minor personages, and the like. In the second are the details of administration and law, disquisitions on theology and sectarian issues, the rise of Islam, the Crusades, the descriptions and history of peoples outside the empire, the history of the papacy and of the countries of Europe and Asia after the fall of the empire. Characteristic observations and conclusions are whenever possible included.

As a guide to what is omitted and to facilitate reference to a complete text, Gibbon's chapter headings have been retained intact, even where a whole chapter has been omitted. The Chronology at the end of the volume will supply a skeleton for the story and enable the reader to distinguish personages who bear an identical name.

MOSES HADAS

CONTENTS

GIBBON'S
THE DECLINE
AND
FALL OF THE
ROMAN EMPIRE

CHAPTER ONE

The Extent and Military Force of the Empire in the Age of the Antonines

In the second century of the Christian era, the Empire of Rome comprehended the fairest part of the earth, and the most civilised portion of mankind. The frontiers of that extensive monarchy were guarded by ancient renown and disciplined valour. The gentle but powerful influence of laws and manners had gradually cemented the union of the provinces. Their peaceful inhabitants enjoyed and abused the advantages of wealth and luxury. The image of a free constitution was preserved with decent reverence: the Roman senate appeared to possess the sovereign authority, and devolved on the emperors all the executive powers of government. During a happy period (A.D. 98–180) of more than fourscore years, the public administration was conducted by the virtue and abilities of Nerva, Trajan, Hadrian, and the two Antonines.

The principal conquests of the Romans were achieved under the republic; and the emperors, for the most part, were satisfied with preserving those dominions which had been acquired by the policy of the senate, the active emulation of the consuls, and the martial enthusiasm of the people. The seven first centuries were filled with a rapid succession of triumphs; but it was reserved for Augustus to relinquish the ambitious design of subduing the whole earth, and to introduce a spirit

1

of moderation into the public councils. Inclined to peace by his temper and situation, it was easy for him to discover that Rome, in her present exalted situation, had much less to hope than to fear from the chance of arms; and that, in the prosecution of remote wars, the undertaking became every day more difficult, the event more doubtful, and the possession more precarious, and less beneficial. Happily for the repose of mankind, the moderate system recommended by the wisdom of Augustus was adopted by the fears and vices of his immediate successors.

Such were the maxims of imperial policy from the death of Augustus to the accession of Trajan. Trajan was ambitious of fame; and as long as mankind shall continue to bestow more liberal applause on their destroyers than on their benefactors, the thirst of military glory will ever be the vice of the most exalted characters. The praises of Alexander, transmitted by a succession of poets and historians, had kindled a dangerous emulation in the mind of Trajan. Like him, the Roman emperor undertook an expedition against the natives of the east; every day the astonished senate received the intelligence of new names and new nations, that acknowledged his sway. But the death of Trajan soon clouded the splendid prospect; and it was justly to be dreaded, that so many distant nations would throw off the unaccustomed yoke, when they were no longer restrained by the powerful hand which had imposed it.

It was an ancient tradition, that when the Capitol was founded by one of the Roman kings, the god Terminus (who presided over boundaries, and was represented according to the fashion of that age by a large stone) alone, among all the inferior deities, refused to yield his place to Jupiter himself. A favourable inference was drawn from his obstinacy, which was interpreted by the augurs as a sure presage that the boundaries of the Roman power would never recede. During many ages, the prediction, as it is usual, contributed to its own accomplishment. But though Terminus had resisted the majesty of Jupiter, he submitted to the authority of the emperor Hadrian. The resignation of all the eastern conquests of Trajan was the first measure of his reign.

Notwithstanding this difference in their personal conduct,

the general system of Augustus was equally adopted and uniformly pursued by Hadrian and by the two Antonines. They persisted in the design of maintaining the dignity of the empire, without attempting to enlarge its limits. By every honourable expedient they invited the friendship of the barbarians, and endeavoured to convince mankind that the Roman power, raised above the temptation of conquest, was actuated only by the love of order and justice. The terror of the Roman arms added weight and dignity to the moderation of the emperors. They preserved peace by a constant preparation for war; and while justice regulated their conduct, they announced to the nations on their confines that they were as little disposed to endure as to offer an injury.

That public virtue which among the ancients was denominated patriotism, is derived from a strong sense of our own interest in the preservation and prosperity of the free government of which we are members. Such a sentiment, which had rendered the legions of the republic almost invincible, could make but a very feeble impression on the mercenary servants of a despotic prince; and it became necessary to supply that defect by other motives, of a different, but not less forcible nature; honour and religion. The science of tactics was cultivated with success; and as long as the empire retained any vigour, their military instructions were respected as the most perfect model of Roman discipline.

The safety and honour of the empire were principally entrusted to the legions, but the policy of Rome condescended to adopt every useful instrument of war. Considerable levies were regularly made among the provincials, who had not yet deserved the honourable distinction of Romans. Many dependent princes and communities, dispersed round the frontiers, were permitted, for a while, to hold their freedom and security by the tenure of military service.

CHAPTER TWO

Of the Union and internal Prosperity of the Roman Empire, in the Age of the Antonines

It is not alone by the rapidity, or extent of conquest, that we should estimate the greatness of Rome; the firm edifice of Roman power was raised and preserved by the wisdom of ages. The obedient provinces of Trajan and the Antonines were united by laws and adorned by arts. They might occasionally suffer from the partial abuse of delegated authority; but the general principle of government was wise, simple, and beneficent. They enjoyed the religion of their ancestors, whilst in civil honours and advantages they were exalted, by just degrees, to an equality with their conquerors.

The policy of the emperors and the senate, as far as it concerned religion, was happily seconded by the reflections of the enlightened, and by the habits of the superstitious, part of their subjects. The various modes of worship, which prevailed in the Roman world, were all considered by the people as equally true; by the philosopher, as equally false; and by the magistrate, as equally useful. And thus toleration produced not only mutual indulgence, but even religious concord.

The superstition of the people was not embittered by any mixture of theological rancour; nor was it confined by the chains of any speculative system. The devout polytheist, though fondly attached to his national rites, admitted with implicit faith the different religions of the earth. Fear, gratitude, and curiosity, a dream or an omen, a singular disorder, or a distant journey, perpetually disposed him to multiply the articles of his belief, and to enlarge the list of his protectors. The thin texture of the Pagan mythology was interwoven with various but not discordant materials. As soon as it was allowed that sages and heroes, who had lived, or who had died for the benefit of their country, were exalted to a state of power and immortality, it was universally confessed that they deserved, if not the adoration, at least the reverence of all mankind. The deities of a thousand groves and a thousand streams possessed, in peace, their local and respective influence; nor could the Roman who deprecated the wrath of the Tiber, deride the Egyptian who presented his offering to the beneficent genius of the Nile. The visible powers of Nature, the planets, and the elements, were the same throughout the universe. The invisible governors of the moral world were inevitably cast in a similar mould of fiction and allegory. Every virtue, and even vice, acquired its divine representative; every art and profession its patron, whose attributes, in the most distant ages and countries, were uniformly derived from the character of their peculiar votaries. A republic of gods of such opposite tempers and interest required, in every system, the moderating hand of a supreme magistrate, who, by the progress of knowledge and flattery, was gradually invested with the sublime perfections of an Eternal Parent and an Omnipotent Monarch. Such was the mild spirit of antiquity, that the nations were less attentive to the difference than to the resemblance of their religious worship. The Greek, the Roman, and the Barbarian, as they met before their respective altars, easily persuaded themselves that, under various names and with various ceremonies, they adored the same deities. The elegant mythology of Homer gave a beautiful and almost a regular form to the polytheism of the ancient world.

The narrow policy of preserving, without any foreign mixture, the pure blood of the ancient citizens, had checked the fortune, and hastened the ruin, of Athens and Sparta. The aspiring genius of Rome sacrificed vanity to ambition, and deemed it more prudent, as well as honourable, to adopt virtue and merit for her own wheresoever they were found, among slaves or strangers, enemies or barbarians. Till the privileges of Romans had been progressively extended to all the inhabitants of the empire, an important distinction was preserved between Italy and the provinces. The public authority was everywhere exercised by the ministers of the senate and of the emperors, and that authority was absolute, and without control. But the same salutary maxims of government, which had secured the peace and obedience of Italy, were extended to the most distant conquests. A nation of Romans was gradually formed in the provinces, by the double expedient of introducing colonies, and of admitting the most faithful and deserving of the provincials to the freedom of Rome.

So sensible were the Romans of the influence of language over national manners, that it was their most serious care to extend, with the progress of their arms, the use of the Latin tongue. It is a just though trite observation, that victorious Rome was herself subdued by the arts of Greece. Those immortal writers who still command the admiration of modern Europe, soon became the favourite object of study and imitation in Italy and the western provinces. But the elegant amusements of the Romans were not suffered to interfere with their sound maxims of policy. Whilst they acknowledged the charms of the Greek, they asserted the dignity of the Latin tongue, and the exclusive use of the latter was inflexibly maintained in the administration of civil as well as military government. The two languages exercised at the same time their separate jurisdiction throughout the empire: the former as the natural idiom of science; the latter as the legal dialect of public transactions. Those who united letters with business were equally conversant with both; and it was almost impossible, in any province, to find a Roman subject of a liberal education, who was at once a stranger to the Greek and to the Latin language.

It was by such institutions that the nations of the empire insensibly melted away into the Roman name and people. But there still remained, in the centre of every province and of every family, an unhappy condition of men who endured the weight, without sharing the benefits, of society. In the free states of antiquity the domestic slaves were exposed to the wanton rigour of despotism.

Domestic peace and union were the natural consequences of the moderate and comprehensive policy embraced by the Romans. The obedience of the Roman world was uniform, voluntary, and permanent. The vanquished nations, blended into one great people, resigned the hope, nay even the wish, of resuming their independence, and scarcely considered their own existence as distinct from the existence of Rome. The established authority of the emperors pervaded without an effort the wide extent of their dominions, and was exercised with the same facility on the banks of the Thames, or of the Nile, as on those of the Tiber. The legions were destined to serve against the public enemy, and the civil magistrate seldom required the aid of a military force. In this state of general security, the leisure as well as opulence both of the prince and people were devoted to improve and to adorn the Roman empire.

Among the innumerable monuments of architecture constructed by the Romans, how many have escaped the notice of history, how few have resisted the ravages of time and barbarism! And yet even the majestic ruins that are still scattered over Italy and the provinces, would be sufficient to prove that those countries were once the seat of a polite and powerful empire. Their greatness alone, or their beauty, might deserve our attention; but they are rendered more interesting by two important circumstances, which connect the agreeable history of the arts with the more useful history of human manners. Many of those works were erected at private expense, and almost all were intended for public benefit.

In the commonwealths of Athens and Rome, the modest simplicity of private houses announced the equal condition of freedom; whilst the sovereignty of the people was represented in the majestic edifices destined to the public use; nor was this republican spirit totally extinguished by the introduction of wealth and monarchy. It was in works of national honour and benefit, that the most virtuous of the emperors affected to display their magnificence. All these cities were connected with each other, and with the capital, by the public highways, which issuing from the Forum of Rome, traversed Italy, pervaded the provinces, and were terminated only by the frontiers of the empire. If we carefully trace the distance from the wall of Antoninus to Rome, and from thence to Jerusalem, it will be found that the great chain of communication, from the north-west to the south-east point of the empire, was drawn out to the length of four thousand and eighty Roman miles. The public roads were accurately divided by mile-stones, and ran in a direct line from one city to another, with very little respect for the obstacles either of nature or private property. Mountains were perforated, and bold arches thrown over the broadest and most rapid streams. The middle part of the road was raised into a terrace which commanded the adjacent country, consisted of several strata of sand, gravel, and cement, and was paved with large stones, or in some places, near the capital, with granite. Such was the solid construction of the Roman highways, whose firmness has not entirely yielded to the effort of fifteen centuries. Whatever evils either reason or declamation have imputed to extensive empire, the power of Rome was attended with some beneficial consequences to mankind; and the same freedom of intercourse which extended the vices, diffused likewise the improvements, of social life.

Agriculture is the foundation of manufactures; since the productions of nature are the materials of art. Under the Roman empire, the labour of an industrious and ingenious people was variously, but incessantly employed, in the service of the rich. In their dress, their table, their houses, and their furniture, the favourites of fortune united every refinement of conveniency, of elegance, and of splendour, whatever could soothe their pride or gratify their sensuality. Such refinements, under the odious name of luxury, have been severely arraigned by the moralists of every age; and it might perhaps be more conducive to the virtue, as well as happiness, of mankind, if all possessed the necessaries, and none the superfluities, of life. But in the present imperfect condition of society, luxury, though it may proceed from vice or folly, seems to be the only means that can correct the unequal distribution of property. The diligent mechanic, and the skilful artist, who have obtained no share in the division of the earth, receive a voluntary tax from the possessors of land; and the latter are prompted, by a sense of interest, to improve those estates, with whose produce they may purchase additional pleasures. This operation, the particular effects of which are felt in every society, acted with much more diffusive energy in the Roman world. The provinces would soon have been exhausted of their wealth, if the manufactures and commerce of luxury had not insensibly restored to the industrious subjects the sums which were exacted from them by the arms and authority of Rome. As long as the circulation was confined within the bounds of the empire, it impressed the political machine with a new degree of activity, and its consequences, sometimes beneficial, could never become pernicious.

Notwithstanding the prosperity of mankind to exalt the past, and to deprecate the present, the tranquil and prosperous state of the empire was warmly felt, and honestly confessed, by the provincials as well as Romans. "They acknowledged that the true principles of social life, laws, agriculture, and science, which had been first invented by the wisdom of Athens, were now firmly established by the power of Rome, under whose auspicious influence the fiercest barbarians were united by an equal government and common language. They affirm, that with the improvement of arts, the human species was visibly multiplied. They celebrate the increasing splendour of the cities, the beautiful face of the country, cultivated and adorned like an immense garden; and the long festival of peace, which was enjoyed by so many nations, forgetful of their ancient animosities, and delivered from the apprehension of future danger." Whatever suspicions may be suggested by the air of rhetoric and declamation, which seems to prevail in these passages, the substance of them is perfectly agreeable to historic truth.

The love of letters, almost inseparable from peace and refinement, was fashionable among the subjects of Hadrian and the Antonines, who were themselves men of learning and curiosity. It was diffused over the whole extent of their empire; the most northern tribes of Britons had acquired a taste for rhetoric; Homer as well as Virgil were transcribed and studied on the banks of the Rhine and Danube; and the most liberal rewards sought out the faintest glimmerings of literary merit. The sciences of physic and astronomy were successfully cultivated by the Greeks; the observations of Ptolemy and the writings of Galen are studied by those who have improved their discoveries and corrected their errors; but if we except the inimitable Lucian, this age of indolence passed away without having produced a single writer of original genius, or who excelled in the arts of elegant composition. The authority of Plato and Aristotle, of Zeno and Epicurus, still reigned in the schools; and their systems, transmitted with blind deference from one generation of disciples to another, precluded every generous attempt to exercise the powers, or enlarge the limits, of the human mind. The beauties of the poets and orators, instead of kindling a fire like their own, inspired only cold and servile imitations: or if any ventured to deviate from those models, they deviated at the same time from good sense and propriety. On the revival of letters, the youthful vigour of the imagination, after a long repose, national emulation, a new religion, new languages, and a new world, called forth the genius of Europe. But the provincials of Rome, trained by a uniform artificial foreign education, were engaged in a very unequal competition with those bold ancients, who, by expressing their genuine feelings in their native tongue, had already occupied every place of honour. The name of Poet was almost forgotten; that of Orator was usurped by the sophists. A cloud of critics, of compilers, of commentators darkened the face of learning, and the decline of genius was soon followed by the corruption of taste.

CHAPTER THREE

Of the Constitution of the Roman Empire, in the Age of the Antonines

The obvious definition of a monarchy seems to be that of a state, in which a single person, by whatsoever name he may be distinguished, is entrusted with the execution of the laws, the management of the revenue, and the command of the army. But, unless public liberty is protected by intrepid and vigilant guardians, the authority of so formidable a magistrate will soon degenerate into despotism. The influence of the clergy, in an age of superstition, might be usefully employed to assert the rights of mankind; but so intimate is the connection between the throne and the altar, that the banner of the church has very seldom been seen on the side of the people. A martial nobility and stubborn commons, possessed of arms, tenacious of property, and collected into constitutional assemblies, form the only balance capable of preserving a free constitution against enterprises of an aspiring prince. It was on the dignity of the senate, that Augustus and his successors founded their new empire; and they affected, on every occasion, to adopt the language and principles of Patricians. In the administration of their own powers they frequently consulted the great national council, and *seemed* to refer to its decision the most important concerns of peace and war.

To resume, in a few words, the system of the Imperial

11

government, as it was instituted by Augustus, and maintained by those princes who understood their own interest and that of the people, it may be defined an absolute monarchy disguised by the forms of a commonwealth. The masters of the Roman world surrounded their throne with darkness, concealed their irresistible strength, and humbly professed themselves the accountable ministers of the senate, whose supreme decrees they dictated and obeyed.

The face of the court corresponded with the forms of the administration. The emperors, if we except those tyrants whose capricious folly violated every law of nature and decency, disdained that pomp and ceremony which might offend their countrymen, but could add nothing to their real power. In all the offices of life they affected to confound themselves with their subjects, and maintained with them an equal intercourse of visits and entertainments. Their habit, their palace, their table, were suited only to the rank of an opulent senator. Their family, however numerous or splendid, was composed entirely of their domestic slaves and freedmen. Augustus or Trajan would have blushed at employing the meanest of the Romans in those menial offices, which, in the household and bed-chamber of a limited monarch, are so eagerly solicited by the proudest nobles of Britain.

The deification of the emperors is the only instance in which they departed from their accustomed prudence and modesty. The Asiatic Greeks were the first inventors, the successors of Alexander the first objects, of this servile and impious mode of adulation. It was easily transferred from the kings to the governors of Asia; and the Roman magistrates very frequently were adored as provincial deities, with the pomp of altars and temples, of festivals and sacrifices. It was natural that the emperors should not refuse what the proconsuls had accepted; and the divine honours which both the one and the other received from the provinces, attested rather the despotism than the servitude of Rome. But the conquerors soon imitated the vanquished nations in the arts of flattery; and the imperious spirit of the first Cæsar too easily consented to assume, during his lifetime, a place among the tutelar deities of Rome. The milder temper of his successor declined so dangerous an ambition, which was never afterwards revived, except by the madness of Caligula and Domitian.

In the consideration of the imperial government, we have frequently mentioned the artful founder under his well-known title of Augustus, which was not, however, conferred upon him till the edifice was almost completed. The obscure name of Octavianus he derived from a mean family in the little town of Aricia. It was stained with the blood of the proscription; and he was desirous, had it been possible, to erase all memory of his former life. The tender respect of Augustus for a free constitution which he had destroyed, can only be explained by an attentive consideration of the character of that subtle tyrant. A cool head, an unfeeling heart, and a cowardly disposition, prompted him, at the age of nineteen, to assume the mask of hypocrisy, which he never afterwards laid aside. With the same hand, and probably with the same temper, he signed the proscription of Cicero, and the pardon of Cinna. His virtues, and even his vices, were artificial; and according to the various dictates of his interest, he was at first the enemy, and at last the father, of the Roman world. When he framed the artful system of the Imperial authority, his moderation was inspired by his fears. He wished to deceive the people by an image of civil liberty, and the armies by an image of civil government. Augustus was sensible that mankind is governed by names; nor was he deceived in his expectation, that the senate and people would submit to slavery, provided they were respectfully assured that they still enjoyed their ancient freedom. A feeble senate and enervated people cheerfully acquiesced in the pleasing illusion, as long as it was supported by the virtue, or even by the prudence, of the successors of Augustus.

In elective monarchies, the vacancy of the throne is a moment big with danger and mischief. The Roman emperors, desirous to spare the legions that interval of suspense, and the temptation of an irregular choice, invested their designed successor with so large a share of present power, as should enable him, after their decease, to assume the remainder, without suffering the empire to perceive the change of masters. Thus Augustus, after all his fairer prospects had been snatched from him by untimely deaths, rested his last hopes on Tiberius, obtained for his adopted son the censorial and tribunitian powers, and dictated a law by which the future prince was invested with an authority equal to his own, over the provinces and the armies.

The two Antonines governed the Roman world forty-two years, with the same invariable spirit of wisdom and virtue. Their united reigns are possibly the only period of history in which the happiness of a great people was the sole object of government. Titus Antoninus Pius has been justly denominated a second Numa. The same love of religion, justice, and peace, was the distinguishing characteristic of both princes. But the situation of the latter opened a much larger field for the exercise of those virtues. Numa could only prevent a few neighbouring villages from plundering each other's harvests. Antoninus diffused order and tranquillity over the greatest part of the earth. His reign is marked by the rare advantage of furnishing very few materials for history; which is, indeed, little more than the register of the crimes, follies, and misfortunes of mankind. In private life, he was an amiable as well as a good man. The native simplicity of his virtue was a stranger to vanity or affection. He enjoyed with moderation the conveniencies of his fortune, and the innocent pleasures of society: and the benevolence of his soul displayed itself in a cheerful serenity of temper.

The virtue of Marcus Aurelius Antoninus was of a severer and more laborious kind. It was the well-earned harvest of many a learned conference, of many a patient lecture, and many a midnight lucubration. At the age of twelve years he embraced the rigid system of the Stoics, which taught him to submit his body to his mind, his passions to his reason; to consider virtue as the only good, vice as the only evil, all things external as things indifferent. His meditations, composed in the tumult of a camp, are still extant; and he even condescended to give lessons of philosophy in a more public manner than was perhaps consistent with the modesty of a sage, or the dignity of an emperor. But his life was the noblest commentary on the precepts of Zeno. He was severe to himself, indulgent to the imperfections of others, just and beneficent to all mankind.

If a man were called to fix the period in the history of the world during which the condition of the human race was most happy and prosperous, he would, without hesitation, name that which elapsed from the death of Domitian to the accession of Commodus. The vast extent of the Roman empire was governed by absolute power, under the guidance of virtue and wisdom. The armies were restrained by the firm but gentle hand of four successive emperors whose character and authority commanded involuntary respect. The forms of the civil administration were carefully preserved by Nerva, Trajan, Hadrian, and the Antonines, who delighted in the image of liberty, and were pleased with considering themselves as the accountable ministers of the laws. Such princes deserved the honour of restoring the republic, had the Romans of their days been capable of enjoying a rational freedom.

The labours of these monarchs were overpaid by the immense reward that inseparably waited on their success; by the honest pride of virtue, and by the exquisite delight of beholding the general happiness of which they were the authors. A just, but melancholy reflection embittered, however, the noblest of human enjoyments. They must often have recollected the instability of a happiness which depended on the character of a single man. The fatal moment was perhaps approaching, when some licentious youth, or some jealous tyrant, would abuse, to the destruction, that absolute power which they had exerted for the benefit of their people. The ideal restraints of the senate and the laws might serve to display the virtues, but could never correct the vices, of the emperor. The military force was a blind and irresistible instrument of oppression; and the corruption of Roman manners would always supply flatterers eager to applaud, and ministers prepared to serve the fear or the avarice, the lust or the cruelty, of their masters.

These gloomy apprehensions had been already justified by the experience of the Romans. The annals of the emperors exhibit a strong and various picture of human nature, which we should vainly seek among the mixed and doubtful characters of modern history. In the conduct of those monarchs we may trace the utmost lines of vice and virtue; the most exalted perfection, and the meanest degeneracy of our own species.

The golden age of Trajan and the Antonines had been preceded by an age of iron. It is almost superfluous to enumerate the unworthy successors of Augustus. Their unparalleled vices, and the splendid theatre on which they were acted, have saved them from oblivion. The dark unrelenting Tiberius, the furious Caligula, the feeble Claudius, the profligate and cruel Nero, the beastly Vitellius, and the timid inhuman Domitian, are condemned to everlasting infamy. During fourscore years (excepting only the short and doubtful respite of Vespasian's reign) Rome groaned beneath an unremitting tyranny, which exterminated the ancient families of the republic, and was fatal to almost every virtue, and every talent, that arose in that unhappy period.

Under the reign of these monsters the slavery of the Romans was accompanied with two peculiar circumstances, the one occasioned by their former liberty, the other by their extensive conquests, which rendered their condition more completely wretched than that of the victims of tyranny in any other age or country. From these causes were derived, 1. The exquisite sensibility of the sufferers; and, 2. The impossibility of escaping from the hand of the oppressor.

The division of Europe into a number of independent states, connected, however, with each other, by the general resemblance of religion, language, and manners, is productive of the most beneficial consequences to the liberty of mankind. A modern tyrant, who should find no resistance either in his own breast, or in his people, would soon experience a gentle restraint from the example of his equals, the dread of present censure, the advice of his allies, and the apprehension of his enemies. The object of his displeasure, escaping from the narrow limits of his dominions, would easily obtain, in a happier climate, a secure refuge, a new fortune adequate to his merit, the freedom of complaint, and perhaps the means of revenge. But the empire of the Romans filled the world, and when that empire fell into the hands of a single person, the world became a safe and dreary prison for his enemies. The slave of Imperial despotism, whether he was condemned to drag his gilded chain in Rome and the senate, or to wear out a life of exile on the barren rock of Seriphus, or the frozen banks of the

Danube, expected his fate in silent despair. To resist was fatal, and it was impossible to fly. On every side he was encompassed with a vast extent of sea and land, which he could never hope to traverse without being discovered, seized, and restored to his irritated master. Beyond the frontiers, his anxious view could discover nothing, except the ocean, inhospitable deserts, hostile tribes of barbarians, of fierce manners and unknown language, or dependent kings, who would gladly purchase the emperor's protection by the sacrifice of an obnoxious fugitive. "Wherever you are," said Cicero to the exiled Marcellus, "remember that you are equally within the power of the conqueror."

CHAPTER FOUR

*The Cruelty, Follies, and Murder of Commodus —
Election of Pertinax — His Attempts to Reform the
State — His Assassination by the Prætorian
Guards*

The monstrous vices of Commodus have cast a shade on the
purity of his father's virtues. It has been objected to Marcus,
that he sacrificed the happiness of millions to a fond partiality
for a worthless boy; and that he chose a successor in his own
family, rather than in the republic. Nothing, however, was
neglected by the anxious father, and by the men of virtue and
learning whom he summoned to his assistance, to expand the
narrow mind of young Commodus, to correct his growing
vices, and to render him worthy of the throne, for which he
was designed. But the power of instruction is seldom of much
efficacy, except in those happy dispositions where it is almost
superfluous. The distasteful lesson of a grave philosopher was
in a moment obliterated by the whisper of a profligate favourite; and Marcus himself blasted the fruits of this laboured education, by admitting his son, at the age of fourteen or fifteen,
to a full participation of the Imperial power. He lived but four
years afterwards; but he lived long enough to repent a rash
measure, which raised the impetuous youth above the restraint
of reason and authority.

Most of the crimes which disturb the internal peace of society are produced by the restraints which the necessary, but unequal, laws of property have imposed on the appetites of mankind, by confining to a few the possession of those objects that are coveted by many. Of all our passions and appetites, the love of power is of the most imperious and unsociable nature, since the pride of one man requires the submission of the multitude. In the tumult of civil discord, the laws of society lose their force, and their place is seldom supplied by those of humanity. The ardour of contention, the pride of victory, the despair of success, the memory of past injuries, and the fear of future dangers, all contribute to inflame the mind, and to silence the voice of pity. From such motives almost every page of history has been stained with civil blood; but these motives will not account for the unprovoked cruelties of Commodus, who had nothing to wish and everything to enjoy. The beloved son of Marcus succeeded (A.D. 180) to his father, amidst the acclamations of the senate and armies, and when he ascended the throne the happy youth saw round him neither competitor to remove nor enemies to punish. In this calm elevated station it was surely natural that he should prefer the love of mankind to their detestation, the mild glories of his five predecessors, to the ignominious fate of Nero and Domitian.

During the three first years of his reign, the forms, and even the spirit, of the old administration were maintained by those faithful counsellors, to whom Marcus had recommended his son, and for whose wisdom and integrity Commodus still entertained a reluctant esteem. The young prince and his profligate favourites revelled in all the licence of sovereign power; but his hands were yet unstained with blood; and he had even displayed a generosity of sentiment, which might perhaps have ripened into solid virtue. A fatal incident decided his fluctuating character.

One evening (A.D. 183), as the emperor was returning to the palace through a dark and narrow portico in the amphitheatre, an assassin, who waited his passage, rushed upon him with a drawn sword, loudly exclaiming, *The senate sends you this.* The menace prevented the deed; the assassin was seized by the guards, and immediately revealed the authors of the conspiracy.

But the words of the assassin sunk deep into the mind of Commodus, and left an indelible impression of fear and hatred against the whole body of the senate. Those whom he had dreaded as importunate ministers, he now suspected as secret enemies. The Delators, a race of men discouraged, and almost extinguished, under the former reigns, again became formidable, as soon as they discovered that the emperor was desirous of finding disaffection and treason in the senate. That assembly whom Marcus had ever considered as the great council of the nation, was composed of the most distinguished of the Romans; and distinction of every kind soon became criminal. The possession of wealth stimulated the diligence of the informers; rigid virtue implied a tacit censure of the irregularities of Commodus; important services implied a dangerous superiority of merit; and the friendship of the father always insured the aversion of the son. Suspicion was equivalent to proof; trial to condemnation. The execution of a considerable senator was attended with the death of all who might lament or revenge his fate; and when Commodus had once tasted human blood, he became incapable of pity or remorse.

The tyrant's rage, after having shed the noblest blood of the senate, at length recoiled on the principal instrument of his cruelty. Whilst Commodus was immersed in blood and luxury, he devolved the detail of the public business on Perennis; a servile and ambitious minister, who had obtained his post by the murder of his predecessor, but who possessed a considerable share of vigour and ability. By acts of extortion, and the forfeited estates of the nobles sacrificed to his avarice, he had accumulated an immense treasure. The Prætorian guards were under his immediate command; and his son, who already discovered a military genius, was at the head of the Illyrian legions. Perennis aspired to the empire; or what, in the eyes of Commodus, amounted to the same crime, he was capable of aspiring to it, had he not been prevented, surprised, and (A.D. 186) put to death.

Suspicious princes often promote the last of mankind, from a vain persuasion that those who have no dependence, except on their favour, will have no attachment except to the person of their benefactor. Cleander, the successor of Perennis, was a Phrygian by birth; of a nation over whose stubborn but servile temper, blows only could prevail. He had been sent from his native country to Rome, in the capacity of a slave. As a slave he entered the Imperial palace, rendered himself useful to his master's passions, and rapidly ascended to the most exalted station which a subject could enjoy. His influence over the mind of Commodus was much greater than that of his predecessor; for Cleander was devoid of any ability or virtue which could inspire the emperor with envy or distrust. Avarice was the reigning passion of his soul, and the great principle of his administration. The rank of Consul, of Patrician, of Senator, was exposed to public sale; and it would have been considered as disaffection if any one had refused to purchase these empty and disgraceful honours with the greatest part of his fortune. In the lucrative provincial employments, the minister shared with the governor the spoils of the people. The execution of the laws was venal and arbitrary. A wealthy criminal might obtain, not only the reversal of the sentence by which he was justly condemned; but might likewise inflict whatever punishment he pleased on the accuser, the witnesses, and the judge.

Pestilence and famine contributed to fill up the measure of the calamities of Rome. The first could be only imputed to the just indignations of the gods; but (A.D. 189) a monopoly of corn, supported by the riches and power of the minister, was considered as the immediate cause of the second. The popular discontent, after it had long circulated in whispers, broke out in the assembled circus. The people quitted their favourite amusements for the more delicious pleasure of revenge, rushed in crowds towards a palace in the suburbs, one of the emperor's retirements, and demanded, with angry clamours, the head of the public enemy. Cleander who commanded the Prætorian guards, ordered a body of cavalry to sally forth, and disperse the seditious multitude. The multitude fled with precipitation towards the city; several were slain, and many more were trampled to death: but when the cavalry entered the streets, their pursuit was checked by a shower of stones and darts from the roofs and windows of the houses. The foot guards, who had been long jealous of the prerogatives and insolence of the Prætorian cavalry, embraced the party of the people. The tumult became a regular engagement, and threatened a general massacre. The Prætorians, at length, gave way, oppressed with numbers; and the tide of popular fury returned with redoubled violence against the gates of the palace, where Commodus lay, dissolved in luxury, and alone unconscious of the civil war. It was death to approach his person with the unwelcome news. He would have perished in this supine security, had not two women, his elder sister Fadilla, and Marcia, the most favoured of his concubines, ventured to break into his presence. Bathed in tears, and with dishevelled hair, they threw themselves at his feet; and with all the pressing eloquence of fear, discovered to the affrighted emperor, the crimes of the minister, the rage of the people, and the impending ruin, which, in a few minutes, would burst over his palace and person. Commodus started from his dream of pleasure, and commanded that the head of Cleander should be thrown out to the people. The desired spectacle instantly appeased the tumult; and the son of Marcus might even yet have regained the affection and confidence of his outraged subjects.

But every sentiment of virtue and humanity was extinct in the mind of Commodus. Whilst he thus abandoned the reins of empire to these unworthy favourites, he valued nothing in sovereign power, except the unbounded licence of indulging his sensual appetites. His hours were spent in a seraglio of three hundred beautiful women, and as many boys, of every rank, and of every province; and, wherever the arts of seduction proved ineffectual, the brutal lover had recourse to violence. The ancient historians have expatiated on these abandoned scenes of prostitution, which scorned every restraint of nature or modesty; but it would not be easy to translate their too faithful descriptions into the decency of modern language. The intervals of lust were filled up with the basest amusements. The influence of a polite age, and the labour of an attentive education, had never been able to infuse into his rude and brutish mind the least tincture of learning; and he was the first of the Roman emperors totally devoid of taste for the pleasures of the understanding.

Gradually Commodus' innate sense of shame was so far extinguished that he resolved to exhibit before the eyes of the Roman people those exercises which till then he had decently confined within the walls of his palace and to the presence of a few favourites. On the appointed day the various motives of flattery, fear, and curiosity, attracted to the amphitheatre an innumerable multitude of spectators: and some degree of applause was deservedly bestowed on the uncommon skill of the Imperial performer. Whether he aimed at the head or heart of the animal, the wound was alike certain and mortal. With arrows, whose point was shaped into the form of a crescent, Commodus often intercepted the rapid career, and cut asunder the long bony neck of the ostrich. A panther was let loose; and the archer waited till he had leaped upon a trembling malefactor. In the same instant the shaft flew, the beast dropped dead, and the man remained unhurt. The dens of the amphitheatre disgorged at once a hundred lions; a hundred darts from the unerring hand of Commodus laid them dead as they ran raging around the *Arena*. Neither the huge bulk of the elephant, nor the scaly hide of the rhinoceros, could defend them from his stroke. Ethiopia and India yielded their most extraordinary productions; and several animals were slain in the amphitheatre, which had been seen only in the representations of art, or perhaps of fancy. In all these exhibitions, the securest precautions were used to protect the person of the Roman Hercules from the desperate spring of any savage; who might possibly disregard the dignity of the emperor, and the sanctity of the god.

But the meanest of the populace were affected with shame and indignation when they beheld their sovereign enter the lists as a gladiator, and glory in a profession which the laws and manners of the Romans had branded with the justest note of infamy.

Commodus had now attained the summit of vice and infamy. Amidst the acclamations of a flattering court, he was unable to disguise, from himself, that he had deserved the contempt and hatred of every man of sense and virtue in his empire. His ferocious spirit was irritated by the consciousness of that hatred, by the envy of every kind of merit, by the just apprehension of danger, and by the habit of slaughter, which he contracted in his daily amusements. History has preserved a long list of consular senators sacrificed to his wanton suspicion, which sought out, with peculiar anxiety, those unfortunate persons connected, however remotely, with the family of the Antonines, without sparing even the ministers of his crimes or pleasures. His cruelty proved at last fatal to himself. He had shed with impunity the noblest blood of Rome: he perished as soon as he was dreaded by his own domestics. Marcia his favourite concubine, Eclectus his chamberlain, and Lætus his Prætorian præfect, alarmed by the fate of their companions and predecessors, resolved to prevent the destruction which every hour hung over their heads, either from the mad caprice of the tyrant, or the sudden indignation of the people. Marcia seized the occasion of presenting a draught of wine to her lover, after he had fatigued himself with hunting some wild beasts. Commodus retired to sleep; but whilst he was labouring with the effects of poison and drunkenness, a robust youth, by profession a wrestler, entered his chamber, and strangled him without resistance. The body was secretly conveyed out of the palace, before the least suspicion was entertained in the city, or even in the court, of the emperor's death. Such was the fate of the son of Marcus, and so easy was it to destroy a hated tyrant, who, by the artificial powers of government, had oppressed, during thirteen years, so many millions of subjects, each of whom was equal to their master in personal strength and personal abilities.

The measures of the conspirators were conducted with the deliberate coolness and celerity which the greatness of the occasion required. They resolved instantly to fill the vacant throne with an emperor whose character would justify and maintain the action that had been committed. They fixed on Pertinax, præfect of the city, an ancient senator of consular rank, whose conspicuous merit had broke through the obscurity of his birth, and raised him to the first honours of the state. He had successively governed most of the provinces of the empire; and in all his great employments, military as well as civil, he had uniformly distinguished himself by the firmness, the prudence, and the integrity of his conduct. He now remained almost alone of the friends and ministers of Marcus; and when, at a late hour of the night, he was awakened with the news, that the chamberlain and the præfect were at his door, he received them with intrepid resignation, and desired they would execute their master's orders. Instead of death, they offered him the throne of the Roman world. During some moments he distrusted their intentions and assurances. Convinced at length of the death of Commodus, he accepted the purple with a sincere reluctance, the natural effect of his knowledge both of the duties and of the dangers of the supreme rank.

Lætus conducted without delay his new emperor to the camp of the Prætorians, diffusing at the same time through the city a seasonable report that Commodus died suddenly of an apoplexy; and that the virtuous Pertinax had already succeeded to the throne. The guards were rather surprised than pleased with the suspicious death of a prince whose indulgence and liberality they alone had experienced; but the emergency of the occasion, the authority of their præfect, the reputation of Pertinax, and the clamours of the people, obliged them to stifle their secret discontents, to accept the donative promised of the new emperor, to swear allegiance to him, and with joyful acclamations and laurels in their hands to conduct him to the senate-house, that the military consent might be ratified by the civil authority.

This important night was now far spent; with the dawn of day, and (A.D. 193, 1st January) the commencement of the new year, the senators expected a summons to attend an ignominious ceremony. In spite of all remonstrances, even of those of his creatures, who yet preserved any regard for prudence or decency, Commodus had resolved to pass the night in the gladiators' school, and from thence to take possession of the consulship, in the habit and with the attendance of that infamous crew. On a sudden, before the break of day, the senate was called together in the temple of Concord, to meet the guards, and to ratify the election of a new emperor. For a few minutes they sat in silent suspense, doubtful of their unexpected deliverance, and suspicious of the cruel artifices of Commodus; but when at length they were assured that the tyrant was no more, they resigned themselves to all the transports of joy and indignation. Pertinax, who modestly represented the meanness of his extraction, and pointed out several noble senators more deserving than himself of the empire, was constrained by their dutiful violence to ascend the throne, and received all the titles of Imperial power, confirmed by the most sincere vows of fidelity. The memory of Commodus was branded with eternal infamy. The names of tyrant, of gladiator, of public enemy, resounded in every corner of the house. They decreed in tumultuous votes, that his honours should be reversed, his titles erased from the public monuments, his statues thrown down, his body dragged with a hook into the stripping-room of the gladiators, to satiate the public fury; and they expressed some indignation against those officious servants who had already presumed to screen his remains from the justice of the senate. But Pertinax could not refuse those last rites to the memory of Marcus, and the tears of his first protector Claudius Pompeianus, who lamented the cruel fate of his brother-in-law, and lamented still more that he had deserved it.

To heal, as far as it was possible, the wounds inflicted by the hand of tyranny, was the pleasing, but melancholy, task of Pertinax. The innocent victims, who yet survived, were recalled from exile, released from prison, and restored to the full possession of their honours and fortunes. The unburied bodies of murdered senators (for the cruelty of Commodus endeavoured to extend itself beyond death) were deposited in the sepulchres of their ancestors; their memory was justified; and every consolation was bestowed on their ruined and afflicted families. Among these consolations, one of the most grateful was the punishment of the Delators; the common enemies of their master, of virtue, and of their country. Yet even in the inquisition of these legal assassins, Pertinax proceeded with a steady temper, which gave everything to justice, and nothing to popular prejudice and resentment.

The finances of the state demanded the most vigilant care of the emperor. Though every measure of injustice and extortion had been adopted, which could collect the property of the subject into the coffers of the prince, the rapaciousness of

Commodus had been so very inadequate to his extravagance, that, upon his death, no more than eight thousand pounds were found in the exhausted treasury, to defray the current expenses of government, and to discharge the pressing demand of a liberal donative, which the new emperor had been obliged to promise to the Prætorian guards. Yet under these distressed circumstances, Pertinax had the generous firmness to remit all the oppressive taxes invented by Commodus, and to cancel all the unjust claims of the treasury; declaring, in a decree of the senate, "that he was better satisfied to administer a poor republic with innocence, than to acquire riches by the ways of tyranny and dishonour." Economy and industry he considered as the pure and genuine sources of wealth; and from them he soon derived a copious supply for the public necessities. The expense of the household was immediately reduced to one half. All the instruments of luxury, Pertinax exposed to public auction, gold and silver plate, chariots of a singular construction, a superfluous wardrobe of silk and embroidery, and a great number of beautiful slaves of both sexes; excepting only, with attentive humanity, those who were born in a state of freedom, and had been ravished from the arms of their weeping parents. At the same time that he obliged the worthless favourites of the tyrant to resign a part of their ill-gotten wealth, he satisfied the just creditors of the state, and unexpectedly discharged the long arrears of honest services. He removed the oppressive restrictions which had been laid upon commerce, and granted all the uncultivated lands in Italy and the provinces to those who would improve them; with an exemption from tribute, during the term of ten years.

Such an uniform conduct had already secured to Pertinax the noblest reward of a sovereign, the love and esteem of his people; but a hasty zeal to reform the corrupted state, accompanied with less prudence than might have been expected from the years and experience of Pertinax, proved fatal to himself and his country. Amidst the general joy, the sullen and angry countenance of the Prætorian guards betrayed their inward dissatisfaction. Only eighty-six days after the death of Commodus, a general sedition broke out in the camp, which the officers wanted either power or inclination to suppress. At first the assassins were awed by the venerable aspect and majestic firmness of their sovereign, but despair of pardon revived their fury. Pertinax's head was separated from his body, placed on a lance, and carried in triumph to the Prætorian camp, in the sight of a mournful and indignant people.

CHAPTER FIVE

Public Sale of the Empire to Didius Julianus by the Prætorian Guards—Clodius Albinus in Britain, Pescennius Niger in Syria, and Septimius Severus in Pannonia, declare against the Murderers of Pertinax—Civil Wars and Victory of Severus over his three Rivals—Relaxation of Discipline—New Maxims of Government

The Prætorian bands, whose licentious fury was the first symptom and cause of the decline of the Roman empire, derived their institution from Augustus. That crafty tyrant, sensible that laws might colour, but that arms alone could maintain, his usurped dominion, had gradually formed this powerful body of guards in constant readiness to protect his person, to awe the senate, and either to prevent or to crush the first motions of rebellion. He distinguished these favoured troops by a double pay, and superior privileges; but, as their formidable aspect would at once have alarmed and irritated the Roman people, three cohorts only were stationed in the capital; whilst the remainder was dispersed in the adjacent towns of Italy. But after fifty years of peace and servitude, Tiberius ventured on a decisive measure, which for ever riveted the fetters of his country. Under the fair pretences of relieving Italy from the heavy burthen of military quarters and of introducing a stricter discipline among the guards, he assembled them at Rome, in a permanent camp, which was fortified with skilful care, and placed on a commanding situation.

Such formidable servants are always necessary, but often fatal to the throne of despotism. By thus introducing the Prætorian guards, as it were into the palace and the senate, the emperors taught them to perceive their own strength, and the weakness of the civil government; to view the vices of their masters with familiar contempt, and to lay aside that reverential awe, which distance only, and mystery, can preserve towards an imaginary power. In the luxurious idleness of an opulent city, their pride was nourished by the sense of their irresistible weight; nor was it possible to conceal from them, that the person of the sovereign, the authority of the senate, the public treasure, and the seat of empire, were all in their hands. To divert the Prætorian bands from these dangerous reflections, the firmest and best established princes were obliged to mix blandishments with commands, rewards with punishments, to flatter their pride, indulge their pleasures, connive at their irregularities, and to purchase their precarious faith by a liberal donative; which, since the elevation of Claudius, was exacted as a legal claim, on the accession of every new emperor.

The Prætorians had violated the sanctity of the throne, by the atrocious murder of Pertinax; they dishonoured the majesty of it, by their subsequent conduct. Sulpicianus, the father-in-law of Pertinax, yielded to the dictates of ambition, and had already begun to use the only effectual argument, and to treat for the Imperial dignity; but the more prudent of the Prætorians, apprehensive that, in this private contract, they should not obtain a just price for so valuable a commodity, ran out upon the ramparts; and, with a loud voice, proclaimed that the Roman world was to be disposed of to the best bidder by public auction.

This infamous offer, the most insolent excess of military licence, diffused an universal grief, shame, and indignation throughout the city. It reached at length the ears of Didius Julianus, a wealthy senator, who, regardless of the public calamities, was indulging himself in the luxury of the table. His wife and his daughter, his freedmen and his parasites, easily convinced him that he deserved the throne, and earnestly conjured him to embrace so fortunate an opportunity. The vain old man (A.D. 193, 28th March) hastened to the Prætorian camp, where Sulpicianus was still in treaty with the guards; and began to bid against him from the foot of the rampart. The unworthy negotiation was transacted by faithful emissaries, who passed alternately from one candidate to the other, and acquainted each of them with the offers of his rival. Sulpicianus had already promised a donative of five thousand drachms (above one hundred and sixty pounds) to each soldier; when Julian, eager for the prize, rose at once to the sum of six thousand two hundred and fifty drachms, or upwards of two hundred pounds sterling. The gates of the camp were instantly thrown open to the purchaser; he was declared emperor, and received an oath of allegiance from the soldiers, who retained humanity enough to stipulate that he should pardon and forget the competition of Sulpicianus.

It was now incumbent on the Prætorians to fulfill the conditions of the sale. They placed their new sovereign, whom they served and despised, in the centre of their ranks, surrounded him on every side with their shields, and conducted him in close order of battle through the deserted streets of the city. The senate was commanded to assemble; and those who had been the distinguished friends of Pertinax found it necessary to affect a more than common share of satisfaction at this happy revolution.

The nobility, whose conspicuous station and ample possessions exacted the strictest caution, dissembled their sentiments, and met the affected civility of Julian with smiles of complacency and professions of duty. But the people, secure in their numbers and obscurity, gave a free vent to their passions. The enraged multitude affronted the person of Julian, rejected his liberality, and conscious of the impotence of their own resentment, they called aloud on the legions of the frontiers to assert the violated majesty of the Roman empire.

The public discontent was soon diffused from the centre to the frontiers of the empire. The armies of Britain, of Syria, and of Illyricum, lamented the death of Pertinax, in whose company, or under whose command, they had so often fought and conquered. They received with surprise, with indignation, and perhaps with envy, the extraordinary intelligence that the Prætorians had disposed of the empire by public auction; and they sternly refused to ratify the ignominious bargain. Their immediate and unanimous revolt was fatal to Julian, but it was fatal at the same time to the public peace; as the generals of the respective armies, Clodius Albinus, Pescennius Niger, and Septimius Severus, were still more anxious to succeed than to revenge the murdered Pertinax. Their forces were exactly balanced. Each of them was at the head of three legions, with a numerous train of auxiliaries; and however different in their characters, they were all soldiers of experience and capacity.

The Pannonian army was at this time commanded by Septimius Severus, a native of Africa, who, in the gradual ascent of private honours, had concealed his daring ambition, which was never diverted from its steady course by the allurements of pleasure, the apprehension of danger, or the feelings of humanity. On the first news of the murder of Pertinax, he assembled his troops, painted in the most lively colours the crime, the insolence, and the weakness of the Prætorian guards, and animated the legions to arms and to revenge. He concluded (and the peroration was thought extremely eloquent) with promising every soldier about four hundred pounds; an honourable donative, double in value to the infamous bribe with which Julian had purchased the empire. The acclamations of the army immediately saluted Severus with the names of Augustus, Pertinax, and Emperor; and he (A.D. 193, 13th April) thus attained the lofty station to which he was invited, by conscious merit and a long train of dreams and omens, the fruitful offspring either of his superstition or policy.

The wretched Julian had expected, and thought himself prepared, to dispute the empire with the governor of Syria; but in the invincible and rapid approach of the Pannonian legions, he saw his inevitable ruin. The hasty arrival of every messenger increased his just apprehensions. He was successively informed that Severus had passed the Alps; that the Italian cities, unwilling or unable to oppose his progress, had received him with the warmest professions of joy and duty; that the important place of Ravenna had surrendered without resistance, and that the Hadriatic fleet was in the hands of the conqueror. The enemy was now within two hundred and fifty miles of Rome; and every moment diminished the narrow span of life and empire allotted to Julian. At the bidding of Severus he was apprehended by the Prætorians, conducted into a private apartment of the baths of the palace, and (A.D. 193, 2nd June) beheaded as a common criminal, after having purchased, with an immense treasure, an anxious and precarious reign of only sixty-six days.

The first cares of Severus were bestowed on two measures, the one dictated by policy, the other by decency; the revenge, and the honours, due to the memory of Pertinax. Before the new emperor entered Rome, he issued his commands to the Prætorian guards, directing them to wait his arrival on a large plain near the city, without arms, but in the habits of ceremony, in which they were accustomed to attend their sovereign. He was obeyed by those haughty troops, whose contrition was the effect of their just terrors. A chosen part of the Illyrian army encompassed them with levelled spears. Incapable of flight or resistance, they expected their fate in silent consternation. Severus mounted the tribunal, sternly reproached them with perfidy and cowardice, dismissed them with ignominy from the trust which they had betrayed, despoiled them of their splendid ornaments, and banished them, on pain of death, to the distance of an hundred miles from the capital. During the transaction, another detachment had been sent to seize their arms, occupy their camp, and prevent the hasty consequences of their despair.

In less than four years (A.D. 193–197), Severus subdued the riches of the east and the valour of the west. He vanquished two competitors of reputation and ability, and defeated numerous armies provided with weapons and discipline equal to his own. Yet the deceptions of Severus cannot be justified by the most ample privileges of state reason. He promised only to betray, he flattered only to ruin; and however he might occasionally bind himself by oaths and treaties, his conscience, obsequious to his interest, always released him from the inconvenient obligation.

The civil wars of modern Europe have been distinguished, not only by the fierce animosity, but likewise by the obstinate perseverance, of the contending factions. They have generally been justified by some principle, or, at least, coloured by some pretext, of religion, freedom, or loyalty. The leaders were nobles of independent property and hereditary influence. The troops fought like men interested in a decision of the quarrel; and as military spirit and party zeal were strongly diffused throughout the whole community, a vanquished chief was immediately supplied with new adherents, eager to shed their blood in the same cause. But the Romans, after the fall of the republic, combated only for the choice of masters. Under the standard of a popular candidate for empire, a few enlisted from affection, some from fear, many from interest, none from principle. The legions, uninflamed by party zeal, were allured into civil war by liberal donatives, and still more liberal promises. A defeat, by disabling the chief from the performance of his engagements, dissolved the mercenary allegiance of his followers; and left them to consult their own safety, by a timely desertion of an unsuccessful cause. It was of little moment to the provinces, under whose name they were oppressed or governed; they were driven by the impulsion of the present power, and as soon as that power yielded to a superior force, they hastened to implore the clemency of the conqueror, who, as he had an immense debt to discharge, was obliged to sacrifice the most guilty countries to the avarice of his soldiers. In the vast extent of the Roman empire, there were few fortified cities capable of protecting a routed army; nor was there any person, or family, or order of men, whose natural interest, unsupported by the powers of government, was capable of restoring the cause of a sinking party.

The true interest of an absolute monarch generally coincides with that of his people. Their numbers, their wealth, their order, and their security, are the best and only foundations of his real greatness; and were he totally devoid of virtue, prudence might supply its place, and would dictate the same rule of conduct. Severus considered the Roman empire as his property, and had no sooner secured the possession, than he bestowed his care on the cultivation and improvement of so valuable an acquisition. Salutary laws, executed with inflexible firmness, soon corrected most of the abuses with which, since the death of Marcus, every part of the government had been infected. In the administration of justice, the judgments of the emperor were characterised by attention, discernment, and impartiality; and whenever he deviated from the strict line of equity, it was generally in favour of the poor and oppressed; not so much indeed from any sense of humanity, as from the natural propensity of a despot, to humble the pride of greatness, and to sink all his subjects to the same common level of absolute dependence. His expensive taste for building, magnificent shows, and above all a constant and liberal distribution of corn and provisions, were the surest means of captivating the affection of the Roman people. The misfortunes of civil discord were obliterated. The calm of peace and prosperity was once more experienced in the provinces; and many cities, restored by the munificence of Severus, assumed the title of his colonies, and attested by public monuments their gratitude and felicity. The fame of the Roman arms was revived by that warlike and successful emperor, and he boasted with a just pride, that, having received the empire oppressed with foreign and domestic wars, he left it established in profound universal, and honourable peace.

The Prætorians, who murdered their emperor and sold the empire, had received the just punishment of their treason; but the necessary, though dangerous, institution of guards, was soon restored on a new model by Severus, and increased to four times the ancient number. Formerly these troops had been recruited in Italy; and as the adjacent provinces gradually imbibed the softer manners of Rome, the levies were extended to Macedonia, Noricum, and Spain. In the room of these elegant troops, better adapted to the pomp of courts than to the uses of war, it was established by Severus, that from all the legions of the frontiers, the soldiers most distinguished for strength, valour, and fidelity, should be occasionally draughted; and promoted, as an honour and reward, into the more eligible service of the guards. By this new institution, the Italian youth were diverted from the exercise of arms, and the capital was terrified by the strange aspect and manners of a multitude of barbarians. The command of these favoured and formidable troops soon became the first office of the empire. As the government degenerated into military despotism, the Prætorian Præfect, who in his origin had been a simple captain of the guards, was placed, not only at the head of the army, but of the finances, and even of the law. In every department of administration he represented the person and exercised the authority of the emperor.

Till the reign of Severus, the virtue and even the good sense of the emperors had been distinguished by their zeal or affected reverence for the senate, and by a tender regard to the nice frame of civil policy instituted by Augustus. But the youth of Severus had been trained in the implicit obedience of camps, and his riper years spent in the despotism of military command. His haughty and inflexible spirit could not discover, or would not acknowledge, the advantage of preserving an intermediate power, however imaginary, between the emperor and the army. He disdained to profess himself the servant of an assembly that detested his person and trembled at his frown; he issued his commands, where his request would have proved as effectual; assumed the conduct and style of a sovereign and a conqueror, and exercised, without disguise, the whole legislative as well as the executive power.

CHAPTER SIX

The Death of Severus—Tyranny of Caracalla—
Usurpation of Macrinus—Follies of Elagabalus
—Virtues of Alexander Severus—Licentiousness of
the Army—General State of the Roman Finances

Like most of the Africans, Severus was passionately addicted
to the vain studies of magic and divination, deeply versed in
the interpretation of dreams and omens, and perfectly acquainted with the science of judicial astrology; which, in almost every age, except the present, has maintained its
dominion over the mind of man. He had lost his first wife
whilst he was governor of the Lionnese Gaul. In the choice of
a second, he sought only to connect himself with some favourite of fortune; and as soon as he had discovered that a
young lady of Emesa in Syria had *a royal nativity*, he solicited, and obtained her hand. Julia Domna (for that was her
name) deserved all that the stars could promise her. She possessed, even in an advanced age, the attractions of beauty, and
united to a lively imagination, a firmness of mind, and
strength of judgment, seldom bestowed on her sex. Her amiable qualities never made any deep impression on the dark and
jealous temper of her husband; but in her son's reign she administered the principal affairs of the empire, with a prudence
that supported his authority; and with a moderation that some-

times corrected his wild extravagances. Julia applied herself to letters and philosophy, with some success, and with the most splendid reputation. She was the patroness of every art, and the friend of every man of genius. The grateful flattery of the learned has celebrated her virtue; but, if we may credit the scandal of ancient history, chastity was very far from being the most conspicuous virtue of the empress Julia.

Two sons, Caracalla and Geta, were the fruit of this marriage, and the destined heirs of the empire. The fond hopes of the father, and of the Roman world, were soon disappointed by these vain youths, who displayed the indolent security of hereditary princes; and a presumption that fortune would supply the place of merit and application. Without any emulation of virtue or talents, they discovered, almost from their infancy, a fixed and implacable antipathy for each other. Their aversion, confirmed by years, and fomented by the arts of their interested favourites, broke out in childish, and gradually in more serious, competitions; and, at length, divided the theatre, the circus, and the court, into two factions; actuated by the hopes and fears of their respective leaders. The prudent emperor endeavoured, by every expedient of advice and authority, to allay this growing animosity. The unhappy discord by his sons clouded all his prospects, and threatened to overturn a throne raised with so much labour, cemented with so much blood, and guarded with every defence of arms and treasure.

Upon intelligence of war in Britain and of an invasion (A.D. 208) of the province of the barbarians of the North, Severus, despite his advanced years, accompanied his rival sons upon a successful expedition to that island. The declining health and last illnesses of Severus inflamed the wild ambition and black passions of Caracalla's soul. Impatient of any delay or division of empire, he attempted, more than once, to shorten the small remainder of his father's days, and endeavoured, but without success, to excite a mutiny among the troops. The old emperor had often censured the misguided lenity of Marcus, who, by a single act of justice, might have saved the Romans from the tyranny of his worthless son. Placed in the same situation, he experienced how easily the rigour of a judge dissolves away in the tenderness of a parent. He deliberated, he threatened, but he could not punish; and this last and only instance of mercy was more fatal to the empire than a long series of cruelty. The disorder of his mind irritated the pains of his body; he wished impatiently for death, and hastened the instant of it by his impatience. He expired (A.D. 211, 4th February) at York in the sixty-fifth year of his life, and in the eighteenth of a glorious and successful reign.

Julia attempted to prevent the latent civil war by dividing the sovereignty of the Empire between her sons, Caracalla to retain Europe and Geta to rule Asia and Egypt. Caracalla artfully listened to his mother's entreaties, and consented (A.D. 212, 27th February) to meet his brother in her apartment, on terms of peace and reconciliation. In the midst of their conversation, some centurions, who had contrived to conceal themselves, rushed with draw swords upon the unfortunate Geta. His distracted mother strove to protect him in her arms; but, in the unavailing struggle, she was wounded in the hand, and covered with the blood of her younger son, while she saw the elder animating and assisting the fury of the assassins. As soon as the deed was perpetrated, Caracalla, with hasty steps, and horror in his countenance, ran towards the Prætorian camp as his only refuge, and threw himself on the ground before the statues of the tutelar deities. The soldiers attempted to raise and comfort him. In broken and disordered words he informed them of his imminent danger and fortunate escape; insinuating that he had prevented the designs of his enemy, and declared his resolution to live and die with his faithful troops. Geta had been the favourite of the soldiers; but complaint was useless, revenge was dangerous, and they still reverenced the son of Severus. Their discontent died away in idle murmurs, and Caracalla soon convinced them of the justice of his cause, by distributing in one lavish donative the accumulated treasures of his father's reign.

Caracalla's own reign was marked by capricious and monstrous cruelties, and he was assassinated, near Edessa, 8th March 217. The plot against him had been instigated by Macrinus, a præfect of the Prætorians, who now succeeded to the purple. Macrinus's efforts to reform the relaxed discipline of the soldiery only gained their ill will, and they were soon ready to transfer their sovereignty to another.

The empress Julia had experienced all the vicissitudes of fortune. From an humble station she had been raised to greatness, only to taste the superior bitterness of an exalted rank. She was doomed to weep over the death of one of her sons, and over the life of the other. The cruel fate of Caracalla, though her good sense must have long taught her to expect it, awakened the feelings of a mother and of an empress. Notwithstanding the respectful civility expressed by the usurper toward the widow of Severus, she descended with a painful struggle into the condition of a subject, and soon withdrew herself by a voluntary death from the anxious and humiliating dependence. Julia Mæsa, her sister, was ordered to leave the court and Antioch. She retired to Emesa with an immense fortune, the fruit of twenty years' favour, accompanied by her two daughters, Soæmias, and Mamæa, each of whom was a widow, and each had an only son. Bassianus, for that was the name of the son of Soæmias, was consecrated to the honourable ministry of high priest of the Sun; and this holy vocation, embraced either from prudence or superstition, contributed to raise the Syrian youth to the empire of Rome. A numerous body of troops was stationed at Emesa; and, as the severe discipline of Macrinus had constrained them to pass the winter encamped, they were eager to revenge the cruelty of such unaccustomed hardships. The soldiers, who resorted in crowds to the temple of the Sun, beheld with veneration and delight the elegant dress and figure of a young Pontiff: they recognised, or they thought that they recognised, the features of Caracalla, whose memory they now adored. The artful Mæsa saw and cherished their rising partiality, and readily sacrificing her daughter's reputation to the fortune of her grandson, she insinuated that Bassianus was the natural son of their murdered sovereign. The sums distributed by her emissaries with a lavish hand silenced every objection, and the profusion sufficiently proved the affinity, or at least the resemblance, of Bassianus with the great original. The young Antoninus (for he had assumed and polluted that respectable name) was (A.D. 218, 16th May) declared emperor by the troops of Emesa, asserted his hereditary right, and called aloud on the armies to follow the standard of a young and liberal prince, who had taken up arms to revenge his father's death and the oppression of the military order.

Whilst a conspiracy of women and eunuchs was concerted with prudence, and conducted with rapid vigour, Macrinus, who, by a decisive motion, might have crushed his infant enemy, floated between the opposite extremes of terror and security, which alike fixed him inactive at Antioch. A spirit of rebellion diffused itself through all the camps and garrisons of Syria, successive detachments murdered their officers, and joined the party of the rebels; and the tardy restitution of military pay and privileges was imputed to the acknowledged weakness of Macrinus. At length he marched out of Antioch, to meet the increasing and zealous army of the young pretender. His own troops seemed to take the field with faintness and reluctance; but (A.D. 218, 7th June), in the heat of battle, the Prætorian guards, almost by an involuntary impulse, asserted the superiority of their valour and discipline. The rebel ranks were broken; when the mother and grandmother of the Syrian prince, who, according to their eastern custom, had attended the army, threw themselves from their covered chariots, and, by exciting the compassion of the soldiers, endeavoured to animate their drooping courage. Antoninus himself, who, in the rest of his life, never acted like a man, in this important crisis of his fate approved himself a hero, mounted his horse, and, at the head of his rallied troops, charged sword in hand among the thickest of the enemy; whilst the eunuch Gannys, whose occupations had been confined to female cares and the soft luxury of Asia, displayed the talents of an able and experienced general. The battle still raged with doubtful violence, and Macrinus might have obtained the victory, had he not betrayed his own cause by a shameful and precipitate flight. His cowardice served only to protract his life a few days, and to stamp deserved ignominy on his misfortunes. It is scarcely necessary to add, that his son Diadumenianus was involved in the same fate. As soon as the stubborn Prætorians could be convinced that they fought for a prince who had basely deserted them, they surrendered to the conqueror; the contending parties of the Roman army, mingling tears of joy and tenderness, united under the banners of the imagined son of Caracalla, and the East acknowledged with pleasure the first emperor of Asiatic extraction.

As the attention of the new emperor was diverted by the most trifling amusements, he (A.D. 219) wasted many months in his luxurious progress from Syria to Italy, passed at Nicomedia his first winter after his victory, and deferred till the ensuing summer his triumphal entry into the capital. A faithful picture, however, which preceded his arrival, and was placed by his immediate order over the altar of Victory in the senate-house, conveyed to the Romans the just but unworthy resemblance of his person and manners. He was drawn in his sacerdotal robes of silk and gold, after the loose flowing fashion of the Medes and Phœnicians; his head was covered with a lofty tiara, his numerous collars and bracelets were adorned with gems of an inestimable value. His eyebrows were tinged with black, and his cheeks painted with an artificial red and white. The grave senators confessed with a sigh, that, after having long experienced the stern tyranny of their own countrymen, Rome was at length humbled beneath the effeminate luxury of Oriental despotism.

The Sun was worshipped at Emesa, under the name of Elagabalus, and under the form of a black conical stone, which, as it was universally believed, had fallen from heaven on that sacred place. To his protecting deity, Antoninus, not without some reason, ascribed his elevation to the throne. The display of superstitious gratitude was the only serious business of his reign. The triumph of the God of Emesa over all the religions of the earth, was the great object of his zeal and vanity: and the appellation of Elagabalus (for he presumed as pontiff and favourite to adopt that sacred name) was dearer to him than all the titles of Imperial greatness. In a solemn procession through the streets of Rome, the way was strewed with gold dust; the black stone, set in precious gems, was placed on a chariot drawn by six milk-white horses richly caparisoned. The pious emperor held the reins, and, supported by his ministers, moved slowly backwards, that he might perpetually enjoy the felicity of the divine presence. In a magnificent temple raised on the Palatine Mount, the sacrifices of the god of Elagabalus were celebrated with every circumstance of cost and solemnity. The richest wines, the most extraordinary victims, and the rarest aromatics, were profusely consumed on his altar. Around the altar a chorus of Syrian damsels performed their lascivious dances to the sound of barbarian music, whilst the gravest personages of the state and army, clothed in long Phœnician tunics, officiated in the meanest functions, with affected zeal and secret indignation.

A rational voluptuary adheres with invariable respect to the temperate dictates of nature, and improves the gratifications of sense by social intercourse, endearing connections, and the soft colouring of taste and the imagination. But Elagabalus (I speak of the emperor of that name), corrupted by his youth, his country, and his fortune, abandoned himself to the grossest pleasures with ungoverned fury, and soon found disgust and satiety in the midst of his enjoyments. The inflammatory powers of art were summoned to his aid: the confused multitude of women, of wines, and of dishes, and the studied variety of attitudes and sauces, served to revive his languid appetites. New terms and new inventions in these sciences, the only ones cultivated and patronised by the monarch, signalised his reign, and transmitted his infamy to succeeding times. A capricious prodigality supplied the want of taste and elegance; and whilst Elagabalus lavished away the treasures of his people in the wildest extravagance, his own voice and that of his flatterers applauded a spirit and magnificence unknown to the tameness of his predecessors. To confound the order of seasons and climates, to sport with the passions and prejudices of his subjects, and to subvert every law of nature and decency, were in the number of his most delicious amusements. A long train of concubines, and a rapid succession of wives, among whom was a vestal virgin, ravished by force from her sacred asylum, were insufficient to satisfy the impotence of his passions. The master of the Roman world affected to copy the dress and manners of the female sex, preferred the distaff to the sceptre, and dishonoured the principal dignities of the empire by distributing them among his numerous lovers; one of whom was publicly invested with the title and authority of the emperor's, or, as he more properly styled himself, of the empress's husband.

A demonstration of affection, for his cousin Alexander provoked the jealousy of Elagabalus, and the unseasonable severity he showed in consequence proved instantly fatal to his minions, his mother, and himself. Elagabalus was (A.D. 222, 10th March) massacred by the indignant Prætorians, his mutilated corpse dragged through the streets of the city, and thrown into the Tiber. His memory was branded with eternal infamy by the senate; the justice of whose decree has been ratified by posterity.

In the room of Elagabalus, his cousin Alexander was raised to the throne by the Prætorian guards. But as Alexander was a modest and dutiful youth, of only seventeen years of age, the reins of government were in the hands of two women, of his mother Mamæa, and of Mæsa, his grandmother. After the death of the latter, who survived but a short time the elevation of Alexander, Mamæa remained the sole regent of her son and of the empire.

In every age and country, the wiser, or at least the stronger of the two sexes, has usurped the powers of the state, and confined the other to the cares and pleasures of domestic life. In hereditary monarchies, however, and especially in those of modern Europe, the gallant spirit of chivalry, and the law of succession, have accustomed us to allow a singular exception; and a woman is often acknowledged the absolute sovereign of a great kingdom, in which she would be deemed incapable of exercising the smallest employment, civil or military. But as the Roman emperors were still considered as the generals and magistrates of the republic, their wives and mothers, although distinguished by the name of Augusta, were never associated to their personal honours; and a female reign would have appeared an inexplicable prodigy in the eyes of those primitive Romans who married without love, or loved with delicacy and respect.

The substances, not the pageantry, of power was the object of Mamæa's manly ambition. She maintained an absolute and lasting empire over the mind of her son, and in his affection

the mother could not brook a rival. Alexander, with her consent, married the daughter of a Patrician; but his respect for
his father-in-law, and love for the empress, were inconsistent
with the tenderness or interest of Mamæa. The Patrician was
executed on the ready accusation of treason, and the wife of
Alexander driven with ignominy from the palace, and banished into Africa.

The simple journal of his ordinary occupations exhibits a
pleasing picture of an accomplished emperor, and with some
allowance for the difference of manners, might well deserve
the imitation of modern princes. Alexander rose early; the first
moments of the day were consecrated to private devotion, and
his domestic chapel was filled with the images of those
heroes, who, by improving or reforming human life, had deserved the grateful reverence of posterity. But, as he deemed
the service of mankind the most acceptable worship of the
gods, the greatest part of his morning hours was employed in
his council, where he discussed public affairs, and determined
private causes, with a patience and discretion above his years.
The dryness of business was relieved by the charms of literature: and a portion of time was always set apart for his favourite studies of poetry, history, and philosophy. The works of
Virgil and Horace, the Republics of Plato and Cicero, formed
his taste, enlarged his understanding, and gave him the noblest
ideas of man and government. The exercises of the body succeeded to those of the mind; and Alexander, who was tall,
active, and robust, surpassed most of his equals in the gym-
nastic arts. Refreshed by the use of the bath and a slight din-
ner, he resumed, with new vigour, the business of the day;
and, till the hour of supper, the principal meal of the Romans,
he was attended by his secretaries, with whom he read and
answered the multitude of letters, memorials, and petitions,
that must have been addressed to the master of the greatest
part of the world. His table was served with the most frugal
simplicity; and whenever he was at liberty to consult his own
inclination, the company consisted of a few select friends,
men of learning and virtue, amongst whom Ulpian was constantly invited.

The Prætorian guards were attached to the youth of Alexander. They loved him as a tender pupil, whom they had saved from a tyrant's fury, and placed on the Imperial throne. That amiable prince was sensible of the obligation; but as his gratitude was restrained within the limits of reason and justice, they soon were more dissatisfied with the virtues of Alexander, than they had ever been with the vices of Elagabalus. Their præfect, the wise Ulpian, was the friend of the laws and of the people; he was considered as the enemy of the soldiers, and to his pernicious counsels every scheme of reformation was imputed. Some trifling accident blew up their discontent into a furious mutiny; and a civil war raged, during three days, in Rome, whilst the life of that excellent minister was defended by the grateful people. Terrified, at length, by the sight of some houses in flames, and by the threats of a general conflagration, the people yielded with a sigh, and left the virtuous, but unfortunate, Ulpian to his fate. He was pursued into the Imperial palace, and massacred at the feet of his master, who vainly strove to cover him with the purple, and to obtain his pardon from the inexorable soldiers. Such was the deplorable weakness of government, that the emperor was unable to revenge his murdered friend and his insulted dignity, without stooping to the arts of patience and dissimulation.

The lenity of the emperor confirmed the insolence of the troops; the legions imitated the example of the guards, and defended their prerogative of licentiousness with the same furious obstinacy. The administration of Alexander was an unavailing struggle against the corruption of his age.

The dissolute tyranny of Commodus, the civil wars occasioned by his death, and the new maxims of policy introduced by the house of Severus, had all contributed to increase the dangerous power of the army, and to obliterate the faint image of laws and liberty that was still impressed on the minds of the Romans. This internal change, which undermined the foundations of the empire, we have endeavoured to explain with some degree of order and perspicuity. The personal characters of the emperors, their victories, laws, follies, and fortunes, can interest us no farther than as they are connected with the general history of the Decline and Fall of the monarchy. Our constant attention to that great object will not suffer us to overlook a most important edict of Antoninus Caracalla, which communicated to all the free inhabitants of the empire the name and privileges of Roman citizens. His unbounded liberality flowed not, however, from the sentiments of a generous mind; it was the sordid result of avarice, and will naturally be illustrated by some observations on the finances of that state, from the victorious ages of the commonwealth to the reign of Alexander Severus.

During more than two hundred years after the conquest of Veii, the victories of the republic added less to the wealth than to the power of Rome. The states of Italy paid their tribute in military service only, and the vast force both by sea and land, which was exerted in the Punic wars, was maintained at the expense of the Romans themselves. That high-spirited people (such is often the generous enthusiasm of freedom) cheerfully submitted to the most excessive but voluntary burdens, in the just confidence that they should speedily enjoy the rich harvest of their labours. Their expectations were not disappointed. In the course of a few years, the riches of Syracuse, of Carthage, of Macedonia, and of Asia, were brought in triumph to Rome. The treasures of Perseus alone amounted to near two millions sterling, and the Roman people, the sovereign of so many nations, was for ever delivered from the weight of taxes. The increasing revenue of the provinces was found sufficient to defray the ordinary establishment of war and government, and the superfluous mass of gold and silver was deposited in the temple of Saturn, and reserved for any unforeseen emergency of the state.

(The closing pages of Chapter VI are devoted to a full but somewhat antiquated analysis of the revenues of the Roman Empire.)

CHAPTER SEVEN

The Elevation and Tyranny of Maximin—Rebellion in Africa and Italy, under the Authority of the Senate—Civil Wars and Seditions—Violent Deaths of Maximin and his Son, of Maximus and Balbinus, and of the three Gordians—Usurpation and secular Games of Philip

Of the various forms of government which have prevailed in the world, an hereditary monarchy seems to present the fairest scope for ridicule. Is it possible to relate, without an indignant smile, that, on the father's decease, the property of a nation, like that of a drove of oxen, descends to his infant son, as yet unknown to mankind and to himself; and that the bravest warriors and the wisest statesmen, relinquishing their natural right to empire, approach the royal cradle with bended knees and protestations of inviolable fidelity? Satire and declamation may paint these obvious topics in the most dazzling colours, but our more serious thoughts will respect a useful prejudice, that establishes a rule of succession, independent of the passions of mankind; and we shall cheerfully acquiesce in any expedient which deprives the multitude of the dangerous, and indeed the ideal, power of giving themselves a master.

In the cool shade of retirement, we may easily devise imaginary forms of government, in which the sceptre shall be

constantly bestowed on the most worthy, by the free and in-
corrupt suffrage of the whole community. Experience over-
turns these airy fabrics, and teaches us that, in a large society,
the election of a monarch can never devolve to the wisest, or
to the most numerous, part of the people. The army is the only
order of men sufficiently united to concur the same sentiments, and powerful enough to impose them on the rest of
their fellow-citizens: but the temper of soldiers, habituated at
once to violence and to slavery, renders them very unfit guardians of a legal, or even a civil, constitution. Justice, humanity,
or political wisdom, are qualities they are too little acquainted
with in themselves, to appreciate them in others. Valour will
acquire their esteem, and liberality will purchase their suffrage; but the first of these merits is often lodged in the most
savage breasts; the latter can only exert itself at the expense of
the public; and both may be turned against the possessor of the
throne, by the ambition of a daring rival.

The superior prerogative of birth, when it has obtained the
sanction of time and popular opinion, is the plainest and least
invidious of all distinctions among mankind. The acknowledged right extinguishes the hopes of faction, and the conscious security disarms the cruelty of the monarch. To the firm
establishment of this idea, we owe the peaceful succession,
and mild administration, of European monarchies. To the defect of it, we must attribute the frequent civil wars, through
which an Asiatic despot is obliged to cut his way to the throne
of his fathers. In Rome the right to the throne, which none
could claim from birth, every one assumed from merit. The
daring hopes of ambition were set loose from the salutary
restraints of law and prejudice; and the meanest of mankind
might, without folly, entertain a hope of being raised by valour and fortune to a rank in the army, in which a single crime
would enable him to wrest the sceptre of the world from his
feeble and unpopular master. After the murder of Alexander
Severus, and the elevation of Maximin, no emperor could
think himself safe upon the throne, and every barbarian peasant of the frontier might aspire to that august, but dangerous
station.

About thirty-two years before that event, the emperor Severus, returning from an eastern expedition, halted in Thrace, to celebrate, with military games, the birthday of his younger son, Geta. The country flocked in crowds to behold their sovereign, and a young barbarian of gigantic stature earnestly solicited, in his rude dialect, that he might be allowed to contend for the prize of wrestling. As the pride of discipline would have been disgraced in the overthrow of a Roman soldier by a Thracian peasant, he was matched with the stoutest followers of the camp, sixteen of whom he successively laid on the ground. His victory was rewarded by some trifling gifts, and a permission to enlist in the troops. The next day, the happy barbarian was distinguished above a crowd of recruits, dancing and exulting after the fashion of his country. As soon as he perceived that he had attracted the emperor's notice, he instantly ran up to his horse, and followed him on foot, without the least appearance of fatigue, in a long and rapid career. "Thracian," said Severus, with astonishment, "art thou disposed to wrestle after thy race?" "Most willingly, Sir," replied the unwearied youth, and, almost in a breath, overthrew seven of the strongest soldiers in the army. A gold collar was the prize of his matchless vigour and activity, and he was immediately appointed to serve in the horse-guards who always attended on the person of the sovereign.

Maximin, for that was his name, though born on the territories of the empire, descended from a mixed race of barbarians. His father was a Goth, and his mother of the nation of the Alani. He displayed, on every occasion, a valour equal to his strength; and his native fierceness was soon tempered or disguised by the knowledge of the world. Under the reign of Severus and his son, he obtained the rank of centurion, with the favour and esteem of both those princes, the former of whom was an excellent judge of merit. Gratitude forbade Maximin to serve under the assassin of Caracalla. Honour taught him to decline the effeminate insults of Elagabalus. On the accession of Alexander he returned to court, and was placed by the prince in a station useful to the service and honourable to himself. The fourth legion, to which he was appointed tribune, soon became, under his care, the best disciplined of the whole army. With the general applause of the soldiers, who bestowed on their favourite hero the names of Ajax and Hercules, he was successively promoted to the first military command; and had not he still retained too much of his savage origin, the emperor might perhaps have given his own sister in marriage to the son of Maximin.

Instead of securing his fidelity, these favours served only to inflame the ambition of the Thracian peasant, who deemed his fortune inadequate to his merit, as long as he was constrained to acknowledge a superior. Though a stranger to real wisdom, he was not devoid of a selfish cunning, which showed him that the emperor had lost the affection of the army, and taught him to improve their discontent to his own advantage. It is easy for faction and calumny to shed their poison on the administration of the best of princes, and to accuse even their virtues, by artfully confounding them with those vices to which they bear the nearest affinity. The troops listened with pleasure to the emissaries of Maximin. They blushed at their own ignominious patience, which, during thirteen years, had supported the vexatious discipline imposed by an effeminate Syrian, the timid slave of his mother and of the senate. It was time, they cried, to cast away that useless phantom of the civil power, and to elect for their prince and general a real soldier, educated in camps, exercised in war, who would assert the glory, and distribute among his companions the treasures, of the empire. A great army was at that time assembled on the banks of the Rhine, under the command of the emperor himself, who, almost immediately after his return from the Persian war, had been obliged to march against the barbarians of Germany. The important care of training and reviewing the new levies was intrusted to Maximin. One day (A.D. 235, 19th March), as he entered the field of exercise, the troops, either from a sudden impulse or a formed conspiracy saluted him emperor, silenced by their loud acclamations his obstinate refusal, and hastened to consummate their rebellion by the murder of Alexander Severus.

The former tyrants, Caligula and Nero, Commodus and Caracalla, were all dissolute and inexperienced youths, educated in the purple, and corrupted by the pride of empire, the

luxury of Rome, and the perfidious voice of flattery. The cruelty of Maximin was derived from a different source, the fear
of contempt. Though he depended on the attachment of the
soldiers, who loved him for virtues like their own, he was
conscious that his mean and barbarian origin, his savage appearance, and his total ignorance of the arts and institutions of
civil life, formed a very unfavourable contrast with the amiable manners of the unhappy Alexander. He remembered that,
in his humbler fortune, he had often waited before the door of
the haughty nobles of Rome, and had been denied admittance
by the insolence of their slaves. He recollected too the friendship by a few who had relieved his poverty, and assisted his
rising hopes. But those who had spurned, and those who had
protected the Thracian, were guilty of the same crime, the
knowledge of his original obscurity. For this crime many were
put to death; and by the execution of several of his benefactors, Maximin published, in characters of blood, the indelible
history of his baseness and ingratitude.

As long as the cruelty of Maximin was confined to the
illustrious senators, or even to the bold adventurers, who in
the court or army expose themselves to the caprice of fortune,
the body of the people viewed their sufferings with indifference, or perhaps with pleasure. But the tyrant's avarice, stimulated by the insatiate desires of the soldiers, at length
attacked the public property. Every city of the empire was
possessed of an independent revenue, destined to purchase
corn for the multitude, and to supply the expenses of the
games and entertainments. By a single act of authority, the
whole mass of wealth was at once confiscated for the use of
the Imperial treasury. The temples were stripped of their most
valuable offerings of gold and silver, and the statues of gods,
heroes, and emperors, were melted down and coined into
money. These impious orders could not be executed without
tumults and massacres, as in many places the people chose
rather to die in the defence of their altars, than to behold in the
midst of peace their cities exposed to the rapine and cruelty of
war. The soldiers themselves, among whom this sacrilegious
plunder was distributed, received it with a blush; and, hardened as they were in acts of violence, they dreaded the just

reproaches of their friends and relations. Throughout the Roman world a general cry of indignation was heard, imploring vengeance on the common enemy of human kind; and at length, by an act of private oppression, a peaceful and unarmed province was driven into rebellion against him.

The province of Africa, which had been atrociously oppressed by Maximin's procurator, erected the standard of rebellion against the sovereign of the Roman empire. They rested their hopes on the hatred of mankind against Maximin, and they judiciously resolved to oppose to that detested tyrant, an emperor whose mild virtues had already acquired the love and esteem of the Romans, and whose authority over the province would give weight and stability to the enterprise. Gordianus, their proconsul, and the object of their choice, refused, with unfeigned reluctance, and dangerous honour, and begged with tears that they would suffer him to terminate in peace a long and innocent life, without staining his feeble age with civil blood. Their menaces compelled him to accept the Imperial purple, his only refuge indeed against the jealous cruelty of Maximin; since, according to the reasoning of tyrants, those who have been esteemed worthy of the throne deserve death, and those who deliberate have already rebelled.

When Gordian reluctantly accepted the purple, he was above fourscore years old; a last and valuable remains of the happy age of the Antonines, whose virtues he revived in his own conduct and celebrated in an elegant poem of thirty books. With the venerable proconsul, his son, who had accompanied him into Africa as his lieutenant, was likewise declared emperor. His manners were less pure, but his character was equally amiable with that of his father. Twenty-two acknowledged concubines, and a library of sixty-two thousand volumes, attested the variety of his inclinations, and from the productions which he left behind him it appears that the former as well as the latter were designed for use rather that ostentation.

The inclinations of the senate were neither doubtful nor divided. As soon as their resolution was decided, they convoked in the temple of Castor the whole body of the senate, according to an ancient form of secrecy, calculated to awaken their attention, and to conceal their decrees. "Conscript fathers," said the consul Syllanus, "the two Gordians, both of consular dignity, the one your proconsul, the other your lieutenant, have been declared emperors by the general consent of Africa. Let us return thanks," he boldly continued, "to the youth of Thysdrus; let us return thanks to the faithful people of Carthage, our generous deliverers from an horrid monster —why do you hear me thus coolly, thus timidly? Why do you cast those anxious looks on each other? why hesitate? Maximin is a public enemy! may his enmity soon expire with him, and may we long enjoy the produce and felicity of Gordian the father, the valour and constancy of Gordian the son!" The noble ardour of the consul revived the languid spirit of the senate. By an unanimous decree the election of the Gordians was ratified, Maximin, his son, and his adherents, were pronounced enemies of their country and liberal rewards were offered to whomsoever had the courage and good fortune to destroy them.

While the cause of the Gordians was embraced with such diffusive ardour, the Gordians themselves (A.D. 237, 3rd July) were no more. The feeble court of Carthage was alarmed with the rapid approach of Capelianus, governor of Mauritania, who, with a small band of veterans, and a fierce host of barbarians, attacked a faithful but unwarlike province. The younger Gordian sallied out to meet the enemy at the head of a few guards, and a numerous undisciplined multitude, educated in the peaceful luxury of Carthage. His useless valour served only to procure him an honourable death, in the field of battle. His aged father, whose reign had not exceeded thirty-six days, put an end to his life on the first news of the defeat. Carthage, destitute of defence, opened her gates to the conqueror, and Africa was exposed to the rapacious cruelty of a slave, obliged to satisfy his unrelenting master with a large account of blood and treasure.

The fate of the Gordians filled Rome with just, but unexpected terror. The senate convoked in the temple of Concord, affected to transact the common business of the day, and seemed to decline, with trembling anxiety the consideration of their own and the public danger. A silent consternation prevailed on the assembly, till a senator, of the name and family of Trajan, awakened his brethren from their fatal lethargy. He represented to them, that the choice of cautious dilatory measures had been long since out of their power; that Maximin, implacable by nature, and exasperated by injuries, was advancing towards Italy, at the head of the military force of the empire; and that their only remaining alternative was either to meet him bravely in the field, or tamely to expect the tortures and ignominious death reserved for unsuccessful rebellion. "We have lost," continued he, "two excellent princes; but unless we desert ourselves, the hopes of the republic have not perished with the Gordians. Many are the senators, whose virtues have deserved, and whose abilities would sustain, the Imperial dignity. Let us elect two emperors, one of whom may conduct the war against the public enemy, whilst his colleague remains at Rome to direct the civil administration. I cheerfully expose myself to the dangers and envy of the nomination, and give my vote in favour of Maximus and Balbinus. Ratify my choice, conscript fathers, or appoint, in their place, others more worthy of the empire." The general apprehension silenced the whispers of jealousy; the merit of the candidates was universally acknowledged; and the house resounded with the sincere acclamations, of "long life and victory to the emperors Maximus and Balbinus. You are happy in the judgment of the senate; may the republic be happy under your administration!" The two colleagues had both been consuls (Balbinus had twice enjoyed that honourable office), both had been named among the twenty lieutenants of the senate; and since the one was sixty and the other seventy-four years old, they had both attained a full maturity of age and experience.

After the senate had conferred on Maximus and Balbinus an equal portion of the consular and tribunitian powers, the title of Fathers of their country, and the joint office of Supreme Pontiff, they ascended to the Capitol, to return thanks to the gods, protectors of Rome. The solemn rites of sacrifice were disturbed by a sedition of the people. The licentious multitude neither loved the rigid Maximus, nor did they sufficiently fear the mild and humane Balbinus. Their increasing numbers surrounded the temple of Jupiter; with obstinate cla-

mours they asserted their inherent right of consenting to the
election of their sovereign; they demanded, with an apparent
moderation, that, besides, the two emperors chosen by the
senate, a third should be added of the family of the Gordians,
as a just return of gratitude to those princes who had sacrificed
their lives for the republic. At the head of the city-guards, and
the youth of the equestrian order, Maximus and Balbinus attempted to cut their way through the seditious multitude. The
multitude, armed with sticks and stones, drove them back into
the Capitol. It is prudent to yield when the contest, whatever
may be the issue of it, must be fatal to both parties. A boy,
only thirteen years of age, the grandson of the elder, and
nephew of the younger, Gordian, was produced to the people,
invested with the ornaments and title of Cæsar. The tumult
was appeased by this easy condescension; and the two emperors, as soon as they had been peaceably acknowledged in
Rome, prepared to defend Italy against the common enemy.

Whilst in Rome and Africa revolutions succeeded each
other with such amazing rapidity, the mind of Maximin was
agitated by the most furious passions. He is said to have received the news of the rebellion of the Gordians, and of the
decree of the senate against him, not with the temper of a
man, but the rage of a wild beast; which, as it could not
discharge itself on the distant senate, threatened the life of his
son, of his friends, and of all who ventured to approach his
person. The grateful intelligence of the death of the Gordians
was quickly followed by the assurance that the senate, laying
aside all hopes of pardon or accommodation, had substituted
in their room two emperors, with whose merit he could not be
unacquainted. Revenge was the only consolation left to Maximin, and revenge could only be obtained by arms.

In the campaign against Maximus which ensued, Maximin's fierce temper was exasperated by disappointments,
which he computed to the cowardice of his army; and his
wanton and ill-timed cruelty, instead of striking terror, inspired hatred and a just desire of revenge. A party of Prætorian guards, who trembled for their wives and children in the
camp of Alba, near Rome, executed the sentence of the senate. Maximin, abandoned by his guards, was (A.D. 238,

April) slain in his tent, with his son (whom he had associated to the honours of the purple), Anulinus the præfect, and the principal ministers of his tyranny. Such was the deserved fate of a brutal savage, destitute, as he has generally been represented, of every sentiment that distinguished a civilised, or even a human being. The body was suited to the soul. The stature of Maximin exceeded the measure of eight feet, and circumstances almost incredible are related of his matchless strength and appetite. Had he lived in a less enlightened age, tradition and poetry might well have described him as one of those monstrous giants, whose supernatural power was constantly exerted for the destruction of mankind.

It is easier to conceive than to describe the universal joy of the Roman world on the fall of the tyrant, the news of which is said to have been carried in four days from Aquileia to Rome.

When the senate elected both Maximus and Balbinus as princes, it is probable that, besides the declared reason of providing for the various emergencies of peace and war, they were actuated by the secret desire of weakening by division the despotism of the supreme magistrate. Their policy was effectual, but it proved fatal both to their emperors and to themselves. The jealousy of power was soon exasperated by the difference of character. Maximus despised Balbinus as a luxurious noble, and was in his turn disdained by his colleague as an obscure soldier. Their silent discord was understood rather than seen; but the mutual consciousness prevented them from uniting in any vigorous measures of defence against their common enemies of the Prætorian camp. The whole city was (A.D. 238, 15th July) employed in the Capitoline games, and the emperors were left almost alone in the palace. On a sudden they were alarmed by the approach of a troop of desperate assassins. Ignorant of each other's situation or designs, for they already occupied very distant apartments, afraid to give or to receive assistance, they wasted the important moments in idle debates and fruitless recriminations. The arrival of the guards put an end to the vain strife. They seized on these emperors of the senate, for such they called them with malicious contempt, stripped them of their garments, and dragged them in insolent triumph through the streets of Rome, with a design of inflicting a slow and cruel death on those unfortunate princes. The fear of a rescue from the faithful Germans of the Imperial guards, shortened their tortures; and their bodies, mangled with a thousand wounds, were left exposed to the insults or to the pity of the populace.

In the space of a few months, six princes had been cut off by the sword. Gordian, who had already received the title of Cæsar, was the only person that occurred to the soldiers as proper to fill the vacant throne. They carried him to the camp, and unanimously saluted him Augustus and Emperor. His name was dear to the senate and people; his tender age promised a long impunity of military licence; and the submission of Rome and the provinces to the choice of the Prætorian guards, saved the republic, at the expense indeed of its freedom and dignity, from the horrors of a new civil war in the heart of the capital.

As the third Gordian was only nineteen years of age at the time of his death, the history of his life, were it known to us with greater accuracy than it really is, would contain little more than the account of his education, and the conduct of the ministers, who by turns abused or guided the simplicity of his inexperienced youth. Immediately after his accession, he fell into the hands of his mother's eunuchs, that pernicious vermin of the East, who, since the days of Elagabalus, had infested the Roman palace. By the artful conspiracy of these wretches, an impenetrable veil was drawn between an innocent prince and his oppressed subjects, the virtuous disposition of Gordian was deceived, and the honours of the empire sold without his knowledge, though in very public manner, to the most worthless of mankind. We are ignorant by what fortunate accident the emperor escaped from this ignominious slavery, and devolved his confidence on a minister whose wise counsels had no object except the glory of his sovereign and the happiness of the people. It should seem that (A.D. 240) love and learning introduced Misitheus to the favour of Gordian. The young prince married the daughter of his master of rhetoric, and promoted his father-in-law to the first offices of the empire. Two admirable letters that passed between them are still extant.

The minister, with the conscious dignity of virtue, congratulates Gordian that he is delivered from the tyranny of the eunuchs, and still more that he is sensible of his deliverance. The emperor acknowledges, with an amiable confusion, the errors of his past conduct; and laments, with singular propriety, the misfortune of a monarch, from whom a venal tribe of couriers perpetually labour to conceal the truth.

The prosperity of Gordian expired with Misitheus, who died of flux, not without very strong suspicions of poison. Philip, his successor (A.D. 243) in the præfecture, was an Arab by birth, and consequently, in the earlier part of his life, a robber by profession. His rise from so obscure a station to the first dignities of the empire, seems to prove that he was a bold and able leader. But his boldness prompted him to aspire to the throne, and his abilities were employed to supplant, not to serve, his indulgent master. The minds of the soldiers were irritated by an artificial scarcity, created by his contrivance in the camp; and the distress of the army was attributed to the youth and incapacity of the prince. It is not in our power to trace the successive steps of the secret conspiracy and open sedition, which were at length fatal to Gordian. A sepulchral monument was erected to his memory on the spot where (A.D. 244, March) he was killed, near the conflux of the Euphrates with the little river Aboras. The fortunate Philip, raised to the empire by the votes of the soldiers, found a ready obedience from the senate and the provinces.

(During the third and fourth centuries Persia in the east and Germany in the north became increasingly important factors in the history of the Roman Empire.

CHAPTERS EIGHT and NINE

deal with the geography, antiquities, history, and cultural institutions of these peoples.)

CHAPTER TEN

The Emperors Decius, Gallus, Æmilianus, Valerian, and Gallienus—The general Irruption of the Barbarians—The Thirty Tyrants

From the great secular games celebrated by Philip to the death of the emperor Gallienus there elapsed (A.D. 248–268) twenty years of shame and misfortune. During the calamitous period every instant of time was marked, every province of the Roman world was afflicted by barbarous invaders and military tyrants, and the ruined empire seemed to approach the last and fatal moment of its dissolution. The confusion of the times, and the scarcity of authentic memorials, oppose equal difficulties to the historian, who attempts to preserve a clear and unbroken thread of narration. Surrounded with imperfect fragments, always concise, often obscure, and sometimes contradictory, he is reduced to collect, to compare, and to conjecture: and though he ought never to place his conjectures in the rank of facts, yet the knowledge of human nature, and of the sure operation of its fierce and unrestrained passions, might, on some occasions, supply the want of historical materials.

There is not, for instance, any difficulty in conceiving that the successive murders of so many emperors had loosened all the ties of allegiance between the prince and people; that all

the generals of Philip were disposed to imitate the example of
their master; and that the caprice of armies, long since habituated to frequent and violent revolutions, might any day raise
to the throne of the most obscure of their fellow-soldiers. History can only add that the rebellion against the emperor Philip
broke out in the summer of the year two hundred and forty-
nine, among the legions of Mæsia; and that a subaltern officer,
named Marinus, was the object of their seditious choice. Philip was alarmed. He dreaded lest the treason of the Mæsian
army should prove the first spark of a general conflagration.
Distracted with the consciousness of his guilt and of his
danger, he communicated the intelligence to the senate. A
gloomy silence prevailed, the effect of fear and perhaps of
disaffection: till at length Decius, one of the assembly, assuming a spirit worthy of his noble extraction, ventured to discover more intrepidity than the emperor seemed to possess.
He treated the whole business with contempt, as a hasty and
inconsiderate tumult, and Philip's rival as a phantom of royalty, who in a very few days would be destroyed by the same
inconstancy that had created him. The speedy completion of
the prophecy inspired Philip with a just esteem for so able a
counsellor: and Decius appeared to him the only person capable of restoring peace and discipline to an army whose tumultuous spirit did not immediately subside after the murder of
Marinus. Decius who long resisted his own nomination,
seems to have insinuated the danger of presenting a leader of
merit to the angry and apprehensive minds of the soldiers; and
his prediction was again confirmed by the event. The legion of
Mæsia forced their judge to become (A.D. 249) their accomplice. They left him only the alternative of death or the purple.
His subsequent conduct, after that decisive measure, was un-
avoidable. He conducted or followed his army to the confines
of Italy, whither Philip, collecting all his force to repel the
formidable competitor whom he had raised up, advanced to
meet him. The Imperial troops were superior in number; but
the rebels formed an army of veterans, commanded by an able
and experienced leader. Philip was either killed in the battle or
put to death a few days afterwards at Verona. His son and
associate in the empire was massacred at Rome by the Prætor-

ian guards; and the victorious Decius, with more favourable circumstances than the ambition of that age can usually plead, was universally acknowledged by the senate and provinces. It is reported that, immediately after his reluctant acceptance of the title of Augustus, he had assured Philip, by a private message, of his innocence and loyalty, solemnly protesting that, on his arrival in Italy, he would resign the imperial ornaments and return to the condition of an obedient subject. His professions might be sincere. But in the situation where fortune had placed him it was scarcely possible that he could either forgive or be forgiven.

The emperor Decius had employed a few months in the works of peace and the administration of justice, when (A.D. 250) he was summoned to the banks of the Danube by the invasion of the GOTHS. This is the first considerable occasion in which history mentions that great people, who afterwards broke the Roman power, sacked the Capitol, and reigned in Gaul, Spain, and Italy. So memorable was the part which they acted in the subversion of the Western empire that the name of of GOTHS is frequently but improperly used as a general appellation of rude and warlike barbarism.

Decius found (A.D. 250) the Goths engaged before Nicopolis, on the Jatrus, one of the many monuments of Trajan's victories. On his approach they raised the siege, but with a design only of marching away to a conquest of greater importance, the siege of Philippopolis, a city of Thrace, founded by the father of Alexander, near the foot of mount Hæmus. Decius followed them through a difficult country, and by forced marches; but when he imagined himself at a considerable distance from the rear of the Goths, Cniva, the Gothic king, turned with rapid fury on his pursuers. The camp of the Romans was surprised and pillaged, and, for the first time, their emperor fled in disorder before a troop of half-armed barbarians. After a long resistance, Philippopolis, destitute of succour, was taken by storm. A hundred thousand persons are reported to have been massacred in the sack of that great city. Many prisoners of consequence became a valuable accession to the spoil; and Priscus, a brother of the late emperor Philip, blushed not to assume the purple under the protection of the

barbarous enemies of Rome. The time, however, consumed in
that tedious siege enabled Decius to revive the courage, restore the discipline, and recruit the numbers of his troops. He
intercepted several parties of Carpi, and other Germans, who
were hastening to share the victory of their countrymen, intrusted the passes of the mountains to officers of approved
valour and fidelity; repaired and strengthened the fortifications
of the Danube, and exerted his utmost vigilance to oppose
either the progress or the retreat of the Goths. Encouraged by
the return of fortune, he anxiously waited for an opportunity
to retrieve, by a great and decisive blow, his own glory and
that of the Roman arms.

At the same time when Decius was struggling with the
violence of the tempest, his mind, calm and deliberate amidst
the tumult of war, investigated the more general causes that,
since the age of the Antonines, had so impetuously urged the
decline of the Roman greatness. He soon discovered that it
was impossible to replace that greatness on a permanent basis
without restoring public virtue, ancient principles and manners, and the oppressed majesty of the laws. To execute this
noble but arduous design, he first resolved to revive the obsolete officer of censor; an office which, as long as it had subsisted in its pristine integrity, had so much contributed to the
perpetuity of the state, till it was usurped and gradually neglected by the Cæsars. Conscious that the favour of the sovereign may confer power, but that the esteem of the people
alone bestow authority, he submitted the choice of the censor
to the unbiased voice of the senate. By their unanimous votes,
or rather acclamations, Valerian, who was afterwards emperor, and who then served with distinction in the army of
Decius, was (A.D. 251, 27th Oct.) declared the most worthy
of that exalted honour. As soon as the decree of the senate was
transmitted to the emperor, he assembled a great council in his
camp, and, before the investiture of the censor elect, he ap-
prised him of the difficulty and importance of his great office.
"Happy Valerian," said the prince to his distinguished subject,
"happy in the general approbation of the senate and of the
Roman republic! Accept the censorship of mankind; and judge
of our manners. You will select those who deserve to continue

members of the senate; you will restore the equestrian order to its ancient splendour; you will improve the revenue, yet moderate the public burdens. You will distinguish into regular classes the various and infinite multitude of citizens, and accurately review the military strength, the wealth, the virtue, and the resources of Rome. Your decisions shall obtain the force of laws. The army, the palace, the ministers of justice, and the great officers of the empire, are all subject to your tribunal. None are exempted, excepting only the ordinary consuls, the præfect of the city, the king of the sacrifices, and (as long as she preserves her chastity inviolate) the eldest of the vestal virgins. Even these few, who may not dread the severity, will anxiously solicit the esteem, of the Roman censor."

A magistrate, invested with such extensive powers, would have appeared not so much the minister as the colleague of his sovereign. Valerian justly dreaded an elevation so full of envy and of suspicion. He modestly urged the alarming greatness of the trust, his own insufficiency, and the incurable corruption of the times. He artfully insinuated that the office of censor was inseparable from the Imperial dignity, and that the feeble hands of a subject were unequal to the support of such an immense weight of cares and of power. The approaching event of war soon put an end to the prosecution of a project so specious but so impracticable; and whilst it preserved Valerian from the danger, saved the emperor Decius from the disappointment which would most probably have attended it. A censor may maintain, he can never restore, the morals of a state. It is impossible for such a magistrate to exert his authority with benefit, or even with effect, unless he is supported by a quick sense of honour and virtue in the minds of the people, by a decent reverence for the public opinion, and by a train of useful prejudices combating on the side of national manners. In a period when these principles are annihilated, the censorial jurisdiction must either sink into empty pageantry, or be converted into a partial instrument of vexatious oppression. It was easier to vanquish the Goths than to eradicate the public vices; yet even in the first of these enterprises Decius lost his army and his life.

After initial successes against the Goths, Decius and his

army were trapped in a morass, and so thoroughly defeated that the body of the emperor could not be found. Such was the fate of Decius, in the fiftieth year of his age; together with his son he deserved to be compared, both in life and in death, with the brightest examples of ancient virtue. This fatal blow humbled, for a very little time, the insolence of the legions, and they awaited the decree of the senate for the regulation of the succession. From a just regard for the memory of Decius, the imperial title was conferred on Hostilianus, his only surviving son; but an equal rank, with more effectual power, was granted to Gallus, whose experience and ability seemed equal to the great trust of guardian to the young prince and the distressed empire.

In earlier generations Roman emperors had displayed their greatness, and even their policy, by the regular exercise of a steady and moderate liberality towards the allies of the state. They relieved the poverty of the barbarians, honoured their merit, and recompensed their fidelity. These voluntary marks of bounty were understood to flow not from the fears, but merely from the generosity or the gratitude of the Romans; and whilst presents and subsidies were liberally distributed among friends and suppliants, they were sternly refused to such as claimed them as a debt. But this stipulation of annual payment to a victorious enemy appeared without disguise in the light of an ignominious tribute; the minds of the Romans were not yet accustomed to accept such unequal laws from a tribe of barbarians; and the prince, who by a necessary concession had probably saved his country, became the object of the general contempt and aversion. The death of Hostilianus, though it happened in the midst of a raging pestilence, was interpreted as the personal crime of Gallus; and even the defeat of the late emperor was ascribed by the voice of suspicion to the perfidious counsels of his hated successor. The tranquillity which the empire enjoyed during the first year of his administration served rather to inflame than to appease the public discontent; and, as soon as the apprehensions of war were removed, the infamy of the peace was more deeply and more sensibly felt.

But the Romans were irritated to a still higher degree when

they discovered that they had not even secured their repose, though at the expense of their honour. The dangerous secret of the wealth and weakness of the empire had been revealed to the world. New swarms of barbarians, encouraged (A.D. 253) by the success, and not conceiving themselves bound by the obligation, of their brethren, spread devastation through the Illyrian provinces, and terror as far as the gates of Rome. The defence of the monarchy, which seemed abandoned by the pusillanimous emperor, was assumed by Æmilianus, governor of Pannonia and Mæsia; who rallied the scattered forces, and revived the fainting spirits of the troops. The barbarians were unexpectedly attacked, routed, chased, and pursued beyond the Danube. The victorious leader distributed as a donative the money collected for the tribute, and the acclamations of the soldiers proclaimed him emperor on the field of battle. Gallus, who, careless of the general welfare, indulged himself in the pleasures of Italy, was almost in the same instant informed of the success of the revolt and of the rapid approach of his aspiring lieutenant. He advanced to meet him as far as the plains of Spoleto. When the armies came in sight of each other, the soldiers of Gallus compared the ignominious conduct of their sovereign with the glory of his rival. They admired the valour of Æmilianus; they were attracted by his liberality, for he offered a considerable increase of pay to all deserters. The murder of Gallus, and of his son Volusianus, put an end to the civil war; and the senate (A.D. 253, May) gave a legal sanction to the rights of conquest. The letters of Æmilianus to that assembly displayed a mixture of moderation and vanity. He assured them that he should resign to their wisdom the civil administration; and, contenting himself with the quality of their general, would in a short time assert the glory of Rome, and deliver the empire from all the barbarians both of the North and of the East. His pride was flattered by the applause of the senate; and medals are still extant representing him with the name and attributes of Hercules and Victor and of Mars the Avenger.

If the new monarch possessed the abilities, he wanted the time necessary to fulfil these splendid promises. Less than four months intervened between his victory and his fall. He had vanquished Gallus: he sunk under the weight of a competitor more formidable than Gallus. That unfortunate prince had sent Valerian, already distinguished by the honourable title of censor, to bring the legions of Gaul and Germany to his aid. Valerian executed that commission with zeal and fidelity; and as he arrived too late to save his sovereign, he resolved to revenge him. The troops of Æmilianus, who still lay encamped in the plains of Spoleto, were awed by the sanctity of his character, but much more by the superior strength of his army; and as they were now become as incapable of personal attachment as they had always been of constitutional principle, they (A.D. 253, Aug.) readily imbrued their hands in the blood of a prince who had so lately been the object of their partial choice. The guilt was theirs, but the advantage of it was Valerian's; who obtained the possession of the throne by the means indeed of a civil war, but with a degree of innocence singular in that age of revolutions; since he owned neither gratitude nor allegiance to his predecessor whom he dethroned. Valerian was about sixty years of age when he was invested with the purple, not by the caprice of the populace, or the clamours of the army, but by the unanimous voice of the Roman world.

Instead of making a judicious choice, which would have confirmed his reign and endeared his memory, Valerian, consulting only the dictates of affection or vanity, immediately invested with the supreme honours his son Gallienus, a youth whose effeminate vices had been hitherto concealed by the obscurity of a private station. The joint government of the father and the son subsisted about seven, and the sole administration of Gallienus continued about eight years (A.D. 253-268). But the whole period was one uninterrupted series of confusion and calamity. As the Roman empire was at the same time, and on every side, attacked by the blind fury of foreign invaders, and the wild ambition of domestic usurpers, we shall consult order and perspicuity by pursuing not so much the doubtful arrangement of dates as the more natural distribution of subjects. The most dangerous enemies of Rome, during the reigns of Valerian and Galienus, were, 1. The Franks; 2. The Alemanni; 3. The Goths; and 4. The Persians. Under these general appellations we may comprehend the adventures of less considerable tribes, whose obscure and uncouth names would only serve to oppress the memory and perplex the attention of the reader.

(There follow accounts of the origin, migrations, and inter-actions with Roman interests of the Franks, Suevi, Alemanni, Goths, and Persians. Our account resumes with the victory of the Persian king Sapor over Valerian.)

The voice of history, which is often little more than the organ of hatred or flattery, reproaches Sapor with a proud abuse of the rights of conquest. We are told that Valerian, in chains, but invested with the Imperial purple, was exposed to the multitude, a constant spectacle of fallen greatness; and that whenever the Persian monarch mounted on horseback, he placed his foot on the neck of a Roman emperor. Notwith-standing all the remonstrances of his allies, who repeatedly advised him to remember the vicissitude of fortune, to dread the returning power of Rome, and to make his illustrious cap-tive the pledge of peace, not the object of insult, Sapor still remained inflexible. When Valerian sunk under the weight of shame and grief, his skin, stuffed with straw, and formed into the likeness of a human figure, was preserved for ages in the most celebrated temple of Persia; a more real monument of triumph than the fancied trophies of brass and marble so often erected by Roman vanity. The tale is moral and pathetic, but the truth of it may very fairly be called in question. The letters still extant from the princes of the East to Sapor are manifest forgeries; nor is it natural to suppose that a jealous monarch should, even in the person of a rival, thus publicly degrade the majesty of kings. Whatever treatment the unfortunate Valerian might experience in Persia, it is at least certain that the only emperor of Rome who had ever fallen into the hands of the enemy languished away his life in hopeless captivity.

The emperor Gallienus, who had long supported with im-patience the censorial severity of his father and colleague, received the intelligence of his misfortunes with secret plea-sure and avowed indifference. "I knew that my father was a mortal," said he, "and since he has acted as becomes a brave man, I am satisfied." Whilst Rome lamented the fate of her sovereign, the savage coldness of his son was extolled by the servile courtiers as the perfect firmness of a hero and a stoic. It is difficult to paint the light, the various, the inconstant character of Gallienus, which he displayed without constraint, as soon as he became sole possessor of the empire. In every art that he attempted his lively genius enabled him to succeed; and as his genius was destitute of judgment, he attempted every art except the important ones of war and government. He was a master of several curious but useless sciences, a ready orator and elegant poet, a skilful gardener, an excellent cook, and most contemptible prince. When the great emergencies of the state required his presence and attention, he was engaged in conversation with the philosopher Plotinus, wasting his time in trifling or licentious pleasures, preparing his initiation to the Grecian mysteries, or soliciting a place in the Areopagus of Athens. His profuse magnificence insulted the general poverty; the solemn ridicule of his triumphs impressed a deeper sense of the public disgrace. The repeated intelligence of invasions, defeats, and rebellions, he received with a careless smile; and singling out, with affected contempt, some particular production of the lost province, he carelessly asked whether Rome must be ruined unless it was supplied with linen from Egypt and Arras cloth from Gaul? There were, however, a few short moments in the life of Gallienus when, exasperated by some recent injury, he suddenly appeared the intrepid soldier and the cruel tyrant; till satiated with blood, or fatigued by resistance, he insensibly sunk into the natural mildness and indolence of his character.

At a time when the reins of government were held with so loose a hand, it is not surprising that a crowd of usurpers should start up in every province of the empire against the son of Valerian. It was probably some ingenious fancy, or comparing the thirty tyrants of Rome with the thirty tyrants of Athens, that induced the writers of the Augustan History to select the celebrated number, which has been gradually received into a popular appellation. But in every light the parallel is idle and defective. What resemblance can we discover between a council of thirty persons, the united oppressors of a single city, and an uncertain list of independent rivals, who rose and fell in irregular succession through the extent of a vast empire? Yet if we examine with candour the conduct of these usurpers, it will appear that they were much oftener driven into rebellion by their fears than urged to it by their ambition. They dreaded the cruel suspicions of Gallienus; they equally dreaded the capricious violence of their troops. If the dangerous favour of the army had imprudently declared them deserving of the purple, they were marked for sure destruction; and even prudence would counsel them to secure a short enjoyment of empire, and rather to try the fortune of war than to expect the hand of an executioner. When the clamour of the soldiers invested the reluctant victims with the ensigns of sovereign authority, they sometimes mourned in secret their approaching fate. "You have lost," said Saturninus on the day of his elevation, "you have lost a useful commander, and you have made a very wretched emperor."

The apprehensions of Saturninus were justified by the repeated experience of revolutions. Of the nineteen tyrants who started up under the reign of Gallienus, there was not one who enjoyed a life of peace or a natural death. As soon as they were invested with the bloody purple, they inspired their adherents with the same fears and ambition which had occasioned their own revolt. Italy, Rome, and the senate constantly adhered to the cause of Gallienus, and he alone was considered as the sovereign of the empire. That prince condescended indeed to acknowledge the victorious arms of Odenathus, who deserved the honourable distinction, by the respectful conduct which he always maintained towards the son of Valerian. With the general applause of the Romans, and the consent of Gallienus, the senate conferred the title of Augustus on the brave Palmyrenian and seemed to intrust him with the government of the East, which he already possessed, in so independent a manner, that, like a private succession, he bequeathed it to his illustrious widow Zenobia.

CHAPTER ELEVEN

Reign of Claudius — Defeat of the Goths — Victories, Triumph, and Death of Aurelian

Under the deplorable reigns of Valerian and Gallienus the empire was oppressed and almost destroyed by the soldiers, the tyrants, and the barbarians. It was saved by a series of great princes, who derived their obscure origin from the martial provinces of Illyricum. Within a period of about thirty years, Claudius, Aurelian, Probus, Diocletian and his colleagues, triumphed over the foreign and domestic enemies of the state, re-established, with the military discipline, the strength of the frontiers, and deserved the glorious title of Restorers of the Roman world. The death of Gallienus was resolved in a conspiracy, and, notwithstanding their desire of first terminating the siege of Milan, the extreme danger which accompanied every moment's delay obliged them to hasten the execution of their daring purpose. At a late hour of the night, but while the emperor still protracted the pleasures of the table, an alarm was suddenly given that Aureolus, at the head of all his forces, had made a desperate sally from the town; Gallienus, who was never deficient in personal bravery, started from his silken couch, and, without allowing himself time either to put on his armour or to assemble his guards, he mounted on horseback and rode full speed towards the supposed place of the attack. Encompassed by his declared or concealed enemies, he soon, amidst the nocturnal tumult, received a mortal dart from an uncertain hand. Before he expired, a patriotic sentiment rising in the mind of Gallienus induced him to name a deserving successor, and it was his last request that the Imperial ornaments should be delivered to Claudius, who then commanded a detached army in the neighbourhood of Pavia. On the first news of the emperor's death the troops expressed some suspicion and resentment, till the one was removed and the other assuaged by a donative of twenty pieces of gold to each soldier. They then ratified the election and acknowledged the merit of their new sovereign.

In the arduous task which Claudius had undertaken of restoring the empire to its ancient splendour, it was first necessary to revive among his troops a sense of order and obedience. With the authority of a veteran commander, he represented to them that the relaxation of discipline had introduced a long train of disorders, the effects of which were at length experienced by the soldiers themselves; that a people ruined by oppression, and indolent from despair, could no longer supply a numerous army with the means of luxury, or even of subsistence; that the danger of each individual had increased with the despotism of the military order, since princes who tremble on the throne will guard their safety by the instant sacrifice of every obnoxious subject.

The various nations of Germany and Sarmatia who fought under the Gothic standard had already collected an armament more formidable than any which had yet issued from the Euxine; but by the most signal victories Claudius delivered the empire from the host of barbarians, and was distinguished by posterity under the glorious appellation of Gothicus. During the course of a rigorous winter, in which they were besieged by the emperor's troops, famine and pestilence, desertion and the sword, continually diminished the imprisoned barbarian multitude. On the return of spring nothing appeared in arms except a hardy and desperate band, the remnant of that mighty host which had embarked at the mouth of the Dniester. The pestilence which swept away such numbers of the barbarians at length proved fatal to their conqueror. After a short but glorious reign of two years, Claudius expired at Sirmium, amidst the tears and acclamations of his subjects. In his last illness he convened the principal officers of the state and army, and in their presence recommended Aurelian, one of his generals, as the most deserving of the throne, and the best qualified to execute the great design which he himself had been permitted only to undertake.

The reign of Aurelian lasted only four years and about nine months; but every instant of that short period was filled by some memorable achievement. He put an end to the Gothic war, chastised the Germans who invaded Italy, recovered Gaul, Spain, and Britain out of the hands of Tetricus, and destroyed the proud monarchy which Zenobia had erected in the East on the ruins of the afflicted empire. It was the rigid attention of Aurelian even to the minutest articles of discipline which best owed such uninterrupted success on his arms.

Exhausted by so many calamities, which they had mutually endured and inflicted during a twenty years' war, the Goths and the Romans consented to a lasting and beneficial treaty. It was earnestly solicited by the barbarians, and cheerfully ratified by the legions, to whose suffrage the prudence of Aurelian referred the decision of that important question. The most important condition of peace was understood rather than expressed in the treaty. Aurelian withdrew the Roman forces from Dacia, and tacitly relinquished that great province to the Goths and vandals. His manly judgment convinced him of the solid advantages, and taught him to despise the seeming disgrace, of thus contracting the frontiers of the monarchy. The Dacian subjects, removed from those distant possessions which they were unable to cultivate or defend, added strength and populousness to the southern side of the Danube. A fertile territory, which the repetition of barbarous inroads had changed into a desert, was yielded to their industry, and a new province of Dacia still preserved the memory of Trajan's conquests.

Public consternation at the possibility of a descent of the Alemanni upon the capital induced the Romans to undertake a consultation of the Sibylline books, and to construct fortifications of a grosser and more substantial kind. The seven hills of Rome had been surrounded, by the successors of Romulus, with an ancient wall of more than thirteen miles. The extent of the new walls, erected by Aurelian and finished in the reign of Probus, was reputed to be nearly fifty, but is shown by accurate measurement to be about twenty-one miles. It was a great but melancholy labour, since the defence of the capital betrayed the decline of the monarchy.

Aurelian had no sooner subdued the insurrections which ravaged the west than he turned his arms against Zenobia, the celebrated Queen of Palmyra and the East. Modern Europe has produced several illustrious women who have sustained with glory the weight of empire; nor is our own age destitute of such distinguished characters. But if we except the doubtful achievements of Semiramis, Zenobia is perhaps the only female whose superior genius broke through the servile indolence imposed on her sex by the climate and manners of Asia. She claimed her descent from the Macedonian kings of Egypt, equalled in beauty her ancestor Cleopatra, and far surpassed that princess in chastity and valour. Zenobia was esteemed the most lovely as well as the most heroic of her sex. She was of a dark complexion (for in speaking of a lady these trifles become important). Her teeth were of a pearly whiteness, and her large black eyes sparkled with uncommon fire, tempered by the most attractive sweetness. Her voice was strong and harmonious. Her manly understanding was strengthened and adorned by study. She was not ignorant of the Latin tongue, but possessed in equal perfection the Greek, the Syriac, and the Egyptian languages. She had drawn up for her own use an epitome of oriental history, and familiarly compared the beauties of Homer and Plato under the tuition of the sublime Longinus.

This accomplished woman gave her hand to Odenathus, who, from a private station, raised himself to the dominion of the East. With Zenobia's advice Odenathus won splendid victories over the Great King; the senate and people of Rome revered a stranger who had avenged their captive emperor, and even the insensible son of Valerian accepted Odenathus for his legitimate colleague. But when Odenathus was killed by domestic treason, Zenobia occupied the throne in her own person, without the authorization of Rome, and repelled a Roman army which was sent against her. Instead of the little passions which so frequently perplex a female reign, the steady administration of Zenobia was guided by the most judicious maxims of policy. If it was expedient to pardon, she could calm her resentment; if it was necessary to punish, she could impose silence on the voice of pity. Her strict economy was accused of avarice; yet on every proper occasion she appeared magnificent and liberal. The neighbouring states of Arabia, Armenia, and Persia, dreaded her enmity, and solicited her alliance. To the dominions of Odenathus, which extended from the Euphrates to the frontiers of Bithynia, his widow added the inheritance of her ancestors, the populous and fertile kingdom of Egypt. The emperor Claudius acknowledged her merit, and was content that, while *he* pursued the Gothic war, *she* should assert the dignity of the empire in the east. But with the Gothic peril allayed, it was impossible for Rome to countenance Zenobia's growing control over its eastern appanages.

Aurelian passed over into Asia, reanimated the loyalty of Roman allies, and in battles fought at Antioch and Emesa forced Zenobia to retire within the walls of her capital, where she made every preparation for vigorous resistance. The firmness of Zenobia was supported by the hope that in a very short time famine would compel the Roman army to repass the desert; and by the reasonable expectation that the kings of the East, and particularly the Persian monarch, would arm in the defence of their most natural ally. But fortune and the perseverance of Aurelian overcame every obstacle. The death of Sapor, which happened about this time, distracted the councils of Persia, and the inconsiderable succours that attempted to relieve Palmyra were easily intercepted either by the arms or the liberality of the emperor. From every part of Syria a regular succession of convoys safely arrived in the camp, which was increased by the return of Probus with his victorious troops from the conquest of Egypt. It was then that Zenobia resolved to fly. She mounted the fleetest of her dromedaries, and had already reached the banks of the Euphrates, about sixty miles from Palmyra, when she was overtaken by the pursuit of Aurelian's light horse, seized and brought back a captive to the feet of the emperor.

When the Syrian queen was brought into the presence of Aurelian, he sternly asked her, How she had presumed to rise in arms against the emperors of Rome? The answer of Zenobia was a prudent mixture of respect and firmness. "Because I disdained to consider as Roman emperors an Aureolus or a Gallienus. You alone I acknowledge as my conqueror and my sovereign." But as female fortitude is commonly artificial, so it is seldom steady or consistent. The courage of Zenobia deserted her in the hour of trial; she trembled at the angry clamours of the soldiers, who called aloud for her immediate execution, forgot the generous despair of Cleopatra, which had proposed as her model, and ignominiously purchased life by the sacrifice of her fame and her friends. After one final labour, the suppression of an Egyptian rebel named Firmus, Aurelian could congratulate the senate, the people, and himself, that in little more than three years he had restored universal peace and order to the Roman world.

Since the foundation of Rome no general had more nobly deserved a triumph than Aurelian; nor was a triumph ever celebrated with superior pride and magnificence. The pomp was opened by twenty elephants, four royal tigers, and above two hundred of the most curious animals from every climate of the North, the East, and the South. They were followed by sixteen hundred gladiators, devoted to the cruel amusement of the amphitheatre. The wealth of Asia, the arms and ensigns of so many conquered nations, and the magnificent plate and wardrobe of the Syrian queen, were disposed in exact symmetry or artful disorder. The ambassadors of the most remote parts of the earth, of Æthiopia, Arabia, Persia, Bactriana, India, and China, all remarkable by their rich or singular dresses, displayed the fame and power of the Roman emperor, who exposed likewise to the public view the presents that he had received, and particularly a great number of crowns of gold, the offerings of grateful cities. The victories of Aurelian were attested by the long train of captives who reluctantly attended his triumph—Goths, Vandals, Sarmatians, Alemanni, Franks, Gauls, Syrians, and Egyptians. So long and so various was the pomp of Aurelian's triumph, that, although it opened with the dawn of day, the slow majesty of the proces-

sion ascended not the Capitol before the ninth hour; and it was
already dark when the emperor returned to the palace. The
festival was protracted by theatrical representations, the games
of the circus, the hunting of wild beasts, combats of gladiators, and naval engagements. Liberal donatives were distributed to the army and people, and several institutions,
agreeable or beneficial to the city, contributed to perpetuate
the glory of Aurelian.

It was observed by one of the most sagacious of the Roman
princes, that the talents of his predecessor Aurelian were better suited to the command of an army than to the government
of an empire. Conscious of the character in which nature and
experience had enabled him to excel, he again took the field a
few months after his triumph. It was expedient to exercise the
restless temper of the legions in some foreign war, and the
Persian monarch, exulting in the shame of Valerian, still
braved with impunity the offended majesty of Rome. At the
head of an army, less formidable by its numbers than by its
discipline and valour, the emperor advanced as far as the
Straits which divide Europe from Asia. He there experienced
that the most absolute power is a weak defence against the
effects of despair. He had threatened one of his secretaries
who was accused of extortion, and it was known that he seldom threatened in vain. The last hope which remained for the
criminal was to involve some of the principal officers of the
army in his danger, or at least in his fears. Artfully counter-
feiting his master's hand, he showed them, in a long and
bloody list, their own names devoted to death. Without sus-
pecting or examining the fraud, they resolved to secure their
lives by the murder of the emperor. On his march, between
Byzantium and Heraclea, Aurelian was suddenly attacked by
the conspirators, whose stations gave them a right to surround
his person, and, after a short resistance, fell by the hand of
Mucapor, a general whom he had always loved and trusted.
He died regretted by the army, detested by the senate, but
universally acknowledged as a warlike and fortunate prince,
the useful though severe reformer of a degenerate state.

CHAPTER TWELVE

Conduct of the Army and Senate after the Death of Aurelian—Reigns of Tacitus, Probus, Carus and his Sons

Such was the unhappy condition of the Roman emperors, that, whatever might be their conduct, their fate was commonly the same. A life of pleasure or virtue, of severity or mildness, of indolence or glory, alike led to an untimely grave; and almost every reign is closed by the same disgusting repetition of treason and murder. The death of Aurelian, however, is remarkable by its extraordinary consequences. The chastened legions dutifuly petitioned the senate to name a new emperor, and the fearful senate, mindful of where true power lay, in its turn delegated the choice to the legions. The contention that ensued is one of the best attested but most improbable events in the history of mankind. The troops, as if satiated with the exercise of power, again conjured the senate to invest one of its own body with the Imperial purple. The senate still persisted in its refusal; the army in its request. The reciprocal offer was pressed and rejected at least three times, and, whilst the obstinate modesty of either party was resolved to receive a master from the hands of the other, eight months insensibly elapsed; an amazing period of tranquil anarchy, during which the Roman world remained without a sovereign, without an usurper, and without a sedition. The generals and magistrates appointed by Aurelian continued to execute their ordinary functions; and it is observed that a proconsul of Asia was the only considerable person removed from his office in the whole course of the interregnum.

After each party had shown proper reluctance, the senate agreed to make the nomination; and the consul, addressing himself to Tacitus, the first of the senators, required his opinion on the important subject of a proper candidate for the vacant throne. If we can prefer personal merit to accidental greatness, we shall esteem the birth of Tacitus more truly noble than that of kings. He claimed his descent from the philosophic historian whose writings will instruct the last generations of mankind. The senator Tacitus was then seventy-five years of age. The long period of his innocent life was adorned with wealth and honours. He had twice been invested with the consular dignity, and enjoyed with elegance and sobriety his ample patrimony of between two and three millions sterling. The experience of so many princes, whom he had esteemed or endured, from the vain follies of Elagabalus to the useful rigour of Aurelian, taught him to form a just estimate of the duties, the dangers, and the temptations of their sublime station. From the assiduous study of his immortal ancestor he derived the knowledge of the Roman constitution and of human nature. The voice of the people had already named Tacitus as the citizen the most worthy of empire. The ungrateful rumour reached his ears, and induced him to seek the retirement of one of his villas in Campania. He had passed two months in the delightful privacy of Baiæ, when he reluctantly obeyed the summons of the consul to resume his honourable place in the senate, and to assist the republic with his counsels on this important occasion.

He arose to speak, when, from every quarter of the house, he was saluted with the names of Augustus and Emperor. "Tacitus Augustus, the gods preserve thee! We choose thee for our sovereign, to thy care we entrust the republic and the world. Accept the empire from the authority of the senate. It is due to thy rank, to thy conduct, to thy manners." As soon as the tumult of acclamations subsided, Tacitus attempted to decline the dangerous honour, and to express his wonder that they should elect his age and infirmities to succeed the martial vigour of Aurelian. "Are these limbs, conscript fathers, fitted to sustain the weight of the armour, or to practise the exercises of the camp? The variety of climates, and the hardships of a military life, would soon oppress a feeble constitution, which subsists only by the most tender management. My exhausted strength scarcely enables me to discharge the duty of a senator; how insufficient would it prove to the arduous labours of war and government! Can you hope that the legions will respect a weak old man, whose days have been spent in the shade of peace and retirement? Can you desire that I should ever find reason to regret the favourable opinion of the senate?"

The reluctance of Tacitus, and it might possibly be sincere, was encountered by the affectionate obstinacy of the senate. Five hundred voices repeated at once, in eloquent confusion, that the greatest of the Roman princes, Numa, Trajan, Hadrian, and the Antonines, had ascended the throne in a very advanced season of life; that the mind, not the body, a sovereign, not a soldier, was the object of their choice; and that they expected from him no more than to guide by his wisdom the valour of the legions. The administration of Tacitus was not unworthy of his life and principles. A grateful servant of the senate, he considered that national council as the author, and himself as the subject, of the laws. The expiring senate displayed a sudden lustre, blazed for a moment, and was extinguished for ever. Actually, all that had yet passed at Rome was no more than a theatrical representation, unless it was ratified by the more substantial power of the legions.

But the glory and life of Tacitus were of short duration. Transported in the depth of winter from the soft retirement of Campania to the foot of Mount Caucasus, he sunk under the unaccustomed hardships of a military life. The fatigues of the body were aggravated by the cares of the mind. It may be doubtful whether the soldiers imbrued their hands in the blood of this innocent prince. It is certain that their insolence was the cause of his death. He expired at Tyana in Cappadocia, after a reign of only six months and about twenty days.

The eyes of Tacitus were scarcely closed before his brother Florianus showed himself unworthy to reign by the hasty usurpation of the purple, without expecting the approbation of the senate. The reverence for the Roman constitution, which yet influenced the camp and the provinces, was sufficiently strong to dispose them to censure, but not to provoke them to oppose, the precipitate ambition of Florianus. The discontent would have evaporated in idle murmurs, had not the general of the East, the heroic Probus, boldly declared himself the avenger of the senate.

The perpetual revolutions of the throne had so perfectly erased every notion of hereditary right, that the family of an unfortunate emperor was incapable of exciting the jealousy of his successors. The children of Tacitus and Florianus were permitted to descend into a private station, and to mingle with the general mass of the people. Their poverty indeed became an additional safeguard to their innocence.

The peasants of Illyricum, who had already given Claudius and Aurelian to the sinking empire, had an equal right to glory in the elevation of Probus. Above twenty years before, the emperor Valerian, with his usual penetration, had discovered the rising merit of the young soldier, on whom he conferred the rank of tribune long before the age prescribed by the military regulations. The tribune soon justified his choice by a victory over a great body of Sarmatians, in which he saved the life of a near relation of Valerian; and deserved to receive from the emperor's hand the collars, bracelets, spears, and banners, the mural and the civic crown, and all the honourable rewards reserved by ancient Rome for successful valour. The third, and afterwards the tenth, legion were entrusted to the command of Probus, who, in every step of his promotion, showed himself superior to the station which he filled. Africa and Pontus, the Rhine, the Danube, the Euphrates, and the Nile, by turns afforded him the most splendid occasions of displaying his personal prowess and his conduct in war. Aurelian was indebted to him for the conquest of Egypt, and still more indebted for the honest courage with which he often checked the cruelty of his masters. Tacitus, who desired by the abilities of his generals to supply his own deficiency of military talents, named him commander-in-chief of all the eastern provinces, with five times the usual salary, the promise of the consulship, and the hope of a triumph. When Probus ascended the Imperial throne he was about forty-four years of age; in the full possession of his fame, of the love of the army, and of a mature vigour of mind and body. His acknowledged merit, and the success of his arms against Florianus, left him without an enemy or a competitor. Yet, if we may credit his own professions, very far from being desirous of the empire, he had accepted it with the most sincere reluctance.

The strength of Aurelian had crushed on every side the enemies of Rome. After his death they seemed to revive with an increase of fury and of numbers. They were again vanquished by the active vigour of Probus, who, in a short reign of about six years, equalled the fame of ancient heroes, and restored peace and order to every province of the Roman world. Most of the exploits which distinguished his reign were achieved by the personal valour and conduct of the emperor, insomuch that the writer of his Life expresses some amazement how, in so short a time, a single man could be present in so many distant wars. The remaining actions he entrusted to the care of his lieutenants, the judicious choice of whom forms no inconsiderable part of his glory. Carus, Diocletian, Maximian, Constantius, Galerius, Asclepiodatus, Annibalianus, and a crowd of other chiefs, who afterwards ascended or supported the throne, were trained to arms in the severe school of Aurelian and Probus.

But the most important service which Probus rendered to the republic was the deliverance of Gaul, and the recovery of seventy flourishing cities oppressed by the barbarians of Germany, who, since the death of Aurelian, had ravaged that great province with impunity.

Instead of reducing the warlike natives of Germany Probus contented himself with the humble expedient of constructing a stone wall of considerable height, strengthened by towers placed at convenient intervals, to repel invasion from the north. But the experience of the world, from China to Britain, has exposed the vain attempt of fortifying any extensive tract of country. An active enemy, who can select and vary his points of attack, must in the end discover some feeble spot, or some unguarded moment. The strength, as well as the attention, of the defenders is divided; and such are the blind effects of terror on the firmest troops that a line broken in a single place is almost instantly deserted. The fate of the wall which Probus erected may confirm the general observation. Within a few years after his death it was overthrown by the Alemanni. Its scattered ruins, universally ascribed to the power of the Dæmon, now serve only to excite the wonder of the Swabian peasant.

Among the useful conditions of peace imposed by Probus on the vanquished nations of Germany was the obligation of supplying the Roman army with sixteen thousand recruits, the bravest and most robust of their youth. The emperor dispersed them through all the provinces, and distributed this dangerous reinforcement, in small bands of fifty or sixty each, among the national troops; judiciously observing that the aid which the republic derived from the barbarians should be felt but not seen. Their aid was now become necessary. The feeble elegance of Italy and the internal provinces could no longer support the weight of arms. The hardy frontier of the Rhine and Danube still produced minds and bodies equal to the labours of the camp; but a perpetual series of wars had gradually diminished their numbers. The infrequency of marriage, and the ruin of agriculture, affected the principles of population, and not only destroyed the strength of the present, but intercepted the hope of future generations. The wisdom of Probus embraced a great and beneficial plan of replenishing the exhausted frontiers by new colonies of captive or fugitive barbarians, on whom he bestowed lands, cattle, instruments of husbandry, and every encouragement that might engage them to educate a race of soldiers for the service of the republic.

Notwithstanding the vigilance and activity of Probus, it was almost impossible that he could at once contain in obedience every part of his wide-extended dominions. The barbarians who broke their chains had seized the favourable opportunity of a domestic war. When the emperor marched to the relief of Gaul, he devolved the command of the East on Saturninus. That general, a man of merit and experience, was driven into rebellion by the absence of his sovereign, the levity of the Alexandrian people, the pressing instances of his friends, and his own fears; but from the moment of his elevation he never entertained a hope of empire or even of life. "Alas!" he said, "the republic has lost a useful servant, and the rashness of an hour has destroyed the services of many years. You know not," continued he, "the misery of sovereign power: a sword is perpetually suspended over our head. We dread our very guards, we distrust our companions. The choice of action or of repose is no longer in our disposition, nor is there any age, or character, or conduct, that can protect us from the censure of envy. In thus exalting me to the throne, you have doomed me to a life of cares, and to an untimely fate. The only consolation which remains is the assurance that I shall not fall alone." But as the former part of his prediction was verified by the victory, so the latter was disappointed by the clemency, of Probus.

The military discipline which reigned in the camps of Probus was less cruel than that of Aurelian, but it was equally rigid and exact. Probus exercised his legions in useful agricultural labour, and covered the hills of Gaul and Pannonia with rich vineyards. But, in the prosecution of a favourite scheme, the best of men, satisfied with the rectitude of their intentions, are subject to forget the bounds of moderation; nor did Probus himself sufficiently consult the patience and disposition of his fierce legionaries. The dangers of the military profession seem only to be compensated by a life of pleasure and idleness; but if the duties of the soldier are incessantly aggravated by the labours of the peasant, he will at last sink under the intolerable burden or shake it off with indignation. The imprudence of Probus is said to have inflamed the discontent of his troops. More attentive to the interests of mankind than to those of the army, he expressed the vain hope that, by the establishment of universal peace, he should soon abolish the necessity of a standing and mercenary force. The unguarded expression proved fatal to him. In one of the hottest days of summer, as he severely urged the unwholesome labour of draining the marshes of Sirmium, the soldiers, impatient of fatigue, on a sudden threw down their tools, grasped their arms, and broke out into a furious mutiny. The emperor, conscious of his danger, took refuge in a lofty tower constructed for the purpose of surveying the progress of the work. The tower was instantly forced, and a thousand swords were plunged at once into the bosom of the unfortunate Probus. The rage of the troops subsided as soon as it had been gratified. They then lamented their fatal rashness, forgot the severity of the emperor whom they had massacred, and hastened to perpetuate, by an honorable monument, the memory of his virtues and victories. When the legions had indulged their grief and repentance for the death of Probus, their unanimous consent declared Carus, his Prætorian Præfect, the most deserving of the imperial throne. When Carus assumed the purple he was about sixty years of age, and his two sons, Carinus and Numerian, had already attained the season of manhood.

The authority of the senate expired with Probus; nor was the repentance of the soldiers displayed by the same dutiful regard for the civil power which they had testified after the unfortunate death of Aurelian. The election of Carus was decided without expecting the approbation of the senate, and the new emperor contented himself with announcing, in a cold and stately epistle, that he had ascended the vacant throne. A behaviour so very opposite to that of his amiable predecessor afforded no favourable presage of the new reign: and the Romans, deprived of power and freedom, asserted their privilege of licentious murmurs.

Carus's first care was the long-suspended design of the Persian war. Before his departure for this distant expedition he conferred on his sons Carinus and Numerian the title of Cæsar, investing the former with almost an equal share of the imperial power. The Persian king, Varanes or Bahram, was alarmed at the approach of the Romans, and endeavoured to retard their progress by a negotiation of peace. His ambassadors entered the camp about sunset, at the time when the troops were satisfying their hunger with a frugal repast. The Persians expressed their desire of being introduced to the presence of the Roman emperor. They were at length conducted to a soldier who was seated on the grass. A piece of stale bacon and a few hard peas composed his supper. A coarse woollen garment of purple was the only circumstance that announced his dignity. The conference was conducted with the same disregard of courtly elegance. Carus, taking off a cap which he wore to conceal his baldness, assured the ambassadors that, unless their master acknowledged the superiority of Rome, he would speedily render Persia as naked of trees as his own head was destitute of hair. Notwithstanding some traces of art and preparation, we may discover in this scene the manners of Carus, and the severe simplicity which the martial princes who succeeded Gallienus had already restored in the Roman camps. The ministers of the Great King trembled and retired.

The threats of Carus were not without effect. He ravaged Mesopotamia, cut in pieces whatever opposed his passage, made himself master of the great cities of Seleucia and Ctesiphon (which seem to have surrendered without resistance), and carried his victorious arms beyond the Tigris. He had seized the favourable moment for an invasion. The Persian councils were distracted by domestic factions, and the greater part of their forces were detained on the frontiers of India. Rome and the East received with transport the news of such important advantages. Flattery and hope painted in the most lively colours the fall of Persia, the conquest of Arabia, the submission of Egypt, and a lasting deliverance from the inroads of the Scythian nations. But the reign of Carus was destined to expose the vanity of predictions. They were scarcely uttered before they were contradicted by his death. The vacancy of the throne was not productive of any disturbance. The ambition of the aspiring generals was checked by their mutual fears; and young Numerian, with his absent brother Carinus, were unanimously acknowledged as Roman emperors.

The intelligence of the mysterious fate of the late emperor was soon carried from the frontiers of Persia to Rome; and the senate, as well as the provinces, congratulated the accession of the sons of Carus. These fortunate youths were strangers, however, to that conscious superiority, either of birth or of merit, which can alone render the possession of a throne easy, and as it were natural. Born and educated in a private station, the election of their father raised them at once to the rank of princes; and his death, which happened about sixteen months afterwards, left them the unexpected legacy of a vast empire. To sustain with temper this rapid elevation, an uncommon share of virtue and prudence was requisite; and Carinus, the elder of the brothers, was more than commonly deficient in those qualities. In the Gallic war he discovered some degree of personal courage; but from the moment of his arrival at Rome he abandoned himself to the luxury of the capital, and to the abuse of his fortune. He was soft, yet cruel; devoted to pleasure, but destitute of taste; and, though exquisitely susceptible of vanity, indifferent to the public esteem. In the course of a few months he successively married and divorced nine wives, most of whom he left pregnant; and, notwithstanding this legal inconstancy, found time to indulge such a variety of irregular appetites as brought dishonour on himself and on the noblest houses of Rome. He beheld with inveterate hatred all those who might remember his former obscurity, or censure his present conduct. He banished or put to death the friends and counsellors whom his father had placed about him to guide his inexperienced youth; and he persecuted with the meanest revenge his schoolfellows and companions who had not sufficiently respected the latent majesty of the emperor. With the senators Carinus affected a lofty and regal demeanour, frequently declaring that he designed to distribute their estates among the populace of Rome. From the dregs of that populace he selected his favourites, and even his ministers. The palace, and even the Imperial table, was filled with singers, dancers, prostitutes, and all the various retinue of vice and folly. One of his doorkeepers he intrusted with the government of the city. In the room of the Prætorian Præfect, whom he put to death, Carinus substituted one of the ministers of his looser pleasures. Another, who possessed the same or even a more infamous title to favour, was invested with the consulship. A confidential secretary, who had acquired uncommon skill in the art of forgery, delivered the indolent emperor, with his own consent, from the irksome duty of signing his name.

When the emperor Carus undertook the Persian war, he was induced, by motives of affection as well as policy, to secure the fortunes of his family by leaving in the hands of his eldest son the armies and provinces of the West. The intelligence which he soon received of the conduct of Carinus filled him with shame and regret; nor had he concealed his resolution of satisfying the republic by a severe act of justice, and of adopting, in the place of an unworthy son, the brave and virtuous Constantius, who at that time was governor of Dalmatia. But the elevation of Constantius was for a while deferred; and as soon as the father's death had released Carinus from the control of fear or decency, he displayed to the Romans the extravagancies of Elegabalus, aggravated by the cruelty of Domitian.

The spectacles of Carinus may be best illustrated by the observation of some particulars which history has condescended to relate concerning those of his predecessors. If we confine ourselves solely to the hunting of wild beasts, however we may censure the vanity of the design or the cruelty of the execution, we are obliged to confess that neither before nor since the time of the Romans so much art and expense have ever been lavished for the amusement of the people. By the order of Probus, a great quantity of large trees, torn up by the roots, were transplanted into the midst of the circus. The spacious and shady forest was immediately filled with a thousand ostriches, a thousand stags, a thousand fallow-deer, and a thousand wild boars; and all this variety of game was abandoned to the riotous impetuosity of the multitude. The tragedy of the succeeding day consisted in the massacre of an hundred lions, an equal number of lionesses, two hundred leopards, and three hundred bears. The collection prepared by the younger Gordian for his triumph, and which his successor exhibited in the secular games, was less remarkable by the number than by the singularity of the animals. Twenty zebras displayed their elegant forms and variegated beauty to the eyes of the Roman people. Ten elks, and as many camelopards, the loftiest and most harmless creatures that wander over the plains of Sarmatia and Æthiopia, were contrasted with thirty African hyænas and ten Indian tigers, the most implacable savages of the torrid zone. The unoffending strength with which Nature has endowed the greater quadrupeds was admired in the rhinoceros, the hippopotamus of the Nile, and a majestic troop of thirty-two elephants. While the populace gazed with stupid wonder on the splendid show, the naturalist might indeed observe the figure and properties of so many different species, transported from every part of the ancient world into the amphitheatre of Rome. But this accidental benefit which science might derive from folly is surely insufficient to justify such a wanton abuse of the public riches. There occurs, however, a single instance in the first Punic war in which the senate wisely connected this amusement of the multitude with the interest of the state. A considerable number of elephants, taken in the defeat of the Carthaginian army, were driven through the circus by a few slaves, armed only with blunt javelins. The useful spectacle served to impress the Roman soldier with a just contempt for those unwieldy animals; and he no longer dreaded to encounter them in the ranks of war.

In the midst of this glittering pageantry, the emperor Carinus, secure of his fortune, enjoyed the acclamations of the people, the flattery of his courtiers, and the songs of the poets, who, for want of a more essential merit, were reduced to celebrate the divine graces of his person. In the same hour, but at the distance of nine hundred miles from Rome, his brother expired; and a sudden revolution transferred into the hands of a stranger the sceptre of the house of Carus.

The sons of Carus never saw each other after their father's death. The jealousy between them must have been inflamed by the opposition of their characters. In the most corrupt of times Carinus was unworthy to live: Numerian deserved to reign in a happier period. But his talents were rather of the contemplative than of the active kind. His constitution was debilitated by the hardships of the Persian war, and he had contracted a weakness in his eyes which obliged him to confine himself to the solitude and darkness of a tent or litter. The administration of affairs was devolved on Arrius Aper, the Prætorian Præfect, who, to the power of his important office, added the honour of being father-in-law to Numerian. The Imperial pavilion was most strictly guarded by his most trusty adherents; and during many days Aper delivered to the army the supposed mandates of their invisible sovereign.

Eight months after the death of Carus the Roman army returning from Mesopotamia reached the Thracian Bosphorus. There was a report circulated through the camp, at first in secret whispers and at length in loud clamours, of the emperor's death, and of the presumption of his ambitious minister, who still exercised the sovereign power in the name of a prince who was no more. With rude curiosity the impatient soldiers broke into the imperial tent, and discovered only the corpse of Numerian. A formal assembly of the army was convoked, and the generals and tribunes announced to the multitude that their choice had fallen on Diocletian, commander of the domestics or bodyguards, as the person the most capable of revenging and succeeding their beloved emperor. The future fortunes of the candidate depended on the chance or conduct of the present hour. Conscious that the station which he had filled exposed him to some suspicions, Diocletian ascended the tribunal, and, raising his eyes towards the Sun, made a solemn profession of his own innocence, in the presence of that all-seeing Deity. Then, assuming the tone of a sovereign and a judge, he commanded that Aper should be brought in chains to the foot of the tribunal. "This man," said he, "is the murderer of Numerian;" and without giving him time to enter on a dangerous justification, drew his sword, and buried it in the breast of the unfortunate præfect. A charge supported by such decisive proof was admitted without contradiction, and the legions, with repeated acclamations, acknowledged the justice and authority of the emperor Diocletian.

CHAPTER THIRTEEN

The Reign of Diocletian and his Three Associates, Maximian, Galerius, and Constantius—General Re-establishment of Order and Tranquility—The Persian War, Victory, and Triumph—The new Form of Administration—Abdication and Retirement of Diocletian and Maximian

As the reign of Diocletian was more illustrious than that of any of his predecessors, so was his birth more abject and obscure. The strong claims of merit and violence had frequently superseded the ideal prerogatives of nobility; but a distinct line of separation was hitherto preserved between the free and the servile part of mankind. The parents of Diocletian had been slaves in the house of Anulinus, a Roman senator; nor was he himself distinguished by any other name than that which he derived from a small town in Dalmatia, from whence his mother deduced her origin. Diocletian was successively promoted to the government of Mæsia, the honours of the consulship, and the important command of the guards of the palace. He distinguished his abilities in the Persian war; and after the death of Numerian, the slave, by the confession and judgment of his rivals, was declared the most worthy of the Imperial throne. His abilities were useful rather than splendid—a vigorous mind improved by the experience and study of mankind; dexterity and application in business; a judicious mixture of liberality and economy, of mildness and rigour; profound dissimulation under the disguise of military frankness; steadiness to pursue his ends; flexibility to vary his means; and, above all, the great art of submitting his own passions, as well as those of others, to the interest of his ambition, and of colouring his ambition with the most specious pretences of justice and public utility. Like Augustus, Diocletian may be considered as the founder of a new empire. Like the adopted son of Cæsar, he was distinguished as a statesman rather than as a warrior; nor did either of those princes employ force, whenever their purpose could be effected by policy.

The victory of Diocletian was remarkable for its singular mildness. A people accustomed to applaud the clemency of the conqueror, if the usual punishments of death, exile, and confiscation were inflicted with any degree of temper and equity, beheld, with the most pleasing astonishment, a civil war, the flames of which were extinguished in the field of battle. The discerning judgment of Aurelian, of Probus, and of Carus, had filled the several departments of the state and army with officers of approved merit, whose removal would have injured the public service, without promoting the interest of the successor. Such a conduct, however, displayed to the Roman world the fairest prospect of the new reign, and the emperor affected to confirm this favourable prepossession by declaring that, among all the virtues of his predecessors, he was the most ambitious of imitating the humane philosophy of Marcus Antoninus.

The first considerable action of his reign seemed to evince his sincerity as well as his moderation. After the example of Marcus, he gave himself a colleague in the person of Maximian, on whom he bestowed at first the title of Cæsar, and afterwards that of Augustus. But the motives of his conduct, as well as the object of his choice, were of a very different nature from those of his admired predecessor. By investing a luxurious youth with the honours of the purple, Marcus had discharged a debt of private gratitude, at the expense, indeed, of the happiness of the state. By associating a friend, and a

fellow-soldier to the favours of government, Diocletian, in a
time of public danger, provided for the defence both of the
East and of the West. Maximian was born a peasant, and, like
Aurelian, in the territory of Sirmium. Ignorant of letters, careless of laws, the rusticity of his appearance and manners still
betrayed in the most elevated fortune the meanness of his extraction. War was the only art which he professed. In a long
course of service he had distinguished himself on every frontier of the empire; and though his military talents were formed
to obey rather than to command, though, perhaps, he never
attained the skill of a consummate general, he was capable, by
his valour, constancy, and experience, of executing the most
arduous undertakings. Nor were the vices of Maximian less
useful to his benefactor. Insensible to pity, and fearless of
consequences, he was the ready instrument of every act of
cruelty which the policy of that artful prince might at once
suggest and disclaim. As soon as a bloody sacrifice had been
offered to prudence or to revenge, Diocletian, by his seasonable intercession, saved the remaining few whom he had never
designed to punish, gently censured the severity of his stern
colleague, and enjoyed the comparison of a golden and an iron
age, which was universally applied to their opposite maxims
of government. Notwithstanding the difference of their characters, the two emperors maintained, on the throne, that
friendship which they had contracted in a private station. The
haughty, turbulent spirit of Maximian, so fatal afterwards to
himself and to the public peace, was accustomed to respect the
genius of Diocletian, and confessed the ascendant of reason
over brutal violence. From a motive either of pride or superstition, the two emperors assumed the titles, the one of Jovius,
the other of Herculius. Whilst the motion of the world (such
was the language of their venal orators) was maintained by the
all-seeing wisdom of Jupiter, the invincible arm of Hercules
purged the earth from monsters and tyrants.

But even the omnipotence of Jovius and Herculius was
insufficient to sustain the weight of the public administration.
The prudence of Diocletian discovered that the empire, as-
sailed on every side by the barbarians, required on every side
the presence of a great army and of an emperor. With this

view, he resolved once more to divide his unwieldy power, and with the inferior title of *Cæsars*, to confer on two generals of approved merit an equal share of the sovereign authority. Galerius, surnamed Armentarius, from his original profession of a herdsman, and Constantius, who from his pale complexion had acquired the denomination of Chlorus, were the two persons invested with the second honours of the Imperial purple.

To strengthen the bonds of political, by those of domestic, union, each of the emperors assumed the character of a father to one of the Cæsars—Diocletian to Galerius, and Maximian to Constantius; and each, obliging them to repudiate their former wives, bestowed his daughter in marriage on his adopted son. The four princes distributed among themselves the wide extent of the Roman empire. The defence of Gaul, Spain, and Britain was intrusted to Constantius: Galerius was stationed on the banks of the Danube, as the safeguard of the Illyrian provinces. Italy and Africa were considered as the department of Maximian; and for his peculiar portion Diocletian reserved Thrace, Egypt, and the rich countries of Asia. Every one was sovereign within his own jurisdiction; but their united authority extended over the whole monarchy, and each of them was prepared to assist his colleagues with his counsels or presence.

The first exploit of Maximian, though it is mentioned in a few words by our imperfect writers, deserves, from its singularity, to be recorded in a history of human manners. He suppressed the peasants of Gaul, who, under the appellation of Bagaudæ, had risen in a general insurrection; very simlar to those which in the fourteenth century successively afflicted both France and England. It should seem that very many of those institutions, referred by an easy solution to the feudal system, are derived from the Celtic barbarians. It was very natural for the plebians, oppressed by debt or apprehensive injuries, to implore the protection of some powerful chief, who acquired over their persons and property the same absolute rights as, among the Greeks and Romans, a master exercised over his slaves. The greatest part of the nation was gradually reduced into a state of servitude; compelled to per-

petual labour on the estates of the Gallic nobles, and confined
to the soil, either by the real weight of fetters, or by the no
less cruel and forcible restraints of the laws. During the long
series of troubles which agitated Gaul, from the reign of Gallienus to that of Diocletian, the condition of those servile
peasants was peculiarly miserable; and they experienced at
once the complicated tyranny of their masters, of the barbarians, of the soldiers, and of the officers of the revenue.

Their patience was at last provoked into despair. On every
side they rose in multitudes, armed with rustic weapons, and
with irresistible fury. The ploughman became a foot soldier,
the shepherd mounted on horseback, the deserted villages and
open towns were abandoned to the flames, and the ravages of
the peasants equalled those of the fiercest barbarians. They
asserted the natural rights of men, but they asserted those
rights with the most savage cruelty. The Gallic nobles, justly
dreading their revenge, either took refuge in the fortified
cities, or fled from the wild scene of anarchy. The peasants
reigned without control; and two of their most daring leaders
had the folly and rashness to assume the Imperial ornaments.
Their power soon expired at the approach of the legions. The
strength of union and discipline obtained an easy victory over
a licentious and divided multitude. A severe retaliation was
inflicted on the peasants who were found in arms: the affrighted remnant returned to their respective habitations, and
their unsuccessful effort for freedom served only to confirm
their slavery.

Maximian had no sooner recovered Gaul from the hands of
the peasants, than he lost Britain by the usurpation of Carausius. During the space of seven years fortune continued propi-
tious to a rebellion supported with courage and ability. The
British emperor defended the frontiers of his dominions
against the Caledonians of the north, and invited assistance
from the continent.

His fleets rode triumphant in the channel, commanded the
mouths of the Seine and of the Rhine, ravaged the coasts of
the ocean, and diffused beyond the Columns of Hercules the
terror of his name. Under his command, Britain, destined in a

future age to obtain the empire of the sea, already assumed its natural and respectable station of a maritime power.

By seizing the fleet of Boulogne, Carausius had deprived his master of the means of pursuit and revenge. And when, after a vast expense of time and labour, a new armament was launched into the water, the Imperial troops, unaccustomed to that element, were easily baffled and defeated by the veteran sailors of the usurper. This disappointed effort was soon productive of a treaty of peace. Diocletian and his colleague, who justly dreaded the enterprising spirit of Carausis, resigned to him the sovereignty of Britain, and reluctantly admitted their perfidious servant to a participation of the Imperial honours. While Constantius was energetically assembling forces to combat the rebel he received news of the death of Carausius and was soon able to recover Britain for the empire. After the pacification of the west, campaigns in Africa, Egypt, and Persia restored other segments of the empire which were restive and wavering in their loyalty to firmer adhesion to Rome.

The arduous work of rescuing the distressed empire from tyrants and barbarians had now been completely achieved by a succession of Illyrian peasants. As soon as Diocletian entered into the twentieth year of his reign, he celebrated that memorable era, as well as the success of his arms, by the pomp of a Roman triumph. Maximian, the equal partner of his power, was his only companion in the glory of that day. The two Cæsars had fought and conquered, but the merit of their exploits was ascribed, according to the rigour of ancient maxim, to the auspicious influence of their fathers and emperors. The triumph of Diocletian and Maximian was less magnificent, perhaps, than those of Aurelian and Probus, but it was dignified by several circumstances of superior fame and good fortune.

The spot on which Rome was founded had been consecrated by ancient ceremonies and imaginary miracles. The presence of some god, or the memory of some hero, seemed to animate every part of the city, and the empire of the world had been promised to the Capitol. The native Romans felt and confessed the power of this agreeable illusion. It was derived from their ancestors, had grown up with their earliest habits of

life, and was protected, in some measure, by the opinion of
political utility. The form and the seat of government were
intimately blended together, nor was it esteemed possible to
transport the one without destroying the other. But the sovereignty of the capital was gradually annihilated in the extent of
conquest; the provinces rose to the same level, and the vanquished nations acquired the name and privileges, without in-
bibing the partial affections, of Romans. During a long
period, however, the remains of the ancient constitution and
the influence of custom perserved the dignity of Rome. The
emperors, though perhaps of African or Illyrian extraction,
respected their adopted country as the seat of their power and
the centre of their extensive dominions. The emergencies of
war very frequently required their presence on the frontiers;
but Diocletian and Maximian were the first Roman princes
who fixed, in time of peace, their ordinary residence in the
provinces; and their conduct, however it might be suggested
by private motives, was justified by the very specious considerations of policy. The court of the emperor of the West was,
for the most part, established at Milan, whose situation, at the
foot of the Alps, appeared far more convenient than that of
Rome, for the important purpose of watching the motions of
the barbarians of Germany. Milan soon assumed the splendour
of an Imperial city. The houses are described as numerous and
well built; the manners of the people as polished and liberal.
A circus, a theatre, a mint, a palace, baths, which bore the
name of their founder Maximian; porticoes adorned with
statues, and a double circumference of walls, contributed to
the beauty of the new capital; nor did it seem oppressed even
by the proximity of Rome. To rival the majesty of Rome was
the ambition likewise of Diocletian, who employed his leisure
and the wealth of the East in the embellishment of Nicomedia,
a city placed on the verge of Europe and Asia, almost at an
equal distance between the Danube and the Euphrates. By the
taste of the monarch, and at the expense of the people, Nicomedia acquired, in the space of a few years, a degree of magnificence which might appear to have required the labour of
ages, and became inferior only to Rome, Alexandria, and Antioch in extent or populousness. The life of Diocletian and

Maximian was a life of action, and a considerable portion of it was spent in camps, or in their long and frequent marches; but whenever the public business allowed them any relaxation, they seem to have retired with pleasure to their favourite residences of Nicomedia and Milan. Till Diocletian, in the twentieth year of his reign, celebrated his Roman triumph, it is extremely doubtful whether he ever visited the ancient capital of the empire. Even on that memorable occasion his stay did not exceed two months. Disgusted with the licentious familiarity of the people, he quitted Rome with precipitation thirteen days before it was expected that he should have appeared in the senate invested with the ensigns of the consular dignity.

The dislike expressed by Diocletian towards Rome and Roman freedom was not the effect of momentary caprice, but the result of the most artful policy. That crafty prince had framed a new system of Imperial government, which was afterwards completed by the family of Constantine; and as the image of the old constitution was religiously preserved in the senate, he resolved to deprive that order of its small remains of power and consideration. But the most fatal though secret wound which the senate received from the hands of Diocletian and Maximian was inflicted by the inevitable operation of their absence. As long as the emperors resided at Rome, that assembly might be oppressed, but it could scarcely be neglected. The name of the senate was mentioned with honour till the last period of the empire; the vanity of its members were still flattered with honorary distinctions; but the assembly which had so long been the source, and so long the instrument of power, was respectfully suffered to sink into oblivion. The senate of Rome, losing all connection with the Imperial court and the actual constitution, was left a venerable but useless monument of antiquity on the Capitoline hill.

When the Roman princes had lost sight of the senate and of their ancient capital, they easily forgot the origin and nature of their legal power. The civil offices of consul, of proconsul, or censor, and of tribune, by the union of which it had been formed, betrayed to the people its republican extraction. Those modest titles were laid aside; and if they still distinguished their high station by the appellation of Emperor, or

IMPERATOR, that word was understood in a new and more dignified sense, and no longer denoted the general of the Roman armies, but the sovereign of the Roman world. The name of Emperor, which was at first of a military nature, was associated with another of a more servile kind. The epithet of DOMINUS, or Lord, in its primitive signification, was expressive not of the authority of a prince over his subjects, or of a commander over his soldiers, but of the despotic power of a master over his domestic slaves. Viewing it in that odious light, it had been rejected with abhorrence by the first Cæsars. Their resistance insensibly became more feeble, and the name less odious; till at length the style of *our Lord and Emperor* was not only bestowed by flattery, but was regularly admitted into the laws and public monuments.

The pride, or rather the policy, of Diocletian, engaged that artful prince to introduce the stately magnificence of the court of Persia. He ventured to assume the diadem, an ornament detested by the Romans as the odious ensign of royalty, and the use of which had been considered as the most desperate act of the madness of Caligula. It was no more than a broad white fillet set with pearls, which encircled the emperor's head. The sumptuous robes of Diocletian and his successors were of silk and gold; and it is remarked with indignation that even their shoes were studded with the most precious gems. The access to their sacred person was every day rendered more difficult by the institution of new forms and ceremonies. The avenues of the palace were strictly guarded by the various *schools*, as they began to be called, of domestic officers. The interior apartments were entrusted to the jealous vigilance of the eunuchs; the increase of whose numbers and influence was the most infallible symptom of the progress of despotism. When a subject was at length admitted to the Imperial presence, he was obliged, whatever might be his rank, to fall prostrate on the ground, and to adore, according to the eastern fashion, the divinity of his lord and master.

Ostentation was the first principle of the new system instituted by Diocletian. The second was division. He divided the empire, the provinces, and every branch of the civil as well as military administration. He multiplied the wheels of the machine of government, and rendered its operations less rapid but more secure. Whatever advantages and whatever defects might attend these innovations, they must be ascribed in a very great degree to the first inventor; but as the new frame of policy was gradually improved and completed by succeeding princes, it will be more satisfactory to delay the consideration of it till the season of its full maturity and perfection.

It was in the twenty-first year of his reign that Diocletian executed his memorable resolution of abdicating the empire; an action more naturally to have been expected from the elder or the younger Antoninus than from a prince who had never practised the lessons of philosophy either in the attainment or in the use of supreme power. On the same day, albeit reluctantly, Maximian made his resignation of the Imperial dignity at Milan. Diocletian, who, from a servile origin had raised himself to the throne, passed the last nine years of his life in a private condition. His tenderness, or at least his pride, was deeply wounded by the misfortunes of his wife and daughter; and the last moments of Diocletian were embittered by some affronts, which Licinius and Constantine might have spared the father of so many emperors and the first author of their own fortune. A report, though of a very doubtful nature, has reached our times, that he prudently withdrew himself from their power by a voluntary death (A.D. 313).

CHAPTER FOURTEEN

*Troubles after the Abdication of Diocletian—
Death of Constantius—Elevation of Constantine
and Maxentius—Six Emperors at the same Time
—Death of Maximian and Galerius—Victories of
Constantine over Maxentius and Licinius—Reunion of the Empire under the Authority of Constantine*

The balance of power established by Diocletian subsisted no
longer than while it was sustained by the firm and dexterous
hand of the founder. It required such a fortunate mixture of
different tempers and abilities as could scarcely be found, or
even expected, a second time; two emperors without jealousy,
two Cæsars without ambition and the same general interest
invariably pursued by four independent princes. The abdication of Diocletian and Maximian was succeeded by eighteen
years of discord and confusion. The empire was afflicted by
five civil wars; and the remainder of the time was not so much
a state of tranquillity as a suspension of arms between several
hostile monarchs, who, viewing each other with an eye of fear
and hatred, strove to increase their respective forces at the
expense of their subjects.

As soon as Diocletian and Maximian had resigned the purple, their station, according to the rules of the new constitution, was filled by the two Cæsars, Constantius and Galerius,

who immediately assumed the title of Augustus. Constantius enjoyed seniority and retained the administration of Gaul, Spain, and Britain. Clemency, temperance, and moderation distinguished the amiable character of Constantius, and his fortunate subjects had frequently occasion to compare the virtues of their sovereign with the passion of Maximian, and even with the arts of Diocletian. The stern temper of Galerius was cast in a very different mould; and while he commanded the esteem of his subjects, he seldom condescended to solicit their affections. After the elevation of Constantius and Galerius to the rank of *Augusti*, two new *Cæsars* were required to supply their place and to complete the system of Imperial government. The two persons whom Galerius promoted to the rank of Cæsar were better suited to serve the views of his ambition and their principal recommendation seems to have consisted in the want of merit or personal consequence. The first of these was Daza, or as he was afterwards called, Maximin, whose mother was the sister of Galerius. At the same time Severus, a faithful servant, addicted to pleasure but not incapable of business, was sent to Milan to receive from the reluctant hands of Maximian the Cæsarian ornaments and the possession of Italy and Africa. But within less than eighteen months two unexpected revolutions overturned the ambitious schemes of Galerius. The hopes of uniting the western provinces to his empire were disappointed by the elevation of Constantine; whilst Italy and Africa were lost by the successful revolt of Maxentius.

Maxentius was the son of the emperor Maximian, and he had married the daughter of Galerius. His birth and alliance seemed to offer him the fairest promise of succeeding to the empire; but his vices and incapacity procured him the same exclusion from the dignity of Cæsar which Constantine had deserved by a dangerous superiority of merit. As a result of intrigues Maxentius was proclaimed emperor and was supported by Maximian, whom the authority of Diocletian had forced to abdicate. At the request of his son and of the senate Maximian condescended to reassume the purple. His ancient dignity, his experience, and his fame in arms added strength as well as reputation to the party of Maxentius.

Though the characters of Constantine and Maxentius had very little affinity with each other, their situation and interest were the same, and prudence seemed to require that they should unite their forces against the common enemy. Notwithstanding the superiority of his age and dignity, the indefatigable Maximian passed the Alps, and, courting a personal interview with the sovereign of Gaul, carried with him his daughter Fausta as the pledge of the new alliance. The marriage was celebrated at Arles with every circumstance of magnificence; and the ancient colleague of Diocletian, who again asserted his claim to the Western empire, conferred on his son-in-law and ally the title of Augustus. By consenting to receive that honour from Maximian, Constantine seemed to embrace the cause of Rome and of the senate; but his professions were ambiguous, and his assistance slow and ineffectual. He considered with attention the approaching contest between the masters of Italy and the emperor of the East, and was prepared to consult his own safety or ambition in the event of the war. The consequence of their and Galerius' rival ambitions was that the Roman world for the first, and indeed the last, time was administered by six emperors. In the West, Constantine and Maxentius affected to reverence their father Maximian. In the East, Licinius and Maximin honoured with more real consideration their benefactor Galerius. The opposition of interest, and the memory of a recent war, divided the empire into two great hostile powers; but their mutual fears produced an apparent tranquillity, and even a feigned reconciliation, till the death of the elder princes, of Maximian, and more particularly of Galerius, gave a new direction to the views and passions of their surviving associates. Maximian, while agitating in Gaul, was driven by Constantine into Marseilles, whose people surrendered him; he is said to have strangled himself. Galerius died of a loathsome disease. Of the four emperors that remained, Constantine and Licinius were connected by a bond of common interest, and a secret alliance was conducted between Maximin and Maxentius.

When Maxentius moved to seize Italy Constantine campaigned against him with energy and determination. The final battle was fought at a place called Saxa Rubra, about nine miles from Rome. After a stubborn resistance, especially on the part of the prætorians, the forces of Maxentius were routed and thousands rushed into the Tiber. The emperor himself attempted to escape back into the city over the Milvian Bridge, but the crowds which pressed together through that narrow passage forced him into the river, where he was immediately drowned by the weight of his armour. Constantine extirpated the family, but pardoned the adherents, of Maxentius. Games and festivals were instituted to preserve the fame of his victory, and several edifices, raised at the expense of Maxentius, were dedicated to the honour of his successful rival. The triumphal arch of Constantine still remains a melancholy proof of the decline of the arts, and a singular testimony of the meanest vanity. As it was not possible to find in the capital of the empire a sculptor who was capable of adorning that public monument, the arch of Trajan, without any respect either for his memory or for the rules of propriety, was stripped of its most elegant figures. The difference of times and persons, of actions and characters, was totally disregarded. The Parthian captives appear prostrate at the feet of a prince who never carried his arms beyond the Euphrates; and curious antiquarians can still discover the head of Trajan on the trophies of Constantine. The new ornaments which it was necessary to introduce between the vacancies of ancient sculpture are executed in the rudest and most unskilful manner.

Before Constantine marched into Italy he had secured the friendship, or at least the neutrality, of Licinius, the Illyrian emperor. He had promised his sister Constantia in marriage to that prince; but the celebration of the nuptials was deferred till after the conclusion of the war, and the interview of the two emperors at Milan, which was appointed for that purpose, appeared to cement the union of their families and interests. In the midst of the public festivity they were suddenly obliged to take leave of each other. An inroad of the Franks summoned Constantine to the Rhine, and the hostile approach of the sovereign of Asia demanded the immediate presence of Licinius. Maximin had been the secret ally of Maxentius and, now moved westward from Syria. Licinius met and defeated him at Heraclea; Maximin fled precipitately and died at Tarsus. The provinces of the east cheerfully acknowledged the authority of Licinius.

The Roman world was now divided between Constantine and Licinius, the former of whom was master of the West, and the latter of the East. It might perhaps have been expected that the conquerors, fatigued with civil war, and connected by a private as well as public alliance, would have renounced, or at least would have suspended, any farther designs of ambition. And yet a year had scarcely elapsed after the death of Maximin, before the victorious emperors turned their arms against each other. Constantine got the better of Licinius in two battles, but prudently decided to come to terms with him before a third encounter. He consented to leave his rival, or, as he again styled Licinius, his friend and brother, in the possession of Thrace, Asia Minor, Syria, and Egypt; but the provinces of Pannonia, Dalmatia, Dacia, Macedonia, and Greece were yielded to the Western empire, and the dominions of Constantine now extended from the confines of Caledonia to the extremity of Peloponnesus. It was stipulated by the same treaty that three royal youths, the sons of the emperors, should be called to the hopes of the succession. Crispus and the young Constantine were soon afterwards declared Cæsars in the West, while the younger Licinius was invested with the same dignity in the East. In this double proportion of honours, the conqueror asserted the superiority of his arms and power.

The reconciliation of Constantine and Licinius, though it was embittered by resentment and jealousy, by the remembrance of recent injuries, and by the apprehension of future dangers, maintained, however, above eight years, the tranquillity of the Roman world. Constantine addressed himself to legislative and administrative reforms and to strengthening the frontiers. But the glory he had won made it impossible that Constantine should any longer endure a partner in the empire. Confiding in the superiority of his genius and military power, he determined, without any previous injury, to exert them for the destruction of Licinius, whose advanced age and unpopular vices seemed to offer a very easy conquest. Constantia, wife of Licinius and sister of Constantine, interceded with her brother and obtained his promise that upon surrendering the purple Licinius would be permitted to pass the remainder of his life in peace and affluence; but he was put under confinement nevertheless, and presently executed. Now the Roman world was again united under the authority of one emperor, thirty-seven years after Diocletian had divided his power and provinces with his associate Maximian.

CHAPTER FIFTEEN

The Progress of the Christian Religion, and the Sentiments, Manners, Numbers, and Condition of the Primitive Christians

A candid but rational inquiry into the progress and establishment of Christianity may be considered as a very essential part of the history of the Roman empire. While that great body was invaded by open violence, or undermined by slow decay, a pure and humble religion gently insinuated itself into the minds of men, grew up in silence and obscurity, derived new vigour from opposition, and finally erected the triumphant banner of the cross on the ruins of the Capitol. Nor was the influence of Christianity confined to the period or to the limits of the Roman empire. After a revolution of thirteen or fourteen centuries, that religion is still professed by the nations of Europe, the most distinguished portion of humankind in arts and learning as well as in arms. By the industry and zeal of the Europeans it has been widely diffused to the most distant shores of Asia and Africa; and by the means of their colonies has been firmly established from Canada to Chile, in a world unknown to the ancients.

But this inquiry, however useful or entertaining, is attended with two peculiar difficulties. The scanty and suspicious materials of ecclesiastical history seldom enable us to dispel the dark cloud that hangs over the first age of the church. The great law of impartiality too often obliges us to reveal the imperfections of the uninspired teachers and believers of the Gospel; and, to a careless observer, *their* faults may seem to cast a shade on the faith which they professed. But the scandal of the pious Christian, and the fallacious triumph of the Infidel, should cease as soon as they recollect not only *by whom*, but likewise *to whom*, the Divine Revelation was given. The theologian may indulge the pleasing task of describing Religion as she descended from heaven, arrayed in her native purity. A more melancholy duty is imposed on the historian. He must discover the inevitable mixture of error and corruption which she contracted in a long residence upon earth, among a weak and degenerate race of beings.

Our curiosity is naturally prompted to inquire by what means the Christian faith obtained so remarkable a victory over the established religions of the earth. To this inquiry an obvious but unsatisfactory answer may be returned: that it was owing to the convincing evidence of the doctrine itself, and to the ruling providence of its great Author. But as truth and reason seldom find so favourable a reception in the world, and as the wisdom of Providence frequently condescends to use the passions of the human heart and the general circumstances of mankind, as instruments to execute its purpose, we may still be permitted, though with becoming submission, to ask, not indeed what were the first, but what were the secondary causes of the rapid growth of the Christian church? It will, perhaps, appear that it was most effectually favoured and assisted by the five following causes:—I. The inflexible, and, if we may use the expression, the intolerant zeal of the Christians, derived, it is true, from the Jewish religion, but purified from the narrow and unsocial spirit which, instead of inviting, had deterred the Gentiles from embracing the law of Moses. II. The doctrine of a future life, improved by every additional circumstance which could give weight and efficacy to that important truth. III. The miraculous powers ascribed to the primitive church. IV. The pure and austere morals of the Christians. V. The union and discipline of the Christian republic, which gradually formed an independent and increasing state in the heart of the Roman empire.

I. The Jewish religion was admirably fitted for defence, but it was never designed for conquest; and it seems probable that the number of proselytes was never much superior to that of apostates. The obligation of preaching to the Gentiles the faith of Moses had never been inculcated as a precept of the law, nor were the Jews inclined to impose it on themselves as a voluntary duty. Their peculiar distinctions of days, of meats, and a variety of trivial though burdensome observances, were objects of aversion for other nations. The painful and even dangerous rite of circumcision was alone capable of repelling a willing proselyte from the door of the synagogue. Under these circumstances, Christianity offered itself to the world armed with the strength of the Mosaic law and delivered from the weight of its fetters.

II. Since the most sublime efforts of philosophy can extend no farther than feebly to point out the desire, the hope, or at most the probability of a future state, there is nothing except a divine revelation that can ascertain the existence and describe the condition of the invisible country which is destined to receive the souls of men after their separation from the body. When the promise of eternal happiness was proposed to mankind on condition of adopting the faith, and of observing the precepts of the Gospel, it is no wonder that so advantageous an offer should have been accepted by great numbers of every religion, of every rank, and of every province in the Roman empire. The ancient Christians were animated by a contempt for their present existence, and by a just confidence of immortality, of which the doubtful and imperfect faith of modern ages cannot give us any adequate notion. In the primitive church the influence of truth was very powerfully strengthened by an opinion which, however it may deserve respect for its usefulness and antiquity, has not been found agreeable to experience. It was universally believed that the end of the world, and the kingdom of heaven, were at hand. The near approach of this wonderful event had been predicted by the apostles; the tradition of it was preserved by their earliest disciples, and those who understood in their literal sense the discourses of Christ himself were obliged to expect the second and glorious coming of the Son of Man in the clouds, before that generation was totally extinguished which had beheld his humble condition upon earth, and which might still be witness of the calamities of the Jews under Vespasian or Hadrian. And while the happiness and glory of a temporal reign were promised to the disciples of Christ, the most dreadful calamities were denounced against an unbelieving world.

III. The supernatural gifts, which even in this life were ascribed to the Christians above the rest of mankind, must have conduced to their own comfort, and very frequently to the conviction of infidels. From the first of the fathers to the last of the popes, a succession of bishops, of saints, of martyrs, and of miracles, is continued without interruption, and the progress of superstition was so gradual and almost imperceptible, that we know not in what particular link we should break the chain of tradition. Every age bears testimony to the wonderful events by which it was distinguished, and its testimony appears no less weighty and respectable than that of the preceding generation, till we are insensibly led on to accuse our own inconsistency if, in the eighth or in the twelfth century, we deny to the venerable Bede, or to the holy Bernard, the same degree of confidence which, in the second century, we had so liberally granted to Justin or to Irenæus.

IV. The primitive Christian demonstrated his faith by his virtue; the desire of perfection became the ruling passion of his soul. A doctrine so extraordinary and so sublime must inevitably command veneration. The Christians acknowledged that governmental institutions might be necessary to the present system of the world, and submitted to the authority of their pagan governors. But while they inculcated the maxims of passive obedience, they refused to take any active part in the civil administration or the military defence of the empire.

V. The primitive Christians were dead to the business and pleasures of the world; but their love of action soon found a new occupation in the government of the church. The public functions of religion were solely entrusted to the established ministers of the church, the *bishops* and the *presbyters*. Provincial synods were soon instituted, and a regular correspondence between them communicated and approved their respective proceedings. Soon the Catholic church assumed the form and acquired the strength of a great fœderative republic. The progress of ecclesiastical authority gave birth to the memorable distinction of the laity and of the clergy, which had been unknown to the Greeks and Romans. (The remainder of Chapter XV considers the classes of population and the areas of the empire in which Christianity spread most rapidly.)

CHAPTER SIXTEEN

The Conduct of the Roman Government towards the Christians, from the Reign of Nero to that of Constantine

If we recollect the universal toleration of Polytheism as it was invariably maintained by the faith of the people, the incredulity of philosophers, and the policy of the Roman senate and emperors, we are at a loss to discover what offence the Christians had committed, what new provocation could exasperate the mild indifference of antiquity, and what new motives could urge the Roman princes, who beheld without concern a thousand forms of religion subsisting in peace under their gentle sway to inflict a severe punishment on any part of their subjects who had chosen for themselves a singular but an inoffensive mode of faith and worship.

The guilt of the Christian consisted in his preferring his private sentiment to the national religion. The new converts seemed to renounce their family and country that they might connect themselves in an indissoluble band of union with a peculiar society, which everywhere assumed a different character from the rest of mankind. Their gloomy and austere aspect, their abhorrence of the common business and pleasures of life, and their frequent predictions of impending calamities, inspired the Pagans with the apprehension of some

113

danger which would arise from the new sect, the more alarming as it was the more obscure. "Whatever," says Pliny, "may be the principle of their conduct, their inflexible obstinacy appeared deserving of punishment." The first instance of Roman persecution of Christians is that of Nero in the tenth year of his reign (A.D. 64). A great fire had levelled most of Rome to the ground, and the voice of rumour accused the emperor as the incendiary of his own capital, and to divert a suspicion which the power of despotism was unable to suppress, the emperor resolved to substitute in his own place some fictitious criminals and chose the Christians for the purpose. "The guilt of the Christians," Tacitus writes, "deserved indeed the most exemplary punishment, but the public abhorrence was changed into commiseration, from the opinion that those unhappy wretches were sacrificed, not so much to the public welfare as to the cruelty of a jealous tyrant."

The emperor Domitian condemned his relatives Clemens and Domitilla, together with others he suspected of conspiracy, on a charge of *Atheism* and *Jewish manners*, an association of ideas which could be properly applied only to Christians. But this persecution (if it deserves that epithet) was of no long duration. Under the reign of Trajan, information was laid against Christians before the younger Pliny, who was governor of Bithynia. Pliny appealed to Trajan for guidance; the answer of Trajan, to which the Christians of the succeeding age have frequently appealed, discovers as much regard for justice and humanity as could be reconciled with his mistaken notions of religious policy. Instead of displaying the implacable zeal of an Inquisitor, anxious to discover the most minute particles of heresy, and exulting in the number of his victims, the emperor expresses much more solicitude to protect the security of the innocent than to prevent the escape of the guilty. He acknowledges the difficulty of fixing any general plan; but he lays down two salutary rules, which often afforded relief and support to the distressed Christians. Though he directs the magistrates to punish such persons as are legally convicted, he prohibits them, with a very humane inconsistency, from making any inquiries concerning the supposed criminals. Nor was the magistrate allowed to proceed on every kind of information. Anonymous charges the emperor rejects, as too repugnant to the equity of his government; and he strictly requires, for the conviction of those to whom the guilt of Christianity is imputed, the positive evidence of a fair and open accuser.

During the whole course of his reign Marcus Aurelius despised the Christians as a philosopher, and punished them as a sovereign. By a singular fatality, the hardships which they had endured under the government of a virtuous prince immediately ceased on the accession of a tyrant; and as none except themselves had experienced the injustice of Marcus, so they alone were protected by the lenity of Commodus. When the empire was established in the house of Severus, Christians formed a more honourable connection with the new court. In consequence of an altercation, Severus published an edict designed to restrain the progress of Christians; but his laws expired along with the _emperor's authority, and after this accidental tempest the Christians enjoyed a calm of thirty-eight years. The reign of those princes who derived their extraction from the Asiatic provinces proved the most favourable to the Christians. The fall of Philip the Arab introduced a new system so oppressive to the Christians that their former condition, ever since the time of Domitian, was represented as a state of perfect freedom and security, if compared with the rigorous treatment which they experienced under the short reign of Decius.

Valerian, in the first part of his reign, surpassed in clemency those princes who had been suspected of an attachment to the Christian faith; in the last three years and a half he adopted the maxims and imitated the severity of his predecessor Decius. The accession of Gallienus, which increased the calamities of the empire, restored peace to the church; the disciples of Christ passed above forty years in a state of prosperity far more dangerous to their virtue than the severest trials of persecution. Although the policy of Diocletian and the humanity of Constantius inclined them to preserve inviolate the maxims of toleration, it was soon discovered that their two associates, Maximian and Galerius, entertained the most implacable aversion for the name and religion of the Christians.

The Christians (it might speciously be alleged), renouncing the gods and the institutions of Rome, had constituted a distinct republic, which might yet be suppressed before it had acquired any military force; but which was already governed by its own laws and magistrates, was possessed of a public treasure, and was intimately connected in all its parts by the frequent assemblies of the bishops, to whose decrees their numerous and opulent congregations yielded an implicit obedience. Arguments like these may seem to have determined the reluctant mind of Diocletian to embrace a new system of persecution. Diocletian had no sooner published his edicts against the Christians than he divested himself of the Imperial purple. The elevation of Constantius gave free scope to the exercise of his virtues, and the shortness of his reign did not prevent him from establishing a system of toleration of which he left the precept and example to his son Constantine. His fortunate son, from the first moment of his accession declaring himself the protector of the church, at length deserved the appellation of the first emperor who publicly professed and established the Christian religion.

We shall conclude this chapter by a melancholy truth which obtrudes itself on the reluctant mind; that, even admitting, without hesitation or inquiry, all that history has recorded, or devotion has feigned, on the subject of martyrdoms, it must still be acknowledged that the Christians, in the course of their intestine dissensions, have inflicted far greater severities on each other than they had experienced from the zeal of infidels.

CHAPTER SEVENTEEN

Foundation of Constantinople—Political System of Constantine and his Successors—Military Discipline—The Palace—The Finances

After the defeat and abdication of Licinius his victorious rival proceeded to lay the foundations of a city destined to reign in future times the mistress of the East, and to survive the empire and religion of Constantine. In the choice of an advantageous situation he preferred the confines of Europe and Asia; to curb with a powerful arm the barbarians who dwelt between the Danube and the Tanais; to watch with an eye of jealousy the Persian monarch, who indignantly supported the yoke of an ignominious treaty. During the late operations of the war against Licinius he had sufficient opportunity to contemplate, both as a soldier and as a statesman, the incomparable position of Byzantium; and to observe how strongly it was guarded by nature against an hostile attack, whilst it was accessible on every side to the benefits of commercial intercourse. (There follow full descriptions of the topography and structures of Constantinople.)

The foundation of a new capital is naturally connected with the establishment of a new form of civil and military administration. The distinct view of the complicated system of policy introduced by Diocletian, improved by Constantine, and com-

117

pleted by his immediate successors, may not only amuse the
fancy by the singular picture of a great empire, but will tend to
illustrate the secret and internal causes of its rapid decay. In
the pursuit of any remarkable institution, we may be frequently led into the more early or the more recent times of the
Roman history; but the proper limits of this inquiry will be
included within a period of about one hundred and thirty
years, from the accession of Constantine to the publication of
the Theodosian code; from which, as well as from the *Notitia*
of the East and West, we derive the most copious and authentic information of the state of the empire. This variety of objects will suspend, for some time, the course of the narrative;
but the interruption will be censured only by those readers
who are insensible to the importance of laws and manners,
while they peruse, with eager curiosity, the transient intrigues
of a court, or the accidental event of a battle.

The manly pride of the Romans, content with substantial
power, had left to the vanity of the East the forms and ceremonies of ostentatious greatness. But when they lost even the
semblance of those virtues which were derived from their ancient freedom, the simplicity of Roman manners was insensibly corrupted by the stately affectation of the courts of Asia.
The distinctions of personal merit and influence, so conspicuous in a republic, so feeble and obscure under a monarchy,
were abolished by the despotism of the emperors; who substituted in their room a severe subordination of rank and office,
from the titled slaves who were seated on the steps of the
throne, to the meanest instruments of arbitrary power. This
multitude of abject dependents was interested in the support of
the actual government, from the dread of a revolution which
might at once confound their hopes and intercept the reward of
their services. In this divine hierarchy (for such it is frequently
styled) every rank was marked with the most scrupulous
exactness, and its dignity was displayed in a variety of trifling
and solemn ceremonies, which it was a study to learn, and a
sacrilege to neglect. The purity of the Latin language was
debased, by adopting, in the intercourse of pride and flattery,
a profusion of epithets which Tully would scarcely have un-

derstood, and which Augustus would have rejected with indignation. The principal officers of the empire were saluted, even by the sovereign himself, with the deceitful titles of your *Sincerity*, your *Gravity*, your *Excellency*, your *Eminence*, your *sublime and wonderful Magnitude*, your *illustrious and magnificent Highness*. All the magistrates of sufficient importance to find a place in the general state of the empire were accurately divided into three classes—1. The *Illustrious*; 2. The *Spectabiles*, or Respectable; and, 3. The *Clarissimi*, whom we may translate by the word *Honourable*.

As long as the Roman consuls were the first magistrates of a free state, they derived their right to power from the choice of the people. As long as the emperors condescended to disguise the servitude which they imposed, the consuls were still elected by the real or apparent suffrage of the senate. From the reign of Diocletian even these vestiges of liberty were abolished, and the successful candidates, who were invested with the annual honours of the consulship, affected to deplore the humiliating condition of their predecessors. The Scipios and the Catos had been reduced to solicit the votes of plebians, to pass through the tedious and expensive forms of a popular election, and to expose their dignity to the shame of a public refusal; while their own happier fate had reserved them for an age and government in which the rewards of virtue were assigned by the unerring wisdom of a gracious sovereign. Their names and portraits, engraved on gilt tablets of ivory, were dispersed over the empire as presents to the provinces, the cities, the magistrates, the senate, and the people. On the morning of the first of January the consuls assumed the ensigns of their dignity. Their dress was a robe of purple, embroidered in silk and gold, and sometimes ornamented with costly gems. On this solemn occasion they were attended by the most eminent officers of the state and army in the habit of senators; and the useless faces, armed with the once formidable axes, were borne before them by the lictors. The procession moved from the palace to the Forum or principal square of the city; where the consuls ascended their tribunal, and seated themselves in the curule chairs, which were framed after the fashion of ancient times. They immediately exercised an act of jurisdiction, by the manumission of a slave who was brought before them for that purpose; and the ceremony was intended to represent the celebrated action of the elder Brutus, the author of liberty and of the consulship, when he admitted among his fellow-citizens the faithful Vindex, who had revealed the conspiracy of the Tarquins. The public festival was continued during several days in all the principal cities; in Rome, from custom; in Constantinople, from imitation; in Carthage, Antioch, and Alexandria, from the love of pleasure and the superfluity of wealth.

As soon as the consuls had discharged these customary duties, they were at liberty to retire into the shade of private life, and to enjoy during the remainder of the year the undisturbed contemplation of their own greatness. They no longer presided in the national councils; they no longer executed the resolutions of peace or war. The title of consul was still the most splendid object of ambition, the noblest reward of virtue and loyalty. The emperors themselves, who disdained the faint shadow of the republic, were conscious that they acquired an additional splendour and majesty as often as they assumed the annual honours of the consular dignity.

The distinction between patrician and plebeian, which was scrupulously observed during the early Republic, had long become empty of meaning. Little more was left when Constantine ascended the throne than a vague and imperfect tradition that the Patricians had once been the first of the Romans. To form a body of nobles, whose influence may restrain while it secures the authority of the monarch, would have been very inconsistent with the character and policy of Constantine; but, had he seriously entertained such a design, it might have exceeded the measure of his power to ratify by an arbitrary edict an institution which must expect the sanction of time and of opinion. He revived, indeed, the title of PATRICIANS, but he revived it as a personal, not as an hereditary distinction. They yielded only to the transient superiority of the annual consuls; but they enjoyed the pre-eminence over all the great officers of state, with the most familiar access to the person of the prince. This honourable rank was bestowed on them for life; and, as they were usually favourites and ministers who had grown old in the Imperial court, the true etymology of the word was perverted by ignorance and flattery; and the Patricians of Constantine were reverenced as the adopted *Fathers* of the emperor and the republic.

The fortunes of the Prætorian præfects were essentially different from those of the consuls and Patricians. The latter saw their ancient greatness evaporate in a vain title. The former, rising by degrees from the most humble condition were invested with the civil and military administration of the Roman world. After the Prætorian præfects had been dismissed from all military command, the civil functions which they were ordained to exercise over so many subject nations were adequate to the ambition and abilities of the most consummate ministers. To their wisdom was committed the supreme administration of justice and of the finances, the two objects which, in a state of peace, comprehend almost all the respective duties of the sovereign and of the people; of the former, to protect the citizens who are obedient to the laws; of the latter, to contribute the share of their property which is required for the expenses of the state. The coin, the highways, the posts, the granaries, the manufactures, whatever could interest the public prosperity, was moderated by the authority of the Prætorian præfects. As the immediate representatives of the Imperial majesty, they were empowered to explain, to enforce, and on some occasions to modify, the general edicts by their discretionary proclamations. They watched over the conduct of the provincial governors, removed the negligent, and inflicted punishments on the guilty. From all the inferior jurisdictions an appeal in every matter of importance, either civil or criminal, might be brought before the tribunal of the præfect: but *his* sentence was final and absolute; and the emperors themselves refused to admit any complaints against the judgment or the integrity of a magistrate whom they honoured with such unbounded confidence. His appointments were suitable to his dignity; and, if avarice was his ruling passion, he enjoyed frequent opportunities of collecting a rich harvest of fees, of presents, and of perquisites. Though the emperors no longer dreaded the ambition of their præfects, they were attentive to counterbalance the power of this great office by the uncertainty and shortness of its duration. From their superior importance and dignity, Rome and Constantinople were alone excepted from the jurisdiction of the Prætorian præfects.

The civil government of the empire was distributed into thirteen great DIOCESES, each of which equalled the just measure of a powerful kingdom. As the spirit of jealousy and ostentation prevailed in the councils of the emperors, they proceeded with anxious diligence to divide the substance and to multiply the titles of power. The vast countries which the Roman conquerors had united under the same simple form of administration were imperceptibly crumbled into minute fragments, till at length the whole empire was distributed into one hundred and sixteen provinces, each of which supported an expensive and splendid establishment.

All the civil magistrates were drawn from the profession of the law. The celebrated Institutes of Justinian are addressed to the youth of his dominions who had devoted themselves to the study of Roman jurisprudence; and the sovereign condescends to animate their diligence by the assurance that their skill and ability would in time be rewarded by an adequate share in the government of the republic. The first experiment was made of their judicial talents by appointing them to act occasionally as assessors to the magistrates; from thence they were often raised to preside in the tribunals before which they had pleaded. They obtained the government of a province; and, by the aid of merit, of reputation, or of favour, they ascended, by successive steps, to the *illustrious* dignities of the state.

In the system of policy introduced by Augustus, the governors, those at least of the Imperial provinces, were invested with the full powers of the sovereign himself. From the time of Commodus to the reign of Constantine near one hundred governors might be enumerated, who, with various success, erected the standard of revolt; and though the innocent were too often sacrificed, the guilty might be sometimes prevented, by the suspicious cruelty of their master. To secure his throne and the public tranquillity from these formidable servants, Constantine resolved to divide the military from the civil administration, and to establish, as a permanent and professional distinction, a practice which had been adopted only as an occasional expedient. The supreme jurisdiction exercised by the Prætorian præfects over the armies of the empire was transferred to the two *masters general* whom he instituted the one for the *cavalry*, the other for the *infantry*; and though each of these *illustrious* officers was more peculiarly responsible for the discipline of those troops which were under his immediate inspection, they both indifferently commanded in the field the several bodies, whether of horse or foot, which were united in the same army. Their number was soon doubled by the division of the East and West; and as separate generals of the same rank and title were appointed on the four important frontiers of the Rhine, of the Upper and the Lower Danube, and of the Euphrates, the defence of the Roman empire was at length committed to eight masters general of the cavalry and infantry. Under their orders, thirty-five military commanders were stationed in the provinces: three in Britain, six in Gaul, one in Spain, one in Italy, five on the Upper and four on the Lower Danube, in Asia eight, three in Egypt, and four in Africa. The titles of *counts* and *dukes*, by which they were properly distinguished, have obtained a very different sense in modern languages.

The emulation, and sometimes the discord, which reigned between two professions of opposite interests and incompatible manners, was productive of beneficial and of pernicious consequences. It was seldom to be expected that the general and the civil governor of a province should either conspire for the disturbance, or should unite for the service, of their country. While the one delayed to offer the assistance which the other disdained to solicit, the troops very frequently remained without orders or without supplies, the public safety was betrayed, and the defenceless subjects were left exposed to the fury of the barbarians. The divided administration, which had been formed by Constantine, relaxed the vigour of the state, while it secured the tranquillity of the monarch. From the reign of Constantine a popular and even legal distinction was admitted between the *Palatines* and the *Borderers*; the troops of the court, as they were improperly styled, and the troops of the frontier. The former, elevated by the superiority of their pay and privileges, were permitted, except in the extraordinary emergencies of war, to occupy their tranquil stations in the heart of the provinces. The most flourishing cities were oppressed by the intolerable weight of quarters. The soldiers insensibly forgot the virtues of their profession, and contracted only the vices of civil life. They were either degraded by the industry of mechanic trades, or enervated by the luxury of baths and theatres. They soon became careless of their martial exercises, curious in their diet and apparel, and, while they inspired terror to the subjects of the empire, they trembled at the hostile approach of the barbarians. The chain of fortifications which Diocletian and his colleagues had extended along the banks of the great rivers was no longer maintained with the same care, or defended with the same vigilance. The numbers which still remained under the name of the troops of the frontier might be sufficient for the ordinary defence. But their spirit was degraded by the humiliating reflection that *they*, who were exposed to the hardships and dangers of a perpetual warfare, were rewarded only with about two-thirds of the pay and emoluments which were lavished on the troops of the court.

The timid policy, of dividing whatever is united, of reducing whatever is eminent, of dreading every active power, and of expecting that the most feeble will prove the most obedient, seems to pervade the institutions of several princes, and particularly those of Constantine. The martial pride of the legions, whose victorious camps had so often been the scene of rebellion, was nourished by the memory of their past exploits, and the consciousness of their actual strength. As long as they maintained their ancient establishment of six thousand men, they subsisted, under the reign of Diocletian, each of them singly, a visible and important object in the military history of the Roman empire. A few years afterwards these gigantic bodies were shrunk to a very diminutive size; and when *seven* legions, with some auxiliaries, defended the city of Amida against the Persians, the total garrison, with the inhabitants of both sexes, and the peasants of the deserted country, did not exceed the number of twenty thousand persons. From this fact, and from similar examples, there is reason to believe that the constitution of the legionary troops, to which they partly owed their valour and discipline, was dissolved by Constantine; and that the bands of Roman infantry, which still assumed the same names and the same honours, consisted only of one thousand or fifteen hundred men. The conspiracy of so many separate detachments, each of which was awed by the sense of its own weakness, could easily be checked; and the successors of Constantine might indulge their love of ostentation, by issuing their orders to one hundred and thirty-two legions inscribed on the muster-roll of their numerous armies. The resources of the Roman treasury were exhausted by the increase of pay, by the repetition of donatives, and by the invention of new emoluments and indulgences, which, in the opinion of the provincial youth, might compensate the hardships and dangers of a military life. Yet, although the stature was lowered, although slaves, at least by a tacit connivance, were indiscriminately received into the ranks, the insurmountable difficulty of procuring a regular and adequate supply of volunteers obliged the emperors to adopt more effectual and coercive methods. The lands bestowed on the veterans, as the free reward of their valour, were henceforwards granted under a condition which contains the first rudiments of the feudal tenures—that their sons, who succeeded to the inheritance, should devote themselves to the profession of arms as soon as they attained the age of manhood; and their cowardly refusal was punished by the loss of honour, of fortune, or even of life. But as the annual growth of the sons of the veterans bore a very small proportion to the demands of the service, levies of men were frequently required from the provinces, and every proprietor was obliged either to take up arms, or to procure a substitute, or to purchase his exemption by the payment of a heavy fine. The sum of forty-two pieces of gold, to which it was *reduced*, ascertains the exhorbitant price of volunteers, and the reluctance with which the government admitted of this alternative. Such was the horror for the profession of a soldier which had affected the minds of the degenerate Romans that many of the youth of Italy and the provinces chose to cut off the fingers of their right hand to escape from being pressed into the service; and this strange expedient was so commonly practised as to deserve the severe animadversion of the laws, and a peculiar name in the Latin language. The introduction of barbarians into the Roman armies became every day more universal, more necessary, and more fatal.

Besides the magistrates and generals to whom the emperor delegated authority over provinces and armies, he conferred the rank of *Illustrious* on seven of his more immediate servants, to whose fidelity he intrusted his safety, or his counsels, or his treasures: the chamberlain, the master of the offices, the quaestor (a species of chancellor), the count of the sacred largesses (or public treasurer), the count of the private estate, and two counts of the domestics. The perpetual intercourse between the court and the provinces was facilitated by the construction of roads and the institution of posts. But these beneficial establishments were accidentally connected with a pernicious and intolerable abuse. Two or three hundred *agents* or messengers were employed, under the jurisdiction of the master of the offices, to announce the names of the annual consuls, and the edicts or victories of the emperors. They insensibly assumed the licence of reporting whatever they could observe of the conduct either of magistrates or of private citizens; and were soon considered as the eyes of the monarch and the scourge of the people. Under the warm influence of a feeble reign they multiplied to the incredible number of ten thousand, disdained the mild though frequent admonitions of the laws, and exercised in the profitable management of the posts a rapacious and insolent oppression. These official spies, who regularly corresponded with the palace, were encouraged, by favour and reward, anxiously to watch the progress of every treasonable design, from the faint and latent symptoms of disaffection, to the actual preparation of an open revolt. Their careless or criminal violation of truth and justice was covered by the consecrated mask of zeal; and they might securely aim their poisoned arrows at the breast either of the guilty or the innocent, who had provoked their resentment, or refused to purchase their silence. A faithful subject, of Syria perhaps, or of Britain, was exposed to the danger, or at least to the dread, of being dragged in chains to the court of Milan or Constantinople, to defend his life and fortune against the malicious charge of these privileged informers. The ordinary administration was conducted by those methods which extreme necessity can alone palliate; and the defects of evidence were diligently supplied by the use of torture.

The agriculture of the Roman provinces was insensibly ruined, and, in the progress of despotism, which tends to disappoint its own purpose, the emperors were obliged to derive some merit from the forgiveness of debts, or the remission of tributes, which their subjects were utterly incapable of paying. According to the new division of Italy, the fertile and happy province of Campania, the scene of the early victories and of the delicious retirements of the citizens of Rome, extended between the sea and the Apennine from the Tiber to the Silarus. Within sixty years after the death of Constantine, and on the evidence of an actual survey, an exemption was granted in favour of three hundred and thirty thousand English acres of desert and uncultivated land, which amounted to one-eighth of the whole surface of the province. As the footsteps of the barbarians had not yet been seen in Italy, the cause of this amazing desolation, which is recorded in the laws, can be ascribed only to the administration of the Roman emperors.

General taxes were imposed and levied by the absolute authority of the monarch; but the occasional offerings of the *coronary gold* still retained the name and semblance of popular consent. It was an ancient custom that the allies of the republic, who ascribed their safety or deliverance to the success of the Roman arms, and even the cities of Italy, who admired the virtues of their victorious general, adorned the pomp of his triumph by their voluntary gifts of crowns of gold, which, after the ceremony, were consecrated in the temple of Jupiter, to remain a lasting monument of his glory to future ages. The progress of zeal and flattery soon multiplied the number, and increased the size, of these popular donations.

A people elated by pride, or soured by discontent, is seldom qualified to form a just estimate of their actual situation. The subjects of Constantine were incapable of discerning the decline of genius and manly virtue, which so far degraded them below the dignity of their ancestors; but they could feel and lament the rage of tyranny, the relaxation of discipline, and the increase of taxes. The impartial historian, who acknowledges the justice of their complaints, will observe some favourable circumstances which tended to alleviate the misery of their condition. The threatening tempest of barbarians, which so soon subverted the foundations of Roman greatness, was still repelled, or suspended, on the frontiers. The arts of luxury and literature were cultivated, and the elegant pleasures of society were enjoyed, by the inhabitants of a considerable portion of the globe. The forms, the pomp, and the expense of the civil administration contributed to restrain the irregular licence of the soldiers; and although the laws were violated by power, or perverted by subtlety, the sage principles of the Roman jurisprudence preserved a sense of order and equity unknown to the despotic governments of the East. The rights of mankind might derive some protection from religion and philosophy; and the name of freedom, which could no longer alarm, might sometimes admonish, the successors of Augustus, that they did not reign over a nation of Slaves or Barbarians.

CHAPTER EIGHTEEN

Character of Constantine—Gothic War—Death of Constantine—Division of the Empire among his three sons—Persian War—Tragic Deaths of Constantine the Younger and Constans—Usurpation of Magnentius—Civil War—Victory of Constantius

In the life of Augustus we behold the tyrant of the republic converted almost by imperceptible degrees into the father of his country and of human kind. In that of Constantine we may contemplate a hero, who had so long inspired his subjects with love and his enemies with terror, degenerating into a cruel and dissolute monarch, corrupted by his fortune, or raised by conquest above the necessity of dissimulation. The general peace which he maintained during the last fourteen years of his reign was a period of apparent splendour rather than of real prosperity; and the old age of Constantine was disgraced by the opposite yet reconcilable vices of rapaciousness and prodigality. A secret but universal decay was felt in every part of the public administration, and the emperor himself, though he still retained the obedience, gradually lost the esteem of his subjects. The dress and manners which, towards the decline of life, he chose to affect, served only to degrade him in the eyes of mankind. The Asiatic pomp which had been adopted by the

pride of Diocletian assumed an air of softness and effeminacy
in the person of Constantine. He is represented with false hair
of various colours, laboriously arranged by the skilful artists
of the times; a diadem of a new and more expensive fashion; a
profusion of gems and pearls, of collars and bracelets; and a
variegated flowing robe of silk, most curiously embroidered
with flowers of gold. In such apparel, scarcely to be excused
by the youth and folly of Elagabalus, we are at a loss to
discover the wisdom of an aged monarch and the simplicity of
a Roman veteran. A mind thus relaxed by prosperity and indulgence was incapable of rising to that magnanimity which
disdains suspicion and dares to forgive. The deaths of Maximian and Licinius may perhaps be justified by the maxims of
policy as they are taught in the schools of tyrants; but an
impartial narrative of the executions, or rather murders, which
sullied the declining age of Constantine, will suggest to our
most candid thoughts the idea of a prince who could sacrifice,
without reluctance, the laws of justice and the feelings of nature to the dictates either of his passions or of his interest.

The same fortune which so invariably followed the standard of Constantine seemed to secure the hopes and comforts
of his domestic life.

In less than thirty years Constantine's numerous family was
reduced to the persons of Constantious and Julian. Crispus,
the eldest son of Constantine, deserved the esteem and engaged the affections of the court, the army, and the people.
His dangerous popularity soon excited the attention of Constantine, who, both as a father and as a king, was impatient of
an equal. Instead of attempting to secure the allegiance of his
son by the generous ties of confidence and gratitude, he resolved to prevent the mischief which might be apprehended
from dissatisfied ambition. In the midst of a splendid festival
celebrating the twentieth year of Constantine's reign, the unfortunate Crispus was apprehended by order of the emperor,
who laid aside the tenderness of a father without assuming the
equity of a judge. He was sent under a strong guard to Pola in
Istria, where, soon afterwards, he was put to death, either by

the hand of the executioner or by the more gentle operation of poison.

By the death of Crispus the inheritance of the empire seemed to devolve on the three sons of Fausta—Constantine, Constantius, and Constans. In addition to these Cæsars Constantine bestowed the same title upon his two nephews, Dalmatius and Hannibalianus. The indulgence of Constantine admitted these youths to share the administration of the empire, and they studied the art of reigning, at the expense of the people intrusted to their care. The younger Constantine was appointed to hold his court in Gaul; and his brother Constantius exchanged that department, the ancient patrimony of their father, for the more opulent, but less martial, countries of the East. Italy, the Western Illyricum, and Africa, were accustomed to revere Constans, the third of his sons, as the representative of the great Constantine. He fixed Dalmatius on the Gothic frontier, to which he annexed the government of Thrace, Macedonia, and Greece. The city of Cæsarea was chosen for the residence of Hannibalianus; and the provinces of Pontus, Cappadocia, and the Lesser Armenia, were designed to form the extent of his new kingdom. For each of these princes a suitable establishment was provided. A just proportion of guards, of legions, and of auxiliaries, was allotted for their respective dignity and defence. The ministers and generals who were placed about their persons were such as Constantine could trust to assist, and even to control, these youthful sovereigns in the exercise of their delegated power. As they advanced in years and experience, the limits of their authority were insensibly enlarged: but the emperor always reserved for himself the title of Augustus; and while he showed the *Cæsars* to the armies and provinces, he maintained every part of the empire in equal obedience to its supreme head. It was Constantine himself who subdued the Sarmatians and the Goths and so reasserted the majesty of Rome.

If Constantine reckoned among the favours of fortune the death of his eldest son, of his nephew, and perhaps of his wife, he enjoyed an uninterrupted flow of private as well as public felicity till the thirtieth year of his reign, a period which none of his predecessors, since Augustus, had been permitted to celebrate. Constantine survived that solemn festival about ten months, and at the mature age of sixty-four, after a short illness, he ended his memorable life near Nicomedia, whither he had retired for the benefit of the air. The excessive demonstrations of grief, or at least of mourning, surpassed whatever had been practised on any former occasion. Notwithstanding the claims of the senate and people of ancient Rome, the corpse of the deceased emperor, according to his last request, was transported to the city which was destined to preserve the name and memory of its founder. The body of Constantine, adorned with the vain symbols of greatness, the purple and diadem, was deposited on a golden bed in one of the apartments of the palace, which for that purpose had been splendidly furnished and illuminated.

The voice of the dying emperor had recommended the care of his funeral to the piety of Constantius; and that prince, by the vicinity of his eastern station, could easily prevent the diligence of his brothers, who resided in their distant governments of Italy and Gaul. As soon as he had taken possession of the palace of Constantinople, his first care was to remove the apprehensions of his kinsmen, by a solemn oath which he pledged for their security. His next employment was to find some specious pretence which might release his conscience from the obligation of an imprudent promise. The arts of fraud were made subservient to the designs of cruelty; and a manifest forgery was attested by a person of the most sacred character. From the hands of the bishop of Nicomedia, Constantius received a fatal scroll, affirmed to be the genuine testament of his father; in which the emperor expressed his suspicions that he had been poisoned by his brothers; and conjured his sons to revenge his death, and to consult their own safety, by the punishment of the guilty. Whatever reasons might have been alleged by these unfortunate princes to defend their life and honour against so incredible an accusation, they were silenced by the furious clamours of the soldiers, who declared themselves, at once, their enemies, their judges, and their executioners. The spirit, and even the forms, of legal proceedings were repeatedly violated in a promiscuous massacre; which involved the two uncles of Constantius, seven of his cousins, of whom Dalmatius and Hannibalianus were the most illustrious, the Patrician Optatus, who had married a sister of the late emperor, and the præfect Ablavius, whose power and riches had inspired him with some hopes of obtaining the purple. Of so numerous a family, Gallus and Julian alone, the two youngest children of Julius Constantius, were saved from the hands of the assassins, till their rage, satiated with slaughter, had in some measure subsided.

After the partition of the empire three years had scarcely elapsed before the sons of Constantine seemed impatient to convince mankind that they were incapable of contenting themselves with the dominions which they were unqualified to govern. The eldest of those princes soon complained that he was defrauded of his just proportion of the spoils of their murdered kinsmen; and though he might yield to the superior guilt and merit of Constantius, he exacted from Constans the cession of the African provinces, as an equivalent for the rich countries of Macedonia and Greece which his brother had acquired by the death of Dalmatius. The want of sincerity which Constantine experienced in a tedious and fruitless negotiation exasperated the fierceness of his temper, and he eagerly listened to those favourites who suggested to him that his honour, as well as his interest, was concerned in the prosecution of the quarrel. At the head of a tumultuary band, suited for rapine rather than for conquest, he suddenly broke into the dominions of Constans, by the way of the Julian Alps, and the country round Aquileia felt the first effects of his resentment. The measures of Constans, who then resided in Dacia, were directed with more prudence and ability. On the news of his brother's invasion he detached a select and disciplined body of his Illyrian troops, proposing to follow them in person with the remainder of his forces. But the conduct of his lieutenants soon terminated the unnatural contest. By the artful appearances of flight, Constantine was betrayed into an ambuscade, which had been concealed in a wood, where the rash youth, with a few attendants, was surprised, surrounded and slain. His body, after it had been found in the obscure stream of the

Alsa, obtained the honours of an Imperial sepulchre, but his provinces transferred their allegiance to the conqueror, who, refusing to admit his elder brother Constantius to any share in these new acquisitions, maintained the undisputed possession of more than two-thirds of the Roman empire. The fate of Constans himself was delayed about ten years longer, and the revenge of his brother's death was reserved for the more ignoble hand of a domestic traitor. The pernicious tendency of the system introduced by Constantine was displayed in the feeble administration of his sons, who, by their vices and weakness, soon lost the esteem and affections of their people. After the death of Constans, Magnentius and Vetranio assumed the purple in the west, and Constantius returned from the east to deal with these usurpers. Vetranio was deposed; Magnentius was defeated in two battles and fell upon his sword.

CHAPTER NINETEEN

> *Constantius sole Emperor—Elevation and Death of Gallus—Danger and Elevation of Julian—Sarmatian and Persian Wars—Victories of Julian in Gaul*

The divided provinces of the empire were again united by the victory of Constantious; but as that feeble prince was destitute of personal merit either in peace or war; as he feared his generals, and distrusted his ministers; the triumph of his arms served only to establish the reign of the *eunuchs* over the Roman world. Of these slaves the most distinguished was the chamberlain Eusebius, who ruled the monarch and the palace with such absolute sway, that Constantius, according to the sarcasm of an impartial historian, possessed some credit with this haughty favourite. By his artful suggestions, the emperor was persuaded to subscribe the new condemnation of the unfortunate Gallus, and to add a new crime to the long list of unnatural murders which pollute the honour of the house of Constantine.

When the two nephews of Constantine, Gallus and Julian, were saved from the fury of the soldiers, the former was about twelve, and the latter about six, years of age; and, as the eldest was thought to be of a sickly constitution, they obtained with the less difficulty a precarious and dependent life from

135

the affected pity of Constantius, who was sensible that the execution of these helpless orphans would have been esteemed, by all mankind, an act of the most deliberate cruelty. Different cities of Ionia and Bithynia were assigned for the places of their exile and education; but as soon as their growing years excited the jealousy of the emperor, he judged it more prudent to secure those unhappy youths in the strong castle of Macellum near Cæarea. The treatment which they experienced during a six years' confinement was partly such as they could hope from a careful guardian, and partly such as they might dread from a suspicious tyrant. At length, however, the emergencies of the state compelled the emperor, or rather his eunuchs, to invest Gallus, in the twenty-fifth year of his age, with the title of Cæsar, and to cement this political connection by his marriage with the princess Constantina. In this fortune change, the new Cæsar was not unmindful of his brother Julian, who obtained the honours of his rank, the appearances of liberty, and the restitution of an ample patrimony.

The writers the most indulgent to the memory of Gallus, and even Julian himself, though he wished to cast a veil over the frailties of his brother, are obliged to confess that the Cæsar was incapable of reigning. The ungoverned sallies of his rage were often fatal to those who approached his person, or were subject to his power. Constantina, his wife, is described, not as a woman, but as one of the infernal furies tormented with an insatiate thirst of human blood. As long as the civil war suspended the fate of the Roman world, Constantius dissembled his knowledge of the weak and cruel administration to which his choice had subjected the East; but when the victory was decided in favour of Constantius, his dependent colleague became less useful and less formidable. Gallus behaved with foolish truculence to the emissary Constantius despatched to reform the administration of the eastern marches, but was enticed to march westward, and when he came into Constantius' power he was summarily tried as a malefactor and beheaded.

Besides the reigning emperor, Julian alone survived of all the numerous posterity of Constantius Chlorus. The misfortune of his royal birth involved him in the disgrace of Gallus.

From his retirement in the happy country of Ionia he was conveyed, under a strong guard, to the court of Milan, where he languished above seven months in the continual apprehension of suffering the same ignominious death which was daily inflicted, almost before his eyes, on the friends and adherents of his persecuted family. Through the intercession of his patroness, the empress Eusebia, Julian was admitted into the Imperial presence and heard with favour. Presently Athens was appointed to be the place of his honourable exile; from his earliest youth Julian had discovered a passion for the language, the manners, the learning, and the religion of the Greeks, and he obeyed with pleasure an order so agreeable to his wishes.

In the meanwhile, disturbances in several parts of the empire, and in particular barbarian invasions of Gaul, oppressed Constantius with their accumulated weight. For the first time he sincerely acknowledged that his single strength was unequal to such an extent of care and of dominion. Through the efforts of Eusebia and against the opposition of the eunuchs, it was resolved that Julian, after celebrating his nuptials with Helena, sister of Constantius, should be appointed, with the title of Cæsar, to reign over the countries beyond the Alps. After the investiture of Julian in Milan, Constantius spent some time inspecting the antiquities at Rome, and was then called away to deal with an invasion of Mesopotamia by the Persian king Sapor. His successes in Persia were ambivalent. Julian, on the other hand, delivered Gaul from its invaders by a series of brilliant campaigns, rehabilitated the ruined cities of Gaul, reformed their administration, and won the devoted esteem of the subjects of the empire and of the armies he commanded.

CHAPTER TWENTY

The Motives, Progress, and Effects of the Conversion of Constantine—Legal Establishment and Constitution of the Christian or Catholic Church

CHAPTER TWENTY-ONE

*Persecution of Heresy—The Schism of the Dona-
tists—The Arian Controversy—Athanasius—
Distracted State of the Church and Empire under
Constantine and his Sons—Toleration of Paganism*

(These two chapters are largely occupied with theological
matters which are remote from the interests of the ordinary
reader, which are highly controversial, and which do not lend
themselves to abridgement.)

CHAPTER TWENTY-TWO

*Julian is declared Emperor by the Legions of Gaul
—His March and Success—The Death of Constantius—Civil Administration of Julian*

The praises of Julian were repeated with transport in every
part of the empire, except in the palace of Constantius. The
barbarians of Germany had felt, and still dreaded, the arms of
the young Cæsar; his soldiers were the companions of his
victory; the grateful provincials enjoyed the blessings of his
reign; but the favourites, who had opposed his elevation, were
offended by his virtues, and they justly considered the friend
of the people as the enemy of the court. The personal fears of
Constantius were interpreted by his council as a laudable anxiety for the public safety; whilst in private, and perhaps in his
own breast, he disguised, under the less odious appellation of
fear, the sentiments of hatred and envy which he had secretly
conceived for the inimitable virtues of Julian.

The apparent tranquillity of Gaul, and the imminent danger
of the eastern provinces, offered a specious pretence for the
design which was artfully concerted by the Imperial ministers.
They resolved to disarm the Cæsar; to recall those faithful
troops who guarded his person and dignity; and to employ, in
a distant war against the Persian monarch, the hardy veterans
who had vanquished, on the banks of the Rhine, the fiercest

nations of Germany. While Julian used the laborious hours of his winter quarters at Paris in the administration of power, which, in his hands, was the exercise of virtue, he was surprised by the hasty arrival of a tribune and a notary, with positive orders from the emperor, which *they* were directed to execute, and *he* was commanded not to oppose. Constantius signified his pleasure that four entire legions—the Celtæ and Petulants, the Heruli and the Batavians—should be separated from the standard of Julian, under which they had acquired their fame and discipline; that in each of the remaining bands three hundred of the bravest youths should be selected; and that this numerous detachment, the strength of the Gallic army, should instantly begin their march, and exert their utmost diligence to arrive, before the opening of the campaign, on the frontiers of Persia. If Julian complied with the orders which he had received he subscribed his own destruction, and that of a people who deserved his affection. But a positive refusal was an act of rebellion and a declaration of war. The inexorable jealousy of the emperor, the peremptory, and perhaps insidious, nature of his commands, left not any room for a fair apology or candid interpretation; and the dependent station of the Cæsar scarcely allowed him to pause or to deliberate. Unable to resist, unwilling to comply, Julian expressed in the most serious terms his wish, and even his intention, of resigning the purple, which he could not preserve with honour, but which he could not abdicate with safety.

After a painful conflict, Julian was compelled to acknowledge that obedience was the virtue of the most eminent subject, and that the sovereign alone was entitled to judge of the public welfare. He issued the necessary orders for carrying into execution the commands of Constantius; a part of the troops began their march for the Alps; and the detachments from the several garrisons moved towards their respective places of assembly. On the eve of their departure Julian addressed the soldiers, celebrating their exploits and admonishing them to render prompt obedience to the Augustus. The principal officers he entertained at a banquet. They retired from the feast full of grief and perplexity; and lamented the hardship of their fate, which tore them from their beloved

general and their native country. The only expedient which
could prevent their separation was boldly agitated and approved; the popular resentment was insensibly moulded into a
regular conspiracy; their just reasons of complaint were
heightened by passion, and their passions were inflamed by
wine, as on the eve of their departure the troops were indulged
in licentious festivity. At the hour of midnight the impetuous
multitude, with swords, and bows, and torches in their hands,
rushed into the suburbs; encompassed the palace; and, careless
of future dangers, pronounced the fatal and irrevocable words,
JULIAN AUGUSTUS!

Julian was obliged to maintain the station which had been
thrust upon him, but he was still desirous of saving his country from the calamities of a civil war. He wrote Constantius
requesting in respectful terms confirmation of his title of Augustus; these tenders of peace were accompanied and supported by vigorous preparations for war. The terror of a
foreign invasion obliged Constantius to suspend the punishment of a private enemy; but he did demand that the presumptuous Cæsar should expressly renounce the appellation and
rank of Augustus which he had accepted from the rebels. As
soon as Julian perceived that his moderate and respectful behaviour served only to irritate the pride of an implacable adversary, he boldly resolved to commit his life and fortune to
the chance of a civil war. Conscious that success alone could
justify his attempt, he instantly advanced to attack Sirmium,
the strongest and most populous city of the Illyrian provinces.
The intelligence of the rapid progress of Julian was speedily
transmitted to his rival, who, by the retreat of Sapor, had
obtained some respite from the Persian war.

But the humanity of Julian was preserved from the cruel
alternative which he pathetically laments of destroying or of
being himself destroyed: and the seasonable death of Constantius delivered the Roman empire from the calamities of civil
war. The approach of winter could not detain the monarch at
Antioch; and his favourites durst not oppose his impatient desire of revenge. A slight fever, which was perhaps occasioned
by the agitation of his spirits, was increased by the fatigues of
the journey, and Constantius was obliged to halt at the little

town of Mopsucrene, twelve miles beyond Tarsus, where he expired, after a short illness, in the forty-fifth year of his age, and the twenty-fourth of his reign. As soon as the legions of Aquileia were assured of the death of the emperor, they opened the gates of the city, and, by the sacrifice of their guilty leaders, obtained an easy pardon from the prudence or lenity of Julian; who, in the thirty-second year of his age, acquired the undisputed possession of the Roman empire.

The throne of Julian, which the death of Constantius fixed on an independent basis, was the seat of reason, of virtue, and perhaps of vanity. He despaired the honours, renounced the pleasures, and discharged with incessant diligence the duties of his exalted station: and there were few among his subjects who would have consented to relieve him from the weight of the diadem, had they been obliged to submit their time and their actions to the rigorous laws which their philosophic emperor imposed on himself. In one and the same day he gave audience to several ambassadors, and wrote or dictated a great number of letters to his generals, his civil magistrates, his private friends, and the different cities of his dominions. He listened to the memorials which had been received, considered the subject of the petitions, and signified his intentions more rapidly than they could be taken in shorthand by the diligence of his secretaries. He possessed such flexibility of thought, and such firmness of attention, that he could employ his hand to write, his ear to listen, and his voice to dictate; and pursue at once three several trains of ideas without hesitation, and without error. By this avarice of time he seemed to protract the short duration of his reign; and, if the date were less securely ascertained, we should refuse to believe that only sixteen months elapsed between the death of Constantius and the departure of his successor for the Persian war.

Julian pared down the extravagant luxury of the court and corrected many of its abuses. The numerous army of spies, of agents, and informers enlisted by Constantius to secure the repose of one man, and to interrupt that of millions, was immediately disbanded by his generous successor. He sincerely abhorred the system of oriental despotism which Diocletian, Constantine, and the patient habits of four score years, has established in the empire; he absolutely refused the title of *Dominius* or *Lord*. He abolished, by repeated edicts, the unjust and pernicious exemptions which had withdrawn so many idle citizens from the service of their country; and by imposing an equal distribution of public duties he restored the strength of the expiring cities of his empire.

The generality of princes, if they were stripped of their purple and cast naked into the world, would immediately sink to the lowest rank of society, without a hope of emerging from their obscurity. But the personal merit of Julian was, in some measure, independent of his fortune. Whatever had been his choice of life, by the force of intrepid courage, lively wit, and intense application, he would have obtained, or at least he would have deserved, the highest honours of his profession, and Julian might have raised himself to the rank of minister or general of the state in which he was born a private citizen. After an interval of one hundred and twenty years from the death of Alexander Severus, the Romans beheld an emperor who made no distinction between his duties and his pleasures, who laboured to relieve the distress and to revive the spirit of his subjects, and who endeavoured always to connect authority with merit, and happiness with virtue. Even faction, and religious faction, was constrained to acknowledge the superiority of his genius in peace as well as in war, and to confess, with a sigh, that the apostate Julian was a lover of his country, and that he deserved the empire of the world.

CHAPTER TWENTY-THREE

The Religion of Julian—Universal Toleration—He attempts to restore and reform the Pagan Worship—To rebuild the Temple of Jerusalem—His Artful Persecution of the Christians—Mutual Zeal and Injustice

A devout and sincere attachment for the gods of Athens and Rome constituted the ruling passion of Julian. He had been strictly reared as a Christian, but after Gallus was invested with the purple Julian was permitted to breathe the air of freedom, of literature, and of Paganism. It was at the beginning of the civil war that he declared himself, after a decade of dissimulation, at once the implacable enemy of Christ and of Constantius. Instructed by history and reflection, Julian was persuaded that, if the diseases of the body may sometimes be cured by salutary violence, neither steel nor fire can eradicate the erroneous opinions of the mind. He extended to all the inhabitants of the Roman world the benefits of a free and equal toleration; and the only hardship which he inflicted on the Christians was to deprive them of the power of tormenting their fellow-subjects, whom they stigmatised with the odious titles of idolators and heretics. His extraordinary design of rebuilding the temple of Jerusalem proved futile. He prohibited Christians from teaching the arts of grammar and rhetoric, contending that if they refuse to adore the gods of Homer and Demosthenes, they ought to content themselves with the expounding Luke and Matthew in the churches of the Galileans. His most effectual instrument of oppression was the law that obliged the Christians to make full satisfaction for the temples which they had destroyed under the preceding reign.

CHAPTER TWENTY-FOUR

Residence of Julian at Antioch—His successful Expedition against the Persians—Passage of the Tigris—The Retreat and Death of Julian—Election of Jovian—He saves the Roman Army by a disgraceful Treaty

In the cool moments of reflection, Julian preferred the useful and benevolent virtues of Antoninus; but his ambitious spirit was inflamed by the glory of Alexander, and he solicited, with equal ardour, the esteem of the wise and the applause of the multitude. The only rival whom he deemed worthy of his arms was the successor of Cyrus and Artaxerxes, and he resolved, by the final conquest of Persia, to chastise the haughty nation which had so long resisted and insulted the majesty of Rome. A formidable army was destined for this important service, and Julian, marching from Constantinople through the provinces of Asia Minor, arrived at Antioch about eight months after the death of his predecessor. In order to restore the exhausted strength of the legions of Gaul and the discipline and spirit of the eastern troops, Julian was persuaded to remain, until the following spring, at Antioch, among a people maliciously disposed to deride the haste and censure the delays of their sovereign. Despite ill-concealed tensions between himself and the effeminate people of Antioch, Julian did attempt to relieve a shortage of grain by introducing large quantities imported from abroad; but the Imperial wheat was purchased by the rich merchants, and the small quantities that appeared in the market were secretly sold at an advanced and illegal price.

Julian's brilliant strategy in the Persian campaign was countered by the enemy device of destroying food supplies on his lines of march, and after initial successes Julian was forced to turn back. The hardy veterans, accustomed to the cold climate of Gaul and Germany, fainted under the sultry heat of an Assyrian summer; their vigour was exhausted by the incessant repetition of march and combat; and the progress of the army was suspended by the precautions of a slow and dangerous retreat in the presence of an active enemy. Every day, every hour, as the supply diminished, the value and price of subsistence increased in the Roman camp. Julian, who always contented himself with such food as a hungry soldier would have disdained, distributed, for the use of the troops, the provisions of the Imperial household, and whatever could be spared from the sumpter-horses of the tribunes and generals. But this feeble relief served only to aggravate the sense of the public distress; and the Romans began to entertain the most gloomy apprehensions that, before they could reach the frontiers of the empire, they should all perish, either by famine or by the sword of the barbarians.

In one sudden charge of the enemy Julian, who had laid his protective armor aside because of the heat, was fatally wounded. His last moments he spent with the firm temper of a hero and a sage. In emulation of Socrates he discoursed to his friends on philosophical topics until the end. He died in the thirty-second year of his age, after a reign of one year and about eight months from the death of Constantius. While the generals were debating the choice of a successor, a few voices saluted Jovian, who was no more than *first* of the domestics, with the names of Emperor and Augustus. The tumultuary acclamation was instantly repeated by the guards who surrounded the tent, and passed, in a few minutes, to the extremities of the line. The new prince, astonished with his own fortune, was hastily invested with the Imperial ornaments, and received an oath of fidelity from the generals, whose favour and protection he so lately solicited.

The Persian king detained the Romans with specious negotiations until pressing dearth forced them to accept the humiliating conditions of peace which the irresolute Jovian no longer had it in his power to refuse. The five provinces beyond the Tigris, which had been ceded by the grandfather of Sapor, were restored to the Persian monarchy. Jovian was impatient to secure an empire at the expense of a few provinces, and the respectable names of religion and honour concealed his personal fears and ambitions. The predecessors of Jovian had sometimes relinquished the dominion of distant and unprofitable provinces; but, since the foundation of the city, the genius of Rome, the god Terminus, who guarded the boundaries of the republic, had never retired before the sword of a victorious enemy.

CHAPTER TWENTY-FIVE

The Government and Death of Jovian—Election of
Valentinian, who associates his Brother Valens,
and makes the final Division of the Eastern and
Western Empires—Revolt of Procopius—Civil and
Ecclesiastical Administration—Germany—Brit-
ain—Africa—The East—The Danube—Death
of Valentinian II., succeed to the Western Empire

The death of Julian had left the public affairs of the empire in
a very doubtful and dangerous situation. The Roman army
was saved by an inglorious, perhaps a necessary, treaty; and
the first moments of peace were consecrated by the pious Jo
vian to restore the domestic tranquillity of the church and
state. The indiscretion of his predecessor, instead of reconciling, had artfully fomented the religious war; and the balance
which he affected to preserve between the hostile factions
served only to perpetuate the contest by the vicissitudes of
hope and fear, by the rival claims of ancient possession and
actual favour. The Christians had forgotten the spirit of the
Gospel, and the Pagans had imbibed the spirit of the church.

The slightest force, when it is applied to assist and guide
the natural descent of its object, operates with irresistible
weight; and Jovian had the good fortune to embrace the religious opinions which were supported by the spirit of the

times, and the zeal and numbers of the most powerful sect. Under his reign Christianity obtained an easy and lasting victory; and as soon as the smile of royal patronage was withdrawn, the genius of Paganism, which had been fondly raised and cherished by the arts of Julian, sunk irrecoverably in the dust. In many cities the temples were shut or deserted; the philosophers, who had abused their transient favour, thought it prudent to shave their beards and disguise their profession; and the Christians rejoiced that they were now in a condition to forgive or to revenge the injuries which they had suffered under the preceding reign.

It was at Ancrya, on his way back to Constantinople, that Jovian assumed, with his infant son, the name and ensigns of the consulship. After indulging himself with a plentiful, perhaps intemperate, supper, he retired to rest, and the next morning the emperor Jovian was found dead in his bed. For ten days the throne of the Roman world remained without a master. In a solemn assembly of the civil and military powers of the empire several candidates were proposed and rejected; but as soon as the name of Valentinian was pronounced, the merit of that officer united the suffrages of the whole assembly. Valentinian was handsome, brave, and a proven general; it was without guilt and without intrigue that he was summoned to assume, in the forty-third year of his age, the absolute government of the Roman empire. The choice was approved by the acclamations of the troops, who demanded that he name a colleague forthwith. Valentinian resisted this pressure, but thirty days after his own elevation he bestowed the title of Augustus on his brother Valens, then in the thirty-sixth year of his age. Valens had had no experience in civil or military employment, and his character had not inspired the world with any sanguine expectations. Valentinian bestowed upon his brother the rich præfecture of the *East*, from the lower Danube to the confines of Persia; whilst he reserved for his immediate government the warlike præfectures of *Illyricum*, *Italy*, and *Gaul*, from the extremity of Greece to the Caledonian rampart, and from the rampart of Caledonia to the foot of Mount Atlas. The tranquillity of the East was soon disturbed by the attempt of Procopius, who had been one of

Julian's generals, to usurp the authority of Valens. Procopius was deserted by his followers and beheaded. He suffered the ordinary fate of an unsuccessful usurper, but the acts of cruelty which were exercised by the conqueror, under the forms of legal justice, excited the pity and indignation of mankind.

Such indeed are the common and natural fruits of despotism. The inquisition into the crime of magic came to be rigorously prosecuted under the reign of the two brothers. The dark predictions of the death of an emperor or the success of a conspiracy were calculated only to stimulate the hopes of ambition and to dissolve the ties of fidelity, and the intentional guilt of magic was aggravated by the actual crimes of treason and sacrilege. Such vain terrors disturbed the peace of society and the happiness of individuals, and the harmless flame which insensibly melted a waxen image might derive a powerful and pernicious energy from the affrighted fancy of the person whom it was maliciously designed to represent. From the infusion of those herbs which were supposed to possess a supernatural influence it was an easy step to the use of more substantial poison, and the folly of mankind sometimes became the instrument and the mask of the most atrocious crimes. As soon as the zeal of informers was encouraged by the ministers of Valens and Valentinian, they could not refuse to listen to another charge too frequently mingled in the scenes of domestic guilt, a charge of a softer and less malignant nature, for which the pious though excessive rigour of Constantine had recently decreed the punishment of death. This deadly and incoherent mixture of treason and magic, of poison and adultery, afforded infinite gradations of guilt and innocence, of excuse and aggravation, which in these proceedings appear to have been confounded by the angry or corrupt passions of the judges. They easily discovered that the degree of their industry and discernment was estimated by the Imperial court according to the number of executions that were furnished from their respective tribunals. It was not without extreme reluctance that they pronounced a sentence of acquittal, but they eagerly admitted such evidence as was stained with perjury or procured by torture to prove the most improbable charges against the most respectable characters. The progress of the inquiry continually opened new subjects of criminal prosecution; the audacious informer, whose falsehood was detected, retired with impunity; but the wretched victim who discovered his real or pretended accomplices was seldom permitted to receive the price of his infamy. From the extremity of Italy and Asia the young and the aged were dragged in chains to the tribunals of Rome and Antioch. Senators, matrons, and philosophers expired in ignominious and cruel tortures. The soldiers who were appointed to guard the prisons declared, with a murmur of pity and indignation, that their numbers were insufficient to oppose the flight of resistance of the multitude of captives. The wealthiest families were ruined by fines and confiscations; the most innocent citizens trembled for their safety; and we may form some notion of the magnitude of the evil from the extravagant assertion of an ancient writer, that in the obnoxious provinces the prisoners, the exiles, and the fugitives formed the greatest part of the inhabitants.

Valens was of a timid, and Valentinian of a choleric, disposition. An anxious regard to his personal safety was the ruling principle of the administration of Valens. His favourites obtained, by the privilege of rapine and confiscation, the wealth which his economy would have refused. They urged, with persuasive eloquence, *that*, in all cases of treason, suspicion is equivalent to proof; *that* the power supposes the intention of mischief; *that* the intention is not less criminal than the act; and *that* a subject no longer deserves to live, if his life may threaten the safety, or disturb the repose, of his sovereign. The judgment of Valentinian was sometimes deceived, and his confidence abused; but he would have silenced the informers with a contemptuous smile, had they presumed to alarm his fortitude by the sound of danger. In the government of his household, or of his empire, slight, or even imaginary offences—a hasty word, a casual omission, an involuntary delay—were chastised by a sentence of immediate death. The expressions which issued the most readily from the mouth of the emperor of the West were, "Strike off his head;"—"Burn him alive;"—"Let him be beaten with clubs till he expires;" and his most favoured ministers soon understood that, by a

rash attempt to dispute or suspend the execution of his sanguinary commands, they might involve themselves in the guilt
and punishment of disobedience.

But in the calmer moments of reflection the dispassionate
judgment of Valentinian could clearly perceive and accurately
pursue, his own and the public interest; and Valens imitated
his brother's example. Both princes retained the temperate
simplicity which had adorned their private life, and they reformed many of the abuses of the time of Constantius. Valentinian condemned the exposure of new-born infants,
established physicians in the fourteen quarters of Rome, en-
acted that Greek and Latin grammar and rhetoric be taught in
the metropolis of every province, and instituted *Defensors*,
freely elected as tribunes and advocates of the people, to support their rights before the tribunals of the civil magistrates or
even at the foot of the Imperial throne. But the most honourable circumstance of the character of Valentinian is the firm
and temperate impartiality which he uniformly preserved in an
age of religious contention. By suspending the repetition of
mutual injuries the wise and vigorous government of Valentinian contributed to soften the manners, and abate the prejudices, of the religious factions.

Valentinian had been chosen emperor for his soldierly qualities. The death of Julian had relieved the barbarians of the
terror of his name and excited the nations of the East, of the
South, and of the North with hopes of rapine and conquest.
Their inroads were often vexatious and sometimes formidable;
but during the twelve years of the reign of Valentinian, his
firmness and vigilance protected his own dominions; and his
powerful genius seemed to inspire and direct the feeble counsels of his brother. Upon one occasion Valentinian fell into so
ungovernable a fury while reviling ambassadors of the Quadi,
that he burst a blood vessel and fell speechless into the arms of
his attendants, and presently died. Valentinian was about
fifty-four years of age, and he wanted only one hundred days
to accomplish the twelve years of his reign.

At Valentinian's death his eldest son Gratian, whose
mother was Severa, was in the seventeenth year of his age,
and his virtues already justified the favourable opinion of the

army and people. But Valentinian had a four year old son, also named Valentinian, by the empress Justina; and certain members of the Imperial council, who were ambitious of reigning in the name of the infant, procured that the child should be invested, by military acclamation, with the titles and ensigns of supreme power. The impending dangers of a civil war were seasonably prevented by the wise and moderate conduct of the emperor Gratian. He cheerfully accepted the choice of the army, declared that he should always consider the son of Justina as a brother, not as a rival, and advised the empress, with her son Valentinian, to fix their residence at Milan, in the fair and peaceful province of Italy, while he assumed the more arduous command of the countries beyond the Alps. Gratian dissembled his resentment till he could safely punish or disgrace the authors of the conspiracy; and though he uniformly behaved with tenderness and regard to his infant colleague, he gradually confounded, in the administration of the Western empire, the office of a guardian with the authority of a sovereign. The government of the Roman world was exercised in the united names of Valens and his two nephews; but the feeble emperor of the East, who succeeded to the rank of his elder brother, never obtained any weight or influence in the councils of the West.

CHAPTER TWENTY-SIX

Manners of the Pastoral Nations—Progress of the Huns from China to Europe—Flight of the Goths —They pass the Danube—Gothic War—Defeat and Death of Valens—Gratian invests Theodosius with the Eastern Empire—His Character and Success—Peace and Settlement of the Goths

In the disastrous period of the fall of the Roman empire, which may justly be dated from the reign of Valens, the happiness and security of each individual were personally attacked, and the arts and labours of ages were rudely defaced by the barbarians of Scythia and Germany. The invasion of the Huns precipitated on the provinces of the West the Gothic nation, which advanced, in less than forty years, from the Danube to the Atlantic, and opened a way, by the success of their arms, to the inroads of so many hostile tribes more savage than themselves.

The Huns, who under the reign of Valens threatened the empire of Rome, had been formidable, in a much earlier period, to the empire of China. Their ancient, perhaps their original, seat was an extensive, though dry and barren, tract of country immediately on the north side of the great wall. The dark interval of time which elapsed after the Huns were lost in the eyes of the Chinese and before they showed themselves to those of the Romans is impossible to fill. The Gothic king Hermanric, whose dominions extended from the Baltic to the Euxine, was alarmed by the formidable approach of an host of unknown enemies, on whom his barbarous subjects might, without injustice, bestow the epithet of barbarians. Against these enemies, Hermanric prepared to exert the united forces of the Gothic state; but he soon discovered that his vassal tribes, provoked by oppression, were much more inclined to second than to repel the invasion of the Huns.

After Valens had terminated the Gothic war he spent five years at Antioch, watching, from a secure distance, the hostile designs of the Persian monarch; checking the depredations of the Isaurians and Saracens; enforcing by arguments more prevalent than those of reason and eloquence, the belief of the Arian theology; and satisfying his anxious suspicions by the promiscuous execution of the innocent and the guilty. But the attention of the emperor was most seriously engaged by the important intelligence which he received from the civil and military officers who were intrusted with the defense of the Danube. He was informed that the North was agitated by a furious tempest; that the irruption of the Huns, an unknown and monstrous race of savages, had subverted the power of the Goths; and that the suppliant multitudes of that warlike nation, whose pride was now humbled in the dust, covered a space of many miles along the banks of the river. With outstretched arms and pathetic lamentations they loudly deplored their past misfortunes and their present danger; acknowledged that their only hope of safety was in the clemency of the Roman government; and most solemnly protested that, if the gracious liberality of the emperor would permit them to cultivate the waste lands of Thrace, they should ever hold themselves bound, by the strongest obligations of duty and gratitude, to obey the laws and to guard the limits of the republic. These assurances were confirmed by the ambassadors of the Goths, who impatiently expected from the mouth of Valens an answer that must finally determine the fate of their unhappy countrymen. The emperor of the East was no longer guided by the wisdom and authority of his elder brother, whose death happened towards the end of the preceding year; and as the distressful situation

of the Goths required an instant and peremptory decision, he
was deprived of the favourite resource of feeble and timid
minds, who consider the use of dilatory and ambiguous measures as the most admirable efforts of consummate prudence.
As long as the same passions and interests subsist among
mankind, the questions of war and peace, of justice and policy, which were debated in the councils of antiquity, will frequently present themselves as the subject of modern
deliberation. But the most experienced statesman of Europe
has never been summoned to consider the propriety or the
danger of admitting or rejecting an innumerable multitude of
barbarians, who are driven by despair and hunger to solicit a
settlement on the territories of a civilised nation. When that
important proposition, so essentially connected with the public
safety, was referred to the ministers of Valens, they were per-
plexed and divided; but they soon acquiesced in the flattering
sentiment which seemed the most favourable to the pride, the
indolence, and the avarice of their sovereign. The slaves, who
were decorated with the titles of præfects and generals, dissembled or disregarded the terrors of this national emigration
—so extremely different from the partial and accidental
colonies which had been received on the extreme limits of the
empire. But they applauded the liberality of fortune which had
conducted, from the most distant countries of the globe, a
numerous and invincible army of strangers to defend the
throne of Valens, who might now add to the royal treasures
the immense sums of gold supplied by the provincials to compensate their annual proportion of recruits. The prayers of the
Goths were granted, and their service was accepted by the
Imperial court; and orders were immediately despatched to
the civil and military governors of the Thracian diocese to
make the necessary preparations for the passage and subsistence of a great people, till a proper and sufficient territory
could be allotted for their future residence. The liberality of
the emperor was accompanied, however, with two harsh and
rigorous conditions, which prudence might justify on the side
of the Romans, but which distress alone could extort from the
indignant Goths. Before they passed the Danube they were
required to deliver their arms, and it was insisted that their

children should be taken from them and dispersed through the provinces of Asia, where they might be civilised by the arts of education, and serve as hostages to secure the fidelity of their parents.

At this important crisis the military government of Thrace was exercised by Lupicinus and Maximus, in whose venal minds the slightest hope of private emolument outweighed every consideration of public advantage, and whose guilt was only alleviated by their incapacity of discerning the pernicious effects of their rash and criminal administration. Instead of obeying the orders of their sovereign, and satisfying, with decent liberality, the demands of the Goths, they levied an ungenerous and oppressive tax on the wants of the hungry barbarians. The vilest food was sold at an extravagant price, and, in the room of wholesome and substantial provisions, the markets were filled with the flesh of dogs and of unclean animals who had died of disease. To obtain the valuable acquisition of a pound of bread, the Goths resigned the possession of an expensive though serviceable slave, and a small quantity of meat was greedily purchased with ten pounds of a precious but useless metal. When their property was exhausted, they continued this necessary traffic by the sale of their sons and daughters; and notwithstanding the love of freedom which animated every Gothic breast, they submitted to the humiliating maxim that it was better for their children to be maintained in a servile condition than to perish in a state of wretched and helpless independence. The most lively resentment is excited by the tyranny of pretended benefactors, who sternly exact the debt of gatitude which they have cancelled by subsequent injuries; a spirit of discontent insensibly arose in the camp of the barbarians, who pleaded, without success, the merit of their patient and dutiful behaviour, and loudly complained of the inhospitable treatment which they had received from their new allies. They beheld around them the wealth and plenty of a fertile province, in the midst of which they suffered the intolerable hardships of artificial famine. But the means of relief, and even of revenge, were in their hands, since the rapaciousness of their tyrants had left to an injured people the possession and the use of arms.

Lupicinus so exacerbated the Goths as to drive them to open hostility, and in a battle at Marcianopolis their general Fritigern broke the ranks of the Roman legions. The report of the Gothic victory was soon diffused over the adjacent country; and while it filled the minds of the Romans with terror and dismay, their own hasty imprudence contributed to increase the forces of Fritigern and the calamities of the province. The imprudence of Valens and his ministers had introduced into the heart of the empire a nation of enemies.

Gratian, who had subdued an uprising of the Alemanni in the West, sent word to Valens requesting that every dangerous and decisive measure might be suspended till the junction of the two emperors should ensure the success of the Gothic war. But the feeble sovereign of the East was actuated only by the fatal illusions of pride and jealousy, and rushed into the field to erect his imaginary trophy before the diligence of his colleague could usurp any share of the triumphs of the day. On the 9th of August, a day which has deserved to be marked among the most inauspicious of the Roman calendar, the emperor Valens, leaving, under a strong guard, his baggage and military treasure, marched from Hadrianople to attack the Goths, who were encamped about twelve miles from the city. The event of the battle of Hadrianople, so fatal to Valens and to the empire, may be described in a few words: the Roman cavalry fled; the infantry was abandoned, surrounded, and cut to pieces.

The emperor Gratian was far advanced on his march towards the plains of Hadrianople when he was informed that his impatient colleague had been slain in battle, and that two-thirds of the Roman army were exterminated by the sword of the victorious Goths. Gratian was too late to assist, he was too weak to revenge, his unfortunate colleague; and the valiant and modest youth felt himself unequal to the support of a sinking world. A formidable tempest of the barbarians of Germany seemed ready to burst over the provinces of Gaul, and the mind of Gratian was oppressed and distracted by the administration of the Western empire. In this important crisis the government of the East and the conduct of the Gothic war required the undivided attention of a hero and a statesman.

The choice of Gratian was soon declared in favour of an exile, whose father, only three years before, had suffered, under the sanction of *his* authority, an unjust and ignominious death. The great Theodosius, a name celebrated in history and dear to the catholic church, was summoned to the Imperial court, which had gradually retreated from the confines of Thrace to the more secure station of Sirmium. Five months after the death of Valens, the emperor Gratian produced before the assembled troops *his* colleague and *their* master, who, after a modest, perhaps a sincere resistance, was compelled to accept, amidst the general acclamations, the diadem, the purple, and the equal title of Augustus. The provinces of Thrace, Asia, and Egypt, over which Valens had reigned, were resigned to the administration of the new emperor; but as he was specially intrusted with the conduct of the Gothic war, the Illyrian præfecture was dismembered, and the two great dioceses of Dacia and Macedonia were added to the dominions of the Eastern empire.

From the innocent, but humble, labours of his farm, Theodosius was transported, in less than four months, to the throne of the Eastern empire: and the whole period of the history of the world will not perhaps afford a similar example of an elevation at the same time so pure and so honourable. Theodosius was invested with the purple in the thirty-third year of his age. The vulgar gazed with admiration on the manly beauty of his face and the graceful majesty of his person, which they were pleased to compare with the pictures and medals of the emperor Trajan; whilst intelligent observers discovered, in the qualities of his heart and understanding, a more important resemblance to the best and greatest of the Roman princes.

If Theodosius, hastily collecting his scattered forces, had led them into the field to encounter a victorious enemy, his army would have been vanquished by their own fears; and his rashness could not have been excused by the chance of success. But the *great* Theodosius, an epithet which he honourably deserved on this momentous occasion, conducted himself as the firm and faithful guardian of the republic. The deliverance and peace of the Roman provinces was the work of prudence, rather than of valour: the prudence of Theodosius was seconded by fortune; and the emperor never failed to seize, and to improve, every favourable circumstance. The mixed influence of force, of reason, and of corruption, became every day more powerful and more extensive. Each independent chieftain hastened to obtain a separate treaty, from the apprehension that an obstinate delay might expose *him*, alone and unprotected, to the revenge or justice of the conqueror. The general, or rather the final, capitulation of the Goths, may be dated four years, one month, and twenty-five days, after the defeat and death of the emperor Valens.

By the terms of the treaty an army of forty thousand Goths was maintained for the perpetual service of the empire of the East. Theodosius had the address to persuade his allies that the conditions of peace, which had been extorted from him by prudence and necessity, were the voluntary expressions of his sincere friendship for the Gothic nation; but to every discerning eye it was apparent that the Goths would long remain the enemies, and might soon become the conquerors, of the Roman empire. Their rude and insolent behaviour expressed their contempt of the citizens and provincials, whom they insulted with impunity. To the zeal and valour of the barbarians Theodosius was indebted for the success of his arms: but their assistance was precarious; and they were sometimes seduced, by a treacherous and inconstant disposition, to abandon his standard at the moment when their service was the most essential.

CHAPTER TWENTY-SEVEN

Death of Gratian—Ruin of Arianism—St. Ambrose—First Civil War, against Maximus—Character, Administration, and Penance, of Theodosius—Death of Valentinian II.—Second Civil War, against Eugenius—Death of Theodosius

The fame of Gratian, before he had accomplished the twentieth year of age, was equal to that of the most celebrated princes. His gentle and amiable disposition endeared him to his private friends, the graceful affability of his manners engaged the affection of the people; the men of letters, who enjoyed the liberality, acknowledged the taste and eloquence, of their sovereign; his valour and dexterity in arms were equally applauded by the soldiers; and the clergy considered the humble piety of Gratian as the first and most useful of his virtues. But Gratian survived his reputation; before he fell a victim to rebellion, he had lost, in a great measure, the respect and confidence of the Roman world. As soon as time and accident had removed the faithful counsellors Valentinian had appointed for him, the emperor of the West insensibly descended to the level of his natural genius, abandoned the reins of government to the ambitious hands which were stretched forwards to grasp them, and amused his leisure with the most

frivolous gratifications. A public sale of favour and justice
was instituted, both in the court and in the provinces, by the
worthless delegates of his power, whose merits it was made
sacrilege to question. The conscience of the credulous prince
was directed by saints and bishops, who procured an Imperial
edict to punish, as a capital offense, the violation, the neglect,
or even the ignorance of the divine law.

The behaviour of Gratian, which degraded his character in
the eyes of mankind, could not have disturbed the security of
his reign if the army had not been provoked to resent their
peculiar injuries. The legions of Britain and its provincials
proclaimed Maximus, who was of Spanish birth, emperor; and
Maximus understood that he could not hope to reign, or even
to live, if he confined his moderate ambition within the narrow limits of Britain. The armies of Gaul, instead of opposing
the invasion of Maximus, received him with joyful and loyal
acclamations. The emperor of the West fled toward Lyons
with a train of only three hundred horse. The governor of the
Lyonnese province protested his fidelity to Gratian, but allowed an officer of Maximus to execute the orders or the
intentions of the usurper. Gratian's body was denied to the
pious and pressing entreaties of his brother Valentinian. The
events of this revolution had passed in such rapid succession
that it would have been impossible for Theodosius to march to
the relief of his benefactor before he received the intelligence
of his defeat and death.

Maximus's ambassador offered Theodosius the alternative
of peace or war. The imperious voice of honour and gratitude
called aloud for revenge; but the assassin of Gratian possessed
the most warlike provinces of the empire, the East was exhausted by the Gothic war, and it was seriously to be apprehended that, after the vital strength of the republic had been
wasted in a doubtful and destructive contest, the feeble conqueror would remain an easy prey to the barbarians of the
north. These weighty considerations engaged Theodosius to
dissemble his resentment and to accept the alliance of the tyrant. But he stipulated that Maximus should content himself
with the possession of the countries beyond the Alps. The
brother of Gratian was confirmed and secured in the sover-

eignty of Italy, Africa, and Western Illyricum, and some honourable conditions were inserted in the treaty to protect the memory and the laws of the deceased emperor. According to the custom of the age, the images of the three Imperial colleagues were exhibited to the veneration of the people: nor should it be lightly supposed that, in the moment of a solemn reconciliation, Theodosius secretly cherished the intention of perfidy and revenge.

The contempt of Gratian for the Roman soldiers had exposed him to the fatal effects of their resentment. His profound veneration for the Christian clergy was rewarded by the applause and gratitude of a powerful order, which has claimed in every age the privilege of dispensing honours, both on earth and in heaven. The orthodox bishops bewailed his death, and their own irreparable loss; but they were soon comforted by the discovery that Gratian had committed the sceptre of the East to the hands of a prince whose humble faith and fervent zeal were supported by the spirit and abilities of a more vigorous character.

Theodosius suppressed the insolent reign of Arianism and revenged the injuries which the catholics sustained from the zeal of Constantius and Valens. The orthodox emperor considered every heretic as a rebel against the supreme powers of heaven and of earth; and each of those powers might exercise their peculiar jurisdiction over the soul and body of the guilty. Penal statutes were directed against the ministers, the assemblies, and the persons of heretics. The theory of persecution was established by Theodosius, whose justice and piety have been applauded by the saints; but the practice of it, in the fullest extent, was reserved for his rival and colleague, Maximus, the first among the Christian princes who shed the blood of his Christian subjects on account of their religious opinions.

The reign of Maximus might have ended in peace and prosperity, could he have contented himself with the possession of three ample countries, which now constitute the three most flourishing kingdoms of modern Europe. But he aspired to the conquest of Italy, and having crossed the Alps by a ruse, appeared almost under the walls of Milan before Justina and her son Valentinian had received intelligence of his approach.

Flight was their only hope and Aquileia their only refuge. Justina distrusted the strength of the fortifications, and resolved to implore the protection of the great Theodosius. Instead of inviting his royal guests to the palace of Constantinople, Theodosius fixed their residence at Thessalonica, whither they were conveyed by a secret voyage. The momentous question of peace or war was referred by Theodosius to the deliberation of his council. The persecution of the Imperial family, to which Theodosius himself had been indebted for his fortune, was now aggravated by recent and repeated injuries. Neither oaths nor treaties could restrain the boundless ambition of Maximus; and the delay of vigorous and decisive measures, instead of prolonging the blessings of peace, would expose the Eastern empire to the danger of an hostile invasion. The cause of Valentinian was powerfully promoted by the charms of his sister Galla, which softened the heart of Theodosius. The art of Justina managed and directed the impulse of passion, and the celebration of the royal nuptials was the assurance and signal of the civil war. Maximus was defeated on the banks of the Save, besieged in Aquileia, dragged from his throne by his victorious enemies, and conducted like a malefactor to the presence of Theodosius. The emperor showed some disposition to forgive the tyrant of the West, but his pity was checked by his regard for public justice and the memory of Gratian; and he abandoned the victim to the pious zeal of the soldiers, who drew him out of the Imperial presence and instantly separated his head from his body. Theodosius employed the winter months of his residence at Milan to restore the state of the afflicted provinces; and early in the spring he made, after the example of Constantine and Constantius, his triumphal entry into the ancient capital of the Roman empire.

But the painful virtue which claims the merit of victory is exposed to the danger of defeat; and the reign of a wise and merciful prince was polluted by an act of cruelty which would stain the annals of Nero or Domitian. At Thessalonica a general of Theodosius had imprisoned, for just cause, a popular charioteer, and when their favourite was absent on the day of public games, the mob inhumanly murdered the general and some of his principal officers. The fiery and choleric temper of Theodosius was impatient of the dilatory forms of a judicial inquiry, and the punishment of the Thessalonians was blindly committed to the undistinguishing sword of barbarians. The people were invited, in the name of their sovereign, to the games of the circus, and then promiscuously massacred by soldiers who had been secretly posted round the circus. The news filled Ambrose, bishop of Milan, with horror and anguish. His reproaches affected the emperor deeply; and after he had bewailed the mischievous and irreparable consequences of his rash fury, he proceeded in the accustomed manner to perform his devotions in the great church of Milan. He was stopped in the porch by the archbishop, who, in the tone and language of an ambassador of Heaven, declared to his sovereign that private contrition was not sufficient to atone for a public fault or to appease the justice of the offended Deity. The public penance of the emperor Theodosius has been recorded as one of the most honourable events in the annals of the church of Milan. It was deemed sufficient that the emperor of the Romans, stripped of the ensigns of royalty, should appear in a mournful and suppliant posture; and that, in the midst of the church of Milan, he should humbly solicit, with sighs and tears, the pardon of his sins. After a delay of about eight months Theodosius was restored to the communion of the faithful.

After the defeat and death of the tyrant of Gaul, the Roman world was in the possession of Theodosius. He derived from the choice of Gratian his honourable title to the provinces of the East; he had acquired the West by the right of conquest; and the three years which he spent in Italy were usefully employed to restore the authority of the laws and to correct the abuses which had prevailed with impunity under the usurpation of Maximus and the minority of Valentinian. The name of Valentinian was regularly inserted in the public arts, but the tender age and doubtful faith of the son of Justina appeared to require the prudent care of an orthodox guardian, and his specious ambition might have excluded the unfortunate youth, without a struggle and almost without a murmur, from the administration and even from the inheritance of the empire. If

Theodosius had consulted the rigid maxims of interest and policy, his conduct would have been justified by his friends, but the generosity of his behaviour on this memorable occasion has extorted the applause of his most inveterate enemies. He seated Valentinian on the throne of Milan, and, without stipulating any present or future advantages, restored him to the absolute dominion of all the provinces from which he had been driven by the arms of Maximus. To the restitution of his ample patrimony Theodosius added the free and generous gift of the countries beyond the Alps which his successful valour had recovered from the assassin of Gratian.

But the youthful Valentinian, before he had accomplished the twentieth year of his age, was oppressed by domestic treason, and the empire was again involved in the horrors of a civil war. Arbogastes, a gallant soldier of the nation of the Franks, had been raised by his real merits to the position of master-general of the armies of Gaul, and had so far concentrated power into his own hands that Valentinian insensibly sunk into the precarious and dependent condition of a captive. The emperor, without strength or counsel, too hastily resolved to risk an immediate contest with his powerful general. He received Arbogastes on the throne, and, as the count approached with some appearance of respect, delivered to him a paper which dismissed him from all his employments. "My authority," replied Arbogastes, with insulting coolness, "does not depend on the smile or the frown of a monarch;" and he contemptuously threw the paper on the ground. The indignant monarch snatched at the sword of one of the guards, which he struggled to draw from its scabbard, and it was not without some degree of violence that he was prevented from using the deadly weapon against his enemy or against himself. A few days after this extraordinary quarrel, in which he had exposed his resentment and his weakness, the unfortunate Valentinian was found strangled in his apartment, and some pains were employed to disguise the manifest guilt of Arbogastes, and to persuade the world that the death of the young emperor had been the voluntary effect of his own despair.

Some remains of pride and prejudice still opposed the elevation of Arbogastes himself, and the judicious barbarian thought it more advisable to reign under the name of some dependent Roman. He bestowed the purple on the rhetorician Eugenius, whom he had already raised from the place of his domestic secretary to the rank of master of the offices. Ambassadors of Eugenius communicated to Theodosius, with affected grief, the unfortunate accident of the death of Valentinian, and requested that the monarch of the East would embrace as his lawful colleague the respectable citizen who had obtained the unanimous suffrage of the armies and provinces of the West. As the second conquest of the West was a task of difficulty and danger, Theodosius dismissed, with splendid presents and an ambiguous answer, the ambassadors of Eugenius, and almost two years were consumed in the preparations of the civil war. In a battle fought near Aquileia Arbogastes won a victory, but on the following day many of his soldiers went over to Theodosius, who won a decisive victory. The rhetorician Eugenius, who had almost acquired the dominion of the world, was reduced to implore the mercy of the conqueror, and the unrelenting soldiers separated his head from his body as he lay prostrate at the feet of Theodosius. Arbogastes wandered about the mountains for several days, and then turned his sword against his own breast.

After the defeat of Eugenius, the merit, as well as the authority, of Theodosius was cheerfully acknowledged by all the inhabitants of the Roman world. The experience of his past conduct encouraged the most pleasing expectations of his future reign; and the age of the emperor, which did not exceed fifty years, seemed to extend the prospect of the public felicity. His death, only four months after his victory, was considered by the people as an unforeseen and fatal event, which destroyed in a moment the hopes of the rising generation. But the indulgence of ease and luxury had secretly nourished the principles of disease. The strength of Theodosius was unable to support the sudden and violent transition from the palace to the camp; and the increasing symptoms of a dropsy announced the speedy dissolution of the emperor. The opinion, and perhaps the interest, of the public had confirmed the division of the Eastern and Western empires; and the two royal youths, Arcadius and Honorius, who had already obtained, from the tenderness of their father, the title of Augustus, were destined to fill the thrones of Constantinople and of Rome. Those princes were not permitted to share the danger and glory of the civil war; but as soon as Theodosius had triumphed over his unworthy rivals, he called his younger son, Honorius, to enjoy the fruits of the victory, and to receive the sceptre of the West from the hands of his dying father. The arrival of Honorius at Milan was welcomed by a splendid exhibition of the games of the circus; and the emperor, though he was oppressed by the weight of his disorder, contributed by his presence to the public joy. But the remains of his strength were exhausted by the painful effort which he made to assist at the spectacles of the morning. Honorius supplied, during the rest of the day, the place of his father; and the great Theodosius expired in the ensuing night. Notwithstanding the recent animosities of a civil war, his death was universally lamented. The barbarians, whom he had vanquished, and the churchmen, by whom he had been subdued, celebrated with loud and sincere applause the qualities of the deceased emperor which appeared the most valuable in their eyes. The Romans were terrified by the impending dangers of a feeble and divided administration; and every disgraceful moment of the unfortunate reigns of Arcadius and Honorius revived the memory of their irreparable loss.

CHAPTER TWENTY-EIGHT

Final Destruction of Paganism—Introduction of the Worship of Saints and Relics among the Christians

The ruin of Paganism, in the age of Theodosius, is perhaps the only example of the total extirpation of any ancient and popular superstition, and may therefore deserve to be considered as a singular event in the history of the human mind. The Christians, more especially the clergy, had impatiently supported the prudent delays of Constantine and the equal toleration of the elder Valentinian; nor could they deem their conquest perfect or secure as long as their adversaries were permitted to exist. The influence which Ambrose and his brethren had acquired over the youth of Gratian and the piety of Theodosius was employed to infuse the maxims of persecution into the breasts of their Imperial proselytes. Two specious principles of religious jurisprudence were established, from whence they deduced a direct and rigorous conclusion against the subjects of the empire who still adhered to the ceremonies of their ancestors: *that* the magistrate is, in some measure, guilty of the crimes which he neglects to prohibit or to punish; and *that* the idolatrous worship of fabulous deities and real dæmons is the most abominable crime against the supreme majesty of the Creator. The laws of Moses and the example of Jewish history were hastily, perhaps erroneously, applied by the clergy to the mild and universal reign of Christianity. The zeal of the emperors was excited to vindicate their own honour and that of the Deity; and the temples of the Roman world were subverted about sixty years after the conversion of Constantine.

Even after the pagan temples were destroyed or transformed to more pious uses, Pagans still attempted to elude the prohibitions of Theodosius; but these were made increasingly rigorous, until, only twenty-eight years after the death of Theodosius the faint and minute vestiges were no longer visible to eye of the legislator. But among the Christians the worship of saints and relics and similar practices multiplied; it must ingenuously be confessed that the ministers of the catholic church imitated the profane model which they were impatient to destroy. The most respectable bishops had persuaded themselves that the ignorant rustics would more cheerfully renounce the superstitions of Paganism, if they found some resemblance, some compensation, in the bosom of Christianity. The religion of Constantine achieved, in less than a century, the final conquest of the Roman empire: but the victors themselves were insensibly subdued by the arts of their vanquished rivals.

CHAPTER TWENTY-NINE

*Final Division of the Roman Empire between the
Sons of Theodosius—Reign of Arcadius and Hon-
orius—Administration of Rufinus and Stilicho—
Revolt and Defeat of Gildo in Africa*

The genius of Rome expired with Theodosius, the last of the
successors of Augustus and Constantine who appeared in the
field at the head of their armies, and whose authority was
universally acknowledged throughout the whole extent of the
empire. The memory of his virtues still continued, however,
to protect the feeble and inexperienced youth of his two sons.
After the death of their father, Arcadius and Honorius were
saluted, by the unanimous consent of mankind, as the lawful
emperors of the East and of the West; and the oath of fidelity
was eagerly taken by every order of the state; the senates of
old and new Rome, the clergy, the magistrates, the soldiers,
and the people. Arcadius, who then was about eighteen years
of age, was born in Spain in the humble habitation of a private
family. But he received a princely education in the palace of
Constantinople; and his inglorious life was spent in that peaceful and splendid seat of royalty, from whence he appeared to
reign over the provinces of Thrace, Asia Minor, Syria and
Egypt, from the Lower Danube to the confines of Persia and
Æthiopia. His younger brother, Honorius, assumed, in the

eleventh year of his age, the nominal government of Italy, Africa, Gaul, Spain, and Britain; and the troops which guarded the frontiers of his kingdom were opposed, on one side, to the Caledonians, and on the other to the Moors. The great and martial præfecture of Illyricum was divided between the two princes: the defence and possession of the provinces of Noricum, Pannonia, and Dalmatia, still belonged to the Western empire; but the two large dioceses of Dacia and Macedonia, which Gratian had intrusted to the valour of Theodosius, were for ever united to the empire of the East. The boundary in Europe was not very different from the line which now separates the Germans and the Turks; and the respective advantages of territory, riches, populousness, and military strength, were fairly balanced and compensated in this final and permanent division of the Roman empire. The hereditary sceptre of the sons of Theodosius appeared to be the gift of nature and of their father; the generals and ministers had been accustomed to adore the majesty of the royal infants; and the army and people were not admonished of their rights, and of their power, by the dangerous example of a recent election. The gradual discovery of the weakness of Arcadius and Honorius, and the repeated calamities of their reign, were not sufficient to obliterate the deep and early impressions of loyalty. The subjects of Rome, who still reverenced the persons, or rather the names, of their sovereigns, beheld with equal abhorrence the rebels who opposed, and the ministers who abused, the authority of the throne.

Arcadius was wholly dominated by his odious præfect Rufinus, who considered the emperor as his pupil rather than his sovereign. The person and court of Honorius were subject to Stilicho, the competent master-general of the West. Stilicho lured Rufinus to his death, but his plan to dominate the East as well as the West miscarried. At a time when the only hope of delaying the ruin of the Roman name depended on the firm union and reciprocal aid of all the nations to whom it had been gradually communicated, the subjects of Arcadius and Honorius were instructed, by their respective masters, to view each other in a foreign and even hostile light; to rejoice in their mutual calamities; and to embrace, as their faithful allies, the barbarians whom they excited to invade the territories of their countrymen.

CHAPTER THIRTY

Revolt of the Goths—They plunder Greece—Two great Invasions of Italy by Alaric and Radagaisus —They are repulsed by Stilicho—The Germans overrun Gaul—Usurpation of Constantine in the West—Disgrace and Death of Stilicho

If the subjects of Rome could be ignorant of their obligations to the great Theodosius, they were too soon convinced how painfully the spirit and abilities of their deceased emperor had supported the frail and mouldering edifice of the republic. He died in the month of January; and before the end of the winter of the same year, the Gothic nation, directed by the bold and artful genius of Alaric, was in arms. Alaric ravaged all of Greece, and eluded the army of Stilicho, who had marched into the Peloponnesus to chastise him. As a counter-poise to Stilicho the court of Constantinople promoted Alaric to the rank of master-general of the Eastern Illyricum; and the apprehension of a civil war compelled Stilicho to retire.

Armed with the double power of master-general and king of the Visigoths, and seated on the verge of the two empires, Alaric alternately sold his deceitful promises to the courts of Arcadius and Honorius, till he declared and executed his resolution of invading the dominions of the West. He was especially tempted by the fame, the beauty, the wealth of Italy, and

he secretly aspired to plant the Gothic standard on the walls of
Rome, and to enrich his army with the accumulated spoils of
three hundred triumphs. When Alaric crossed the Alps Honorius fled from Milan to Ravenna. With an army which he had
hastily collected in Gaul, Britain, and Germany Stilicho won a
resounding victory over Alaric at Pollentia, but Alaric crossed
the Appenines with the remnants of his army and marched
upon Rome. The capital was saved by the active and incessant
diligence of Stilicho; but he respected the despair of his
enemy; and, instead of committing the fate of the republic to
the chance of another battle, he proposed to purchase the absence of the barbarians. Alaric would have rejected these
terms, but he submitted to the insistence of his chieftains,
ratified the treaty with the empire of the West, and repassed
the Po with the remains of the flourishing army which he had
led into Italy.

During the games held at Rome to celebrate the repulse of
the Goths, an Asiatic monk named Telemachus descended into
the arena to separate the gladiators; the Romans were provoked by the interruption of their pleasures, and overwhelmed
Telemachus under a shower of stones. But the madness of the
people soon subsided; and they submitted without a murmur,
to the laws of Honorius, which abolished forever the human
sacrifices of the amphitheatre. The recent danger to which the
person of the emperor had been exposed motivated the removal of the royal seat to the inaccessible site of Ravenna;
until the middle of the eighth century Ravenna was considered
as the seat of government and the capital of Italy.

Next the Vandal Radagaisus, with increments of Germans
and Scythians, descended into Italy, ravaged the cities in his
path, and laid seige to Florence. The city was reduced to the
last extremity, but was saved by the energy and skill of Stilicho, who deserved a second time the glorious title of Deliverer of Italy. Radagaisus himself was executed, but his forces
marched north and crossed the Rhine into Gaul. This memorable passage of the Suevi, the Vandals, the Alani, and the Burgundians, who never afterwards retreated, may be considered
as the fall of the Roman empire in the countries beyond the
Alps; and the barriers, which had so long separated the savage

and the civilised nations of the earth, were from that fatal moment levelled with the ground. In Britain a usurper named Constantine assumed the throne, and landed at Boulogne with a small force. The neglect of the court of Ravenna had absolved a deserted people from the duty of allegiance; and the submission of Gaul was followed by that of Spain.

Stilicho maintained communication with Alaric, whether with a view towards augmenting his own power or to averting war, and seconded Alaric's request for a large subsidy to desist from attacking Italy. But the senators now demurred at the disgrace of purchasing a truce, and the crafty Olympius had alienated the confidence of Honorius, who was now twenty-five years of age, in the integrity of Stilicho. Stilicho failed to take the vigorous measures that might have saved him, and was presently executed.

CHAPTER THIRTY-ONE

Invasion of Italy by Alaric—Manners of the Roman Senate and People—Rome is thrice besieged, and at length pillaged, by the Goths—Death of Alaric—The Goths evacuate Italy—Fall of Constantine—Gaul and Spain are occupied by the Barbarians—Independence of Britain

The foreign auxiliaries who had been attached to the person of Stilicho lamented his death; but the desire of revenge was checked by a natural apprehension for the safety of their wives and children, who were detained as hostages in the strong cities of Italy, where they had likewise deposited their most valuable effects. At the same hour, and as if by a common signal, the cities of Italy were polluted by the same horrid scenes of universal massacre and pillage, which involved in promiscuous destruction the families and fortunes of the barbarians. Exasperated by such an injury, which might have awakened the tamest and most servile spirit, they cast a look of indignation and hope towards the camp of Alaric, and unanimously swore to pursue with just and implacable war the perfidious nation that had so basely violated the laws of hospitality. By the imprudent conduct of the ministers of Honorius the republic lost the assistance, and deserved the enmity, of thirty thousand of her bravest soldiers; and the weight of that

179

formidable army, which alone might have determined the
event of the war, was transferred from the scale of the Romans
into that of the Goths.

During a period of six hundred and nineteen years the seat
of empire had never been violated by the presence of a foreign
enemy. The opulent nobles of an immense capital, who were
never excited by the pursuit of military glory, and seldom
engaged in the occupations of civil government, naturally resigned their leisure to the business and amusements of private
life. Their desires were continually gratified by the labour of a
thousand hands; from the earliest times the plebians of Rome
had been oppressed by the weight of debt and usury. And now
Rome was besieged by Alaric. By a skilful disposition of his
numerous forces, who impatiently watched the moment of an
assault, Alaric compassed the walls, commanded the twelve
principal gates, intercepted all communication with the adjacent country, and vigilantly guarded the navigation of the
Tiber, from which the Roman derived the surest and most
plentiful supply of provisions.

The last resource of the Romans was in the clemency, or at
least in the moderation, of the king of the Goths. Ambassadors of the senate introduced into his presence declared, perhaps in a more lofty style than became their abject condition,
that the Romans were resolved to maintain their dignity, either
in peace or war; and that, if Alaric refused them a fair and
honourable capitulation, he might sound his trumpets, and
prepare to give battle to an innumerable people, exercised in
arms and animated by despair. "The thicker the hay, the easier
it is mowed," was the concise reply of the barbarian; and this
rustic metaphor was accompanied by a loud and insulting
laugh, expressive of his contempt for the menaces of an unwarlike populace, enervated by luxury before they were emaciated by famine. He then condescended to fix the ransom
which he would accept as the price of his retreat from the
walls of Rome: *all* the gold and silver in the city, whether it
were the property of the state, or of individuals; *all* the rich
and precious movables; and all the slaves who could prove
their title to the name of *barbarians*. The ministers of the
senate presumed to ask, in a modest and supliant tone, "If

such, O king! are your demands, what do you intend to leave us?" "YOUR LIVES," replied the haughty conqueror: they trembled and retired. Yet before they retired, a short suspension of arms was granted, which allowed some time for a more temperate negotiation. The stern features of Alaric were insensibly relaxed; he abated much of the rigour of his terms; and at length consented to raise the siege, on the immediate payment of five thousand pounds of gold, of thirty thousand pounds of silver, of four thousand robes of silk, of three thousand pieces of fine scarlet cloth, and of three thousand pounds weight of pepper. But the public treasury was exhausted; the annual rents of the great estates in Italy and the provinces were intercepted by the calamities of war; the gold and gems had been exchanged, during the famine, for the vilest sustenance; the hoards of secret wealth were still concealed by the obstinacy of avarice; and some remains of consecrated spoils afforded the only resource that could avert the impending ruin of the city. As soon as the Romans had satisfied the rapacious demands of Alaric, they were restored, in some measure, to the enjoyment of peace and plenty.

By the folly of Honorius's ministers Alaric was exasperated to renew his attacks. His threats to destroy the magazines of grain upon which the life of the Roman people depended made them accede to his proposal that Attalus, præfect of the city, should be placed on the throne of the unworthy Honorius. Rome again fell into tumult when the count of Africa, who was faithful to Honorius, prevented the export of grain. Attalus was degraded from his honors and Alaric advanced towards Ravenna to press the irresolution of the Imperial ministers. The crime and folly of the court of Ravenna was expiated a third time by the calamities of Rome. The proclamation of Alaric, when he forced his entrance into a vanquished city, discovered, however, some regard for the laws of humanity and religion. He encouraged his troops boldly to seize the rewards of valour, and to enrich themselves with the spoils of a wealthy and effeminate people; but he exhorted them at the same time to spare the lives of the unresisting citizens.

The retreat of the victorious Goths, who evacuated Rome

on the sixth day, might be the result of prudence, but it was
not surely the effect of fear. At the head of an army encum-
bered with rich and weighty spoils, their intrepid leader advanced along the Appian Way into the southern provinces of
Italy, destroying whatever dared to oppose his passage, and
contenting himself with the plunder of the unresisting country.
After he had reached the southern extreme of Italy, he prepared to cross over into Sicily, and was already meditating a
campaign in Africa; but these designs were defeated by the
premature death of Alaric.

The Goths elected Alaric's brother-in-law Adolphus to succeed to the throne, and the ministers of Honorius accepted his
services as a general. Adolphus vanquished the successors of
Constantine, the usurper of Gaul, but was himself assassinated
on a campaign in Spain. Adolphus was succeeded by Wallia,
and eventually the Goths settled in Gaul under the nominal
suzerainty of Honorius.

The Britons, during these disturbances, found they could
no longer rely on the tardy and doubtful aid of a declining
monarchy, and rejoiced in the important discovery of their
own strength. Actuated by the same spirit, the Armorican
provinces (a name which comprehended the maritime countries of Gaul between the Seine and the Loire) resolved to
imitate the example of the neighbouring island. They expelled
the Roman magistrates, who acted under the authority of the
usurper Constantine; and a free government was established
among a people who had so long been subject to the arbitrary
will of a master. The independence of Britain and Armorica
was soon confirmed by Honorius himself, the lawful emperor
of the West; and the letters by which he committed to the new
states the care of their own safety might be interpreted as an
absolute and perpetual abdication of the exercise and rights of
sovereignty. This revolution dissolved the artificial fabric of
civil and military government; and the independent country,
during a period of forty years, till the descent of the Saxons,
was ruled by the authority of the clergy, the nobles, and the
municipal towns.

CHAPTER THIRTY-TWO

Arcadius Emperor of the East—Administration and Disgrace of Eutropius—Revolt of Gainas—Persecution of St. John Chrysostom—Theodosius II. Emperor of the East—His Sister Pulcheria—His Wife Eudocia—The Persian War, and Division of Armenia

The division of the Roman world between the sons of Theodosius marks the final establishment of the empire of the East, which, from the reign of Arcadius to the taking of Constantinople by the Turks, subsisted one thousand and fifty-eight years in a state of premature and perpetual decay. The sovereign of that empire assumed and obstinately retained the vain, and at length fictitious, title of Emperor of the ROMANS; and the hereditary appellations of CÆSAR and AUGUSTUS continued to declare that he was the legitimate successor of the first of men, who had reigned over the first of nations. The successors of Constantine established their perpetual residence in the royal city which he had erected on the verge of Europe and Asia. Inaccessible to the menaces of their enemies, and perhaps to the complaints of their people, they received with each wind the tributary productions of every climate; while the impregnable strength of their capital continued for ages to defy the hostile attempts of the barbarians. Their dominions were bounded by the Hadriatic and the Tigris; and the whole interval of twenty-five days' navigation, which separated the extreme cold of Scythia from the torrid zone of Ethiopia, was comprehended within the limits of the empire of the East. The populous countries of that empire were the seat of art and learning, of luxury and wealth; and the inhabitants, who had assumed the language and manners of Greeks, styled themselves, with some appearance of truth, the most enlightened and civilised portion of the human species. The form of government was a pure and simple monarchy; the name of the ROMAN REPUBLIC, which so long preserved a faint tradition of freedom was confined to the Latin provinces; and the princes of Constantinople measured their greatness by the servile obedience of their people. They were ignorant how much this passive disposition enervates and degrades every faculty of the mind. The subjects who had resigned their will to the absolute commands of a master were equally incapable of guarding their lives and fortunes against the assaults of the barbarians, or of defending their reason from the terrors of superstition.

Eutropius, the execrable minister of Arcadius, carried his extortion so far that he posted a price-list for the governorships of provinces and obviated criticism by legislating that thoughts as well as actions were subject to prosecution as treason. Gainas, the Goth who had served Eutropius by despatching Ruffinus, persuaded his countryman Tribigeld to raise the standard of revolt. At the petition of his wife Eudoxia Arcadius first exiled and then executed Eutropius. Gainas overreached himself by introducing his soldiers into Constantinople. He marched off towards the Danube, was slain in a battle with the Huns, and his head was sent to Constantinople. No longer oppressed by hostile terrors, Arcadius resigned himself to the dominion of his wife Eudoxia.

Eudoxia's fame has been sullied by her persecution of St. John Chrysostom, the brilliant bishop of Constantinople who offended her by his outspoken criticism. His imprudence tempted his enemies to inflame the haughty spirit of Eudoxia, by reporting, or perhaps inventing, the famous exordium of a sermon, "Herodias is again furious; Herodias again dances; she once more requires the head of John:" an insolent allusion,

which, as a woman and a sovereign, it was impossible for her
to forgive. An order was despatched for the instant removal of
Chrysostom to the extreme desert of Pityus: and his guards so
faithfully obeyed their cruel instructions, that, before he
reached the sea-coast of the Euxine, he expired at Comana, in
Pontus, in the sixtieth year of his age. In the thirty-first year of
his age, after a reign (if we may abuse that word) of thirteen
years, three months, and fifteen days, Arcadius expired in the
palace of Constantinople, leaving behind a son, Theodosius,
of seven years, who had already been invested with the titles
of Cæsar and Augustus.

The survival of the young emperor proved the merit and
integrity of his guardian Anthemius. Theodosius's sister Pulcheria, who was only two years older than himself, received at
the age of sixteen the title of *Augusta;* and though her favour
might be sometimes clouded by caprice or intrigue, she continued to govern the Eastern empire near forty years; during
the long minority of her brother, and after his death in her own
name, and in the name of Marcian, her nominal husband.
From a motive either of prudence or religion, she embraced a
life of celibacy; and notwithstanding some aspersions on the
chastity of Pulcheria, this resolution, which she communicated to her sisters Arcadia and Marina, was celebrated by the
Christian world as the sublime effort of heroic piety. Yet the
devotion of Pulcheria never diverted her indefatigable attention from temporal affairs; and she alone, among all the descendants of the great Theodosius, appears to have inherited
any share of his manly spirit and abilities. The elegant and
familiar use which she had acquired both of the Greek and
Latin languages was readily applied to the various occasions
of speaking or writing on public business: her deliberations
were maturely weighed; her actions were prompt and decisive;
and while she moved without noise or ostentation the wheel of
government, she discreetly attributed to the genius of the emperor the long tranquility of his reign. In the last years of his
peaceful life Europe was indeed afflicted by the arms of Attila; but the more extensive provinces of Asia still continued to
enjoy a profound and permanent repose. Theodosius the
younger was never reduced to the disgraceful necessity of en-

countering and punishing a rebellious subject: and since we cannot applaud the vigour, some praise may be due to the mildness and prosperity of the administration of Pulcheria.

Pulcheria chose as wife for Theodosius the beautiful Athenais, daughter of the pagan philosopher Leontius. Upon her conversion she received the name Eudocia, and she became the mother of the Eudoxia who was married to the third Valentinian, emperor of the West. Pulcheria soon grew jealous of Eudocia, and banished her from the court. Eudocia passed the remainder of her life in Jerusalem.

It was in the reign of Theodosius that the Kingdom of Armenia was finally divided between the Persians and Romans, the Persians obtaining the eastern and more extensive portion of the country, and the Romans the western province; a territorial acquisition, which Augustus might have despised, reflected some lustre on the declining empire of the younger Theodosius.

CHAPTER THIRTY-THREE

Death of Honorius—Valentinian III. Emperor of the West—Administration of his Mother Placidia —Aëtius and Boniface—Conquest of Africa by the Vandals

During a long and disgraceful reign of twenty-eight years, Honorius, emperor of the West, was separated from the friendship of his brother, and afterwards of his nephew, who reigned over the East; and Constantinople beheld, with apparent indifference and secret joy, the calamities of Rome. Upon the death of Honorius the throne was usurped by John, who filled the confidential office of Primicerius, or principal secretary. Theodosius sent an army into Italy, which easily suppressed the rebellion, and Valentinian, Honorius's nephew, was proclaimed emperor of the West. As a child of six he was betrothed to Eudoxia, daughter of Theodosius, and the marriage was consummated when the two attained puberty. His mother Placidia continued to reign for twenty-five years in the name of Valentinian. Amidst the decay of military spirit Placidia's armies were commanded by two generals, Aëtius and Boniface, who may be deservedly named as the last of the Romans. Their union might have supported a sinking empire; their discord was the fatal and immediate cause of the loss of Africa. While Boniface was in Africa to suppress rebellion

Aëitus secretly persuaded Placidia to recall him and secretly persuaded Boniface to disobey the Imperial summons. To avoid his own destruction Boniface entered into an alliance with Gonderic, king of the Vandals.

Upon Gonderic's death his bastard brother, the terrible Genseric, became king of the Vandals; Genseric is a name which in the destruction of the Roman empire has deserved an equal rank with the names of Alaric and Attila. Genseric transported his army into Africa, where he drove the army of Boniface into Hippo. It was during the Vandal siege of Hippo that St. Augustine, its bishop died. Eventually Carthage itself fell. Armies of unknown barbarians, issuing from the frozen regions of the North, had established their victorious reign over the fairest provinces of Europe and Africa.

CHAPTER THIRTY-FOUR

The Character, Conquests, and Court of Attila, King of the Huns—Death of Theodosius the Younger—Elevation of Marcian to the Empire of the East

The Western world was oppressed by the Goths and Vandals, who fled before the Huns; but the achievements of the Huns themselves were not adequate to their power and prosperity. Their victorious hordes had spread from the Volga to the Danube; but the public force was exhausted by the discord of independent chieftains; their valour was idly consumed in obscure and predatory excursions; and they often degraded their national dignity, by condescending, for the hopes of spoil, to enlist under the banners of their fugitive enemies. In the reign of ATTILA the Huns again became the terror of the world.

Attila deduced his noble, perhaps regal, descent from the ancient Huns, who had formerly contended with the monarchs of China. The extent of his empire affords the only remaining evidence of the number and importance of his victories; he might well lament that his illiterate subjects were destitute of the art which could perpetuate the memory of his exploits. If a line of separation were drawn between the civilised and the savage climates of the globe; between the inhabitants of cities, who cultivated the earth, and the hunters and shepherds, who

189

dwelt in tents, Attila might aspire to the title of supreme and sole monarch of the barbarians. When Attila collected his military force, he was able to bring into the field an army of five, or according to another account, of seven hundred thousand barbarians.

When the courts of Ravenna and Constantinople had concerted an enterprise for the recovery of the valuable province of Africa, the subtle Genseric prevented their designs by exciting the king of the Huns to invade the Eastern empire. Attila's sweep was as irresistible as it was destructive. The military force collected to confront him might have been formidable by their arms and numbers, if the generals had understood the science of command, and their soldiers the duty of obedience. The armies of the Eastern empire were vanquished in three successive engagements. Theodosius might still affect the style as well as the title of *Invincible Augustus*, but he was reduced to solicit the clemency of Attila, who imperiously dictated harsh and humiliating conditions of peace.

It would have been strange, indeed, if Theodosius had purchased, by the loss of honour, a secure and solid tranquility, or if his tameness had not invited repetition of injuries. The Byzantine court was insulted by five or six successive embassies; and the ministers of Attila were uniformly instructed to press the tardy or imperfect execution of the last treaty. One of these, Edecon by name, ostensibly agreed, on the occasion of a visit to Constantinople, to procure the assassination of his master, but then informed Attila of Theodosius's plot against his life. Attila was understandably enraged, yet allowed himself to be mollified. But the new treaty was purchased at an expense which might have supported a vigorous and successful war.

Theodosius did not long survive the most humiliating circumstances of an inglorious life. He died, of a fall from his horse, in the fiftieth year of his age, and the forty-third of his reign. His sister Pulcheria, whose authority had been controlled both in civil and ecclesiastical affairs by the pernicious influence of the eunuchs, was unanimously proclaimed empress of the East. The empress did not forget the prejudice and disadvantage to which her sex was exposed; and she wisely resolved to prevent murmurs by the choice of a colleague who would always respect the superior rank and virgin chastity of his wife. She gave her hand to Marcian, a senator, about sixty years of age; and the nominal husband of Pulcheria was solemnly invested with the Imperial purple. Marcian's mild disposition and useful talents, without alarming jealousy, recommended him to esteem and favour; he had seen, perhaps he had felt, the abuses of a venal and oppressive administration, and his own example gave weight and energy to the laws which he promulgated for the reformation of manners.

CHAPTER THIRTY-FIVE

*Invasion of Gaul by Attila—He is repulsed by
Aëtius and the Visigoths—Attila invades and
evacuates Italy—The Deaths of Attila, Aëtius,
and Valentinian the Third*

It was the opinion of Marcian, that war should be avoided as
long as it is possible to preserve a secure and honourable
peace; but it was likewise his opinion that peace cannot be
honourable or secure, if the sovereign betrays a pusillanimous
aversion to war. This temperate courage dictated his reply to
the demands of Attila, who insolently pressed the payment of
the annual tribute. The emperor signified to the barbarians that
they must no longer insult the majesty of Rome by mention of
a tribute; that he was disposed to reward, with becoming liberality, the faithful friendship of his allies; but that, if they presumed to violate the public peace, they should feel that he
possessed troops, and arms, and resolution, to repel their attacks. Attila threatened to chastise the rash successor of Theodosius, but was more attracted by the wealth and fertility of
Gaul and Italy. The particular motives and provocations of
Attila can only be explained by the state of the Western empire
under the reign of Valentinian, or, to speak more correctly,
under the administration of Aëtius.

After the death of his rival Boniface, Aëtius had prudently

retired to the tents of the Huns; and he was indebted to their alliance for his safety and restoration. Placidia delivered herself, her son Valentinian, and the Western empire, into the hands of an insolent subject. The fortunate Aëtius, who was immediately promoted to the rank of patrician, assumed the whole military power of the state. His prudence, rather than his virtue, engaged him to leave the grandson of Theodosius in the possession of the purple; and Valentinian was permitted to enjoy the peace and luxury of Italy, while the patrician appeared in the glorious light of a hero and a patriot, who supported near twenty years the ruins of the Western empire. From a principle of interest, as well as gratitude, Aëtius assiduously cultivated the alliance of the Huns. While he resided in their tents as a hostage or an exile, he had familiarly conversed with Attila himself, and the two famous antagonists appear to have been connected by a personal and military friendship, which they afterwards confirmed by mutual gifts and frequent embassies. His dexterous policy prolonged the advantages of a salutary peace; and a numerous army of Huns and Alani, whom he had attached to his person, was employed in the defence of Gaul.

The kingdom established by the Visigoths in the southern provinces of Gaul had gradually acquired strength and maturity; and the conduct of those ambitious barbarians, either in peace or war, engaged the perpetual vigilance of Aëtius. After the death of Wallia, the Gothic sceptre devolved to Theodoric, the son of the great Alaric; and his prosperous reign of more than thirty years over a turbulent people may be allowed to prove that his prudence was supported by uncommon vigour, both of mind and body. Theodoric, king of the Visigoths, appears to have deserved the love of his subjects, the confidence of his allies, and the esteem of mankind. His throne was surrounded by six valiant sons, who were educated with equal care in the exercises of the barbarian camp, and in those of the Gallic schools. The two daughters of the Gothic king were given in marriage to the eldest sons of the kings of the Suevi and of the Vandals, who reigned in Spain and Africa; but these illustrious alliances were pregnant with guilt and discord. The queen of the Suevi bewailed the death of an husband, inhu-

manly massacred by her brother. The princess of the Vandals
was the victim of a jealous tyrant, whom she called her father.
The cruel Genseric suspected that his son's wife had conspired
to poison him; the supposed crime was punished by the ampu-
tation of her nose and ears; and the unhappy daughter of
Theodoric was ignominiously returned to the court of Toulouse in that deformed and mutilated condition. Theodoric
was urged, by the feelings of a parent and a king, to revenge
such irreparable injuries. The Imperial ministers, who always
cherished the discord of the barbarians, would have supplied
the Goths with arms, and ships, and treasures, for the African
war; and the cruelty of Genseric might have been fatal to
himself, if the artful Vandal had not armed, in his cause, the
formidable power of the Huns. His rich gifts and pressing
solicitations inflamed the ambition of Attila; and the designs
of Aëtius and Theodoric were prevented by the invasion of
Gaul.

The Franks, whose monarchy was still confined to the
neighbourhood of the Lower Rhine, had wisely established the
right of hereditary succession in the noble family of the Mero-
vingians. The death of Clodion, who was the first of the Merovingian kings, after a reign of twenty years, exposed his
kingdom to the discord and ambition of his two sons. Mer-
veus, the younger, implored the protection of Rome; his elder
brother solicited the formidable aid of Attila, and the king of
the Huns embraced an alliance which facilitated the passage
of the Rhine, and justified by a specious and honourable pretence the invasion of Gaul.

When Atilla declared his resolution of supporting the cause
of his allies the Vandals and the Franks, at the same time, and
almost in the spirit of romantic chivalry, the savage monarch
professed himself the lover and the champion of the princess
Honoria. The sister of Valentinian was educated in the palace
of Ravenna; and as her marriage might be productive of some
danger to the state, she was raised, by the title of *Augusta,*
above the hopes of the most presumptuous subject. But the
fair Honoria had no sooner attained the sixteenth year of her
age than she detested the importunate greatness which must
for ever exclude her from the comforts of honourable love: in

the midst of vain and unsatisfactory pomp Honoria sighed, yielded to the impulse of nature, and threw herself into the arms of her chamberlain Eugenius. Her guilt and shame (such is the absurd language of imperious man) were soon betrayed by the appearances of pregnancy: but the disgrace of the royal family was published to the world by the imprudence of the empress Placidia, who dismissed her daughter, after a strict and shameful confinement, to a remote exile at Constantinople. The unhappy princess passed twelve or fourteen years in the irksome society of the sisters of Theodosius and their chosen virgins, to whose *crown* Honoria could no longer aspire, and whose monastic assiduity of prayer, fasting, and vigils she reluctantly imitated. Her impatience of long and hopeless celibacy urged her to embrace a strange and desperate resolution. The name of Attila was familiar and formidable at Constantinople, and his frequent embassies entertained a perpetual intercourse between his camp and the Imperial palace. In the pursuit of love, or rather of revenge, the daughter of Placidia sacrificed every duty and every prejudice, and offered to deliver her person into the arms of a barbarian of whose language she was ignorant, whose figure was scarcely human, and whose religion and manners she abhorred. By the ministry of a faithful eunuch she transmitted to Attila a ring, the pledge of her affection, and earnestly conjured him to claim her as a lawful spouse to whom he had been secretly betrothed. These indecent advances were received, however, with coldness and disdain; and the king of the Huns continued to multiply the number of his wives till his love was awakened by the more forcible passions of ambition and avarice. The invasion of Gaul was preceded and justified by a formal demand of the princess Honoria, with a just and equal share of the Imperial patrimony. On the discovery of her connection with the king of the Huns, the guilty princess was sent away, as an object of horror, from Constantinople to Italy: her life was spared, but the ceremony of her marriage was performed with some obscure and nominal husband before she was immured in a perpetual prison, to bewail those crimes and misfortunes which Honoria might have escaped had she not been born the daughter of an emperor.

The facility with which Attila had penetrated into the heart of Gaul may be ascribed to his insidious policy as well as to the terror of his arms. His public declarations were skilfully mitigated by his private assurances; he alternately soothed and threatened the Romans and the Goths; and the courts of Ravenna and Toulouse, mutually suspicious of each other's intentions, beheld with supine indifference the approach of their common enemy. When Attila held Orleans under siege, Aëtius and Theodoric advanced by rapid marches to relieve the city, and Attila recalled his troops from the pillage of a city which they had already entered. The valour of Attila was always guided by his prudence; and as he foresaw the fatal consequences of a defeat in the heart of Gaul, he repassed the Seine, and expected the enemy in the plains of Châlons, whose smooth and level surface was adapted to the operations of his Scythian cavalry. The nations from the Volga to the Atlantic were assembled on the plain of Châlons; but many of these nations had been divided by faction, or conquest, or emigration; and the appearance of similar arms and ensigns, which threatened each other, presented the image of a civil war. The numbers reported slain at the battle of Châlons seem incredible. Theodoric himself was slain, but Attila was forced to retreat.

Neither the spirit, nor the forces, nor the reputation of Attila were impaired by the failure of the Gallic expedition. In the ensuing spring he repeated his demand of the princess Honoria and her patrimonial treasures. The demand was again rejected or eluded; and the indignant lover immediately took the field, passed the Alps, invaded Italy, and besieged Aquileia with an innumerable host of barbarians. The Huns mounted to the assault with irresistible fury; and the succeeding generation could scarcely discover the ruins of Aquileia. After this dreadful chastisement, Attila pursued his march; and as he passed, the cities of Altinum, Concordia, and Padua were reduced into heaps of stones and ashes. It is a saying worthy of the ferocious pride of Attila, that the grass never grew on the spot where his horse had trod. Yet the savage destroyer undesignedly laid the foundations of a republic which revived, in the feudal state of Europe, the art and spirit of commercial industry.

The Italians, who had long since renounced the exercise of arms, were surprised, after forty years' peace, by the approach of a formidable barbarian, whom they abhorred as the enemy of their religion as well as of their republic. Amidst the general consternation, Aëtius alone was incapable of fear; if the mind of Valentinian had been susceptible of any generous sentiments, he would have chosen such a general for his example and his guide. But the timid grandson of Theodosius, instead of sharing the dangers, escaped from the sound, of war; and his hasty retreat from Ravenna to Rome, from an impregnable fortress to an open capital, betrayed his secret intention of abandoning Italy as soon as the danger should approach his Imperial person. Leo, bishop of Rome, consented to expose his life for the safety of his flock: his majestic aspect and sacerdotal robes excited the veneration of Attila for the spiritual father of the Christians. Shortly after Leo's intercession had saved Rome, Attila himself suddenly died.

The revolution which subverted the empire of the Huns established the fame of Attila, whose genius alone had sustained the huge and disjointed fabric. After his death the boldest chieftains aspired to the rank of kings: the most powerful kings refused to acknowledge a superior; and the numerous sons whom so many various mothers bore to the deceased monarch divided and disputed like a private inheritance the soverign command of the nations of Germany and Scythia. But the emperor of the West, the feeble and dissolute Valentinian, who had reached his thirty-fifth year without attaining the age of reason or courage, abused this apparent security to undermine the foundations of his own throne by the murder of the patrician Aëtius. From the instinct of a base and jealous mind, he hated the man who was universally celebrated as the terror of the barbarians and the support of the republic; and his new favourite, the eunuch Heraclius, awakened the emperor from the supine lethargy which might be disguised during the life of Placidia by the excuse of filial piety. When the patrician offended his sovereign by insisting upon his own views in a conference, Valentinian, drawing his sword—the first sword he had ever drawn—plunged it in the breast of a general who had saved his empire; his courtiers and eunuchs ambitiously struggled to imitate their master; and Aëtius, pierced with an hundred wounds, fell dead in the royal presence.

The luxury of Rome seems to have attracted the long and frequent visits of Valentinian, who was consequently more despised at Rome than in any other part of his dominions. A republican spirit was insensibly revived in the senate, as their authority, and even their supplies, became necessary for the support of his feeble government. The stately demeanour of an hereditary monarch offended their pride, and the pleasures of Valentinian were injurious to the peace and honour of noble families. The birth of the empress Eudoxia was equal to his own, and her charms and tender affection deserved those testimonies of love which her inconstant husband dissipated in vague and unlawful armours. Petronius Maximus, a wealthy senator of the Anician family, who had been twice consul, was possessed of a chaste and beautiful wife: her obstinate resistance served only to irritate the desires of Valentinian, and he resolved to accomplish them either by stratagem or force. Deep gaming was one of the vices of the court; the emperor, who, by chance or contrivance, had gained from Maximus a considerable sum, uncourteously exacted his ring as a security for the debt, and sent it by a trusty messenger to his wife, with an order in her husband's name that she should immediately attend the empress Eudoxia. The unsuspecting wife of Maximus was conveyed in her litter to the Imperial palace; the emissaries of her impatient lover conducted her to a remote and silent bed-chamber; and Valentinian violated, without remorse, the laws of hospitality. Her tears when she returned home, her deep affliction, and the bitter reproaches against a husband whom she considered as the accomplice of his own shame, excited Maximus to a just revenge; the desire of revenge was stimulated by ambition; and he might reasonably aspire, by the free suffrage of the Roman senate, to the throne of a detested and despicable rival. Valentinian, who supposed that every human breast was devoid like his own of friendship and gratitude, had imprudently admitted among his guards several domestics and followers of Aëtius. Two of these, of barbarian race, were persuaded to execute a sacred and honourable duty by punishing with death the assassin of their patron; and their intrepid courage did not long except a favourable moment. Whilst Valentinian amused himself in the field of Mars with the spectacle of some military sports, they suddenly rushed upon him with drawn weapons, despatched the guilty Heraclius, and stabbed the emperor to the heart, without the least opposition from his numerous train, who seemed to rejoice in the tyrant's death. Such was the fate of Valentinian the Third, the last Roman emperor of the family of Theodosius.

The Roman government appeared every day less formidable to its enemies, more odious and oppressive to its subjects. The severe inquisition, which confiscated their goods and tortured their persons, compelled the subjects of Valentinian to prefer the more simple tyranny of the barbarians, to fly to the woods and mountains, or to embrace the vile and abject condition of mercenary servants. They abjured and abhorred the name of Roman citizens, which had formerly excited the ambition of mankind. If all the barbarian conquerors had been annihilated in the same hour, their total destruction would not have restored the empire of the West: and if Rome still survived, she survived the loss of freedom, of virtue, and of honour.

CHAPTER THIRTY-SIX

Sack of Rome by Genseric, King of the Vandals—His Naval Depredations—Succession of the last Emperors of the West, Maximus, Avitus, Majorian, Severus, Anthemius, Olybrius, Glycerius, Nepos, Augustulus—Total Extinction of the Western Empire—Reign of Odoacer, the first Barbarian King of Italy

The loss or desolation of the provinces from the Ocean to the Alps impaired the glory and greatness of Rome: her internal prosperity was irretrievably destroyed by the separation of Africa. The rapacious Vandals confiscated the patrimonial estates of the senators, and intercepted the regular subsidies which relieved the poverty and encouraged the idleness of the plebeians. The distress of the Romans was soon aggravated by an unexpected attack; and the province, so long cultivated for their use by industrious and obedient subjects, was armed against them by an ambitious barbarian. After an interval of six centuries, the fleets that issued from the port of Carthage again claimed the empire of the Mediterranean. The success of the Vandals, the conquest of Sicily, the sack of Palermo, and the frequent descents on the coast of Lucania, awakened and alarmed the mother of Valentinian and the sister of Theodosius. The revolutions of the palace, which left the Western empire without a defender and without a lawful prince, dispelled the apprehensions and stimulated the avarice of Genseric. He immediately equipped a numerous fleet of Vandals and Moors, and cast anchor at the mouth of the Tiber, about three months after the death of Valentinian and the elevation of Maximus to the Imperial throne.

Maximus had forcibly married Valentinian's widow Eudoxia, who, in order to avenge her first husband, invited Genseric to invade Rome. When the Vandals disembarked at the mouth of the Tiber, the only hope which presented itself to Maximus's astonished mind was precipitate flight; but no sooner did he appear in the streets than he was assaulted by a shower of stones, and his mangled body was ignominiously cast into the Tiber. Rome and its inhabitants were delivered to the licentiousness of the Vandals and Moors, whose blind passions revenged the injuries of Carthage. The pillage lasted fourteen days and nights; and all that yet remained of public or private wealth, of sacred or profane treasure, was diligently transported to the vessels of Genseric. Among the spoils were the holy instruments of the temple at Jerusalem, which had been transported to Rome by the emperor Titus. Eudoxia herself, who advanced to meet her friend and deliverer, soon bewailed the imprudence of her own conduct. She was rudely stripped of her jewels; and the unfortunate empress, with her two daughters, the only surviving remains of the great Theodosius, was compelled, as a captive, to follow the haughty Vandal, who immediately hoisted sail, and returned with a prosperous navigation to the port of Carthage.

Upon receiving intelligence of the death of Maximus, the Goths, at the instance of their king Theodoric, raised Avitus to the purple. Theodoric's successes against the Visigoths in Spain exasperated the powerful Count Ricimer, who deposed Avitus. The successor of Avitus presents the welcome discovery of a great and heroic character, such as sometimes arise, in a degenerate age, to vindicate the honour of the human species.

The private and public actions of Majorian are very imperfectly known: but his laws, remarkable for an original cast of thought and expression, faithfully represent the character of a

sovereign who loved his people, who sympathised in their
distress, who had studied the causes of the decline of the empire, and who was capable of applying (as far as such reformation was practicable) judicious and effectual remedies to
the public disorders. His regulations concerning the finances
manifestly tended to remove, or at least to mitigate, the most
intolerable grievances. I. From the first hour of his reign he
was solicitous (I translate his own words) to relieve the *weary*
fortunes of the provincials, oppressed by the accumulated
weight of indictions and superindictions. With this view, he
granted an universal amnesty, a final and absolute discharge of
all arrears of tribute, of all debts which, under any pretence,
the fiscal officers might demand from the people. This wise
dereliction of obsolete, vexatious, and unprofitable claims,
improved and purified the sources of the public revenue; and
the subject, who could now look back without despair, might
labour with hope and gratitude for himself and for his country.
II. In the assessment and collection of taxes Majorian restored
the ordinary jurisdiction of the provincial magistrates, and
suppressed the extraordinary commissions which had been introduced in the name of the emperor himself or of the Prætorian præfects. III. "The municipal corporations (says the
emperor), the lesser senates (so antiquity has justly styled
them), deserve to be considered as the heart of the cities and
the sinews of the republic. And yet so low are they now reduced, by the injustice of magistrates and the venality of col-
lectors, that many of their members, renouncing their dignity
and their country, have taken refuge in distant and obscure
exile." He urges, and even compels, their return to their respective cities; but he removes the grievance which had forced
them to desert the exercise of their municipal functions.

The spectator who casts a mournful view over the ruins of
ancient Rome is tempted to accuse the memory of the Goths
and Vandals for the mischief which they had neither leisure,
nor power, nor perhaps inclination, to perpetrate. The tempest
of war might strike some lofty turrets to the ground; but the
destruction which undermined the foundations of those massy
fabrics was prosecuted, slowly and silently, during a period of

ten centuries; and the motives of interest, that afterwards operated without shame or control, were severely checked by the taste and spirit of the emperor Majorian. The monuments of consular or Imperial greatness were no longer revered as the immortal glory of the capital; they were only esteemed as an inexhaustible mine of materials, cheaper, and more convenient, than the distant quarry. Majorian, who had often sighed over the desolation of the city, applied severe remedies to the growing evil. The emperor conceived that it was his interest to increase the number of his subjects; that it was his duty to guard the purity of the marriage-bed: but the means which he employed to accomplish these salutary purposes are of an ambiguous, and perhaps exceptionable, kind. The pious maids who consecrated their virginity to Christ were restrained from taking the veil until they had reached their fortieth year. Widows under that age were compelled to form a second alliance within the term of five years, by the forfeiture of half their wealth to their nearest relations or to the state.

While the emperor Majorian assiduously laboured to restore the happiness and virtue of the Romans, he encountered the arms of Genseric, from his character and situation their most formidable enemy. Rome expected from him alone the restitution of Africa, and the design which he formed of attacking the Vandals in their new settlements was the result of bold and judicious policy. Genseric was saved from impending ruin by the treacherous destruction of the fleet Majorian had prepared for the invasion of Africa. Majorian was in the midst of reparing this reverse when a sedition forced him to abdicate; five days after his abdication he died of a dysentery.

At Ricimer's command the obsequious senate of Rome bestowed the Imperial title on Libius Servius, who died as soon as his life became inconvenient to his patron. During the six years between the death of Majorian and the elevation of Anthemius the government was in the hands of Ricimer alone; and although the modest barbarian disclaimed the name of king, he accumulated treasures, formed a separate army, negotiated private alliances, and ruled Italy with the same independent and despotic authority which was afterwards exercised by Odoacer and Theodoric. During his reign the kingdom of Italy, a name to which the Western empire was gradually reduced, was afflicted by the incessant depredations of the Vandal pirates. The haughty Ricimer was at length reduced to address the throne of Constantinople in the humble language of a subject; and Italy submitted, as the price and security of alliance, to accept a master from the choice of the emperor of the East. Leo, who had succeeded Marcian as emperor of the East, nominated Anthemius emperor of the West. A huge armament under the command of Basiliscus, brother of the empress Verina, landed in Africa and won initial victories; but during a truce the fleet was burned and Basiliscus returned to Constantinople with great losses. Genseric again became tyrant of the sea; and before he died, in the fullness of years and of glory, he beheld the final extinction of the empire of the West.

Ricimer, who was apprehensive or impatient of a superior, declared Olybrius emperor of the West; senate and people adhered to the cause of Anthemius, who was nevertheless murdered. Within seven months both Olybrius and Ricimer died natural deaths. Julius Nepos, who was married to a niece of the empress Verina, was next made emperor of the West. Orestes, who had served under Attila and had been made patrician and master-general by Nepos himself, rose against Nepos, and though he refused the purple for himself, he allowed his soldiers to acknowledge his son Augustulus as emperor of the West. When Orestes rejected the exorbitant demands of his soldiers, their leader Odoacer, who was son of Edecon, rose to power.

Royalty was familiar to the barbarians, and the submissive people of Italy was prepared to obey, without a murmur, the authority which he should condescend to exercise as the vicegerent of the emperor of the West. But Odoacer had resolved to abolish that useless and expensive office; and such is the weight of antique prejudice, that it required some boldness and penetration to discover the extreme facility of the enterprise. The unfortunate Augustulus was made the instrument of his own disgrace; he signified his resignation to the senate;

and that assembly, in their last act of obedience to a Roman prince, still affected the spirit of freedom and the forms of the constitution. An epistle was addressed, by their unanimous decree, to the emperor Zeno, the son-in-law and successor of Leo, who had lately been restored, after a short rebellion, to the Byzantine throne. They solemnly "disclaim the necessity, or even the wish, of continuing any longer the Imperial succession in Italy; since, in their opinion, the majesty of a sole monarch is sufficient to pervade and protect, at the same time, both the East and the West. In their own name, and in the name of the people, they consent that the seat of universal empire shall be transferred from Rome to Constantinople; and they basely renounce the right of choosing their master, the only vestige that yet remained of the authority which had given laws to the world. The republic (they repeat that name without a blush) might safely confide in the civil and military virtues of Odoacer; and they humbly request that the emperor would invest him with the title of Patrician, and the administration of the *diocese* of Italy."

The son of Orestes assumed and disgraced the names of Romulus Augustus. Odoacer spared the life of the inoffensive youth and dismissed him with a pension. Odoacer was the first barbarian who reigned in Italy, over a people who had once asserted their just superiority above the rest of mankind. The king of Italy was not unworthy of the high station to which his valour and fortune had exalted him: his savage manners were polished by the habits of conversation; and he respected, though a barbarian, the institutions, and even the prejudices, of his subjects.

Notwithstanding the prudence and success of Odoacer, his kingdom exhibited the sad prospect of misery and desolation. Since the age of Tiberius, the decay of agriculture had been felt in Italy; and it was a just subject of complaint that the life of the Roman people depended on the accidents of the winds and waves. In the division and the decline of the empire, the tributary harvests of Egypt and Africa were withdrawn; the numbers of the inhabitants continually diminished with the means of subsistence; and the country was exhausted by the irretrievable losses of war, famine, and pestilence. After a reign of fourteen years Odoacer was oppressed by the superior genius of Theodoric, king of the Ostrogoths; a hero alike excellent in the arts of war and of government, who restored an age of peace and prosperity, and whose name still excites and deserves the attention of mankind.

CHAPTER THIRTY-SEVEN

Origin, Progress, and Effects of the Monastic Life —Conversion of the Barbarians to Christianity and Arianism—Persecution of the Vandals in Africa—Extinction of Arianism among the Barbarians

The indissoluble connection of civil and ecclesiastical affairs has compelled and encouraged me to relate the progress, the persecutions, the establishment, the divisions, the final triumph, and the gradual corruption of Christianity. I have purposely delayed the consideration of two religious events interesting in the study of human nature, and important in the decline and fall of the Roman empire. I. The institution of the monastic life; and II. The conversion of the Northern barbarians.

Prosperity and peace introduced the distinction of the *vulgar* and the *Ascetic Christians*. The loose and imperfect practice of religion satisfied the conscience of the multitude. The prince or magistrate, the soldier or merchant, reconciled their fervent zeal and implicit faith with the exercise of their profession, the pursuit of their interest, and the indulgence of their passions: but the Ascetics, who obeyed and abused the rigid precepts of the Gospel, were inspired by the savage enthusiasm which represents man as a criminal, and God as a tyrant. They seriously renounced the business and pleasures of the age; abjured the use of wine, of flesh, and of marriage; chastised their body, mortified their affections, and embraced a life of misery, as the price of eternal happiness. In the reign of Constantine the Ascetics fled from a profane and degenerate world to perpetual solitude or religious society.

Egypt, the fruitful parent of superstition, afforded the first example of the monastic life. Antony, an illiterate youth of the lower parts of Thebais, distributed his patrimony, deserted his family and native home, and executed his *monastic* penance with original and intrepid fanaticism. The venerable patriarch (for Antony attained the age of one hundred and five years) beheld the numerous progeny which had been formed by his example and his lessons. The Egyptians, who gloried in his marvellous revolution, were disposed to hope, and to believe, that the number of the monks was equal to the remainder of the people; and posterity might repeat the saying which had formerly been applied to the sacred animals of the same country, that in Egypt it was less difficult to find a god than a man.

The lives of the primitive monks were consumed in penance and solitude, undisturbed by the various occupations which fill the time, and exercise the faculties, of reasonable, active, and social beings. According to their faith and zeal, they might employ the day, which they passed in their cells, either in vocal or mental prayer: they assembled in the evening, and they were awakened in the night, for the public worship of the monastery. Even sleep, the last refuge of the unhappy, was rigorously measured: the vacant hours of the monk heavily rolled along, without business or pleasure; and, before the close of each day, he had repeatedly accused the tedious progress of the sun. In this comfortless state, superstition still pursued and tormented her wretched votaries. The repose which they had sought in the cloister was disturbed by tardy repentance, profane doubts, and guilty desires; and, while they considered each natural impulse as an unpardonable sin, they perpetually trembled on the edge of a flaming and bottomless abyss. From the painful struggles of disease and despair, these unhappy victims were sometimes relieved by madness or death; and, in the sixth century, a hospital was founded at Jerusalem for a small portion of the austere penitents who were deprived of their senses. Their visions, before they attained this extreme and acknowledged term of frenzy, have afforded ample materials of supernatural history. It was their firm persuasion that the air which they breathed was peopled with invisible enemies; with innumerable demons, who watched every occasion, and assumed every form, to terrify, and above all to tempt, their unguarded virtue. The imagination, and even the senses, were deceived by the illusions of distempered fanaticism; and the hermit, whose midnight prayer was oppressed by involuntary slumber, might easily confound the phantoms of horror or delight which had occupied his sleeping and his waking dreams.

The monks were divided into two classes: the *Cænobites*, who lived under a common and regular discipline; and the *Anachorets*, who indulged their unsocial, independent fanaticism. The most devout, or the most ambitious, of the spiritual brethren renounced the convent, as they had renounced the world. The fervent monasteries of Egypt, Palestine, and Syria were surrounded by a *Laura*, a distant circle of solitary cells; and the extravagant penance of the Hermits was stimulated by applause and emulation. They sunk under the painful weight of crosses and chains; and their emaciated limbs were confined by collars, bracelets, gauntlets, and greaves of massy and rigid iron. All superfluous incumbrance of dress they contemptuously cast away; and some savage saints of both sexes have been admired, whose naked bodies were only covered by their long hair. They aspired to reduce themselves to the rude and miserable state in which the human brute is scarcely distinguished above his kindred animals; and the numerous sect of Anachorets derived their name from their humble practice of grazing in the fields of Mesopotamia with the common herd. They often usurped the den of some wild beast whom they affected to resemble; they buried themselves in some gloomy cavern, which art or nature had scooped out of the rock; and the marble quarries of Thebais are still inscribed with the monuments of their penance. The most perfect Hermits are supposed to have passed many days without food, many nights without sleep, and many years without speaking;

and glorious was the *man* (I abuse that name) who contrived any cell, or seat, of a peculiar construction, which might expose him, in the most inconvenient posture, to the inclemency of the seasons.

Among these heroes of the monastic life, the name and genius of Simeon Stylites have been immortalized by the singular invention of an aërial penance. At the age of thirteen the young Syrian deserted the profession of a shepherd, and threw himself into an austere monastery. After a long and painful novitiate, in which Simeon was repeatedly saved from pious suicide, he established his residence on a mountain, about thirty or forty miles to the east of Antioch. Within the space of a *mandra*, or circle of stones, to which he had attached himself by a ponderous chain, he ascended a column, which was successively raised from the height of nine, to that of sixty, feet from the ground. In this last and lofty station, the Syrian Anachoret resisted the heat of thirty summers, and the cold of many winters. Habit and exercise instructed him to maintain his dangerous situation without fear or giddiness, and successively to assume the different postures of devotion. He sometimes prayed in an erect attitude, with his outstretched arms in the figure of a cross; but his most familiar practice was that of bending his meagre skeleton from the forehead to the feet; and a curious spectator, after numbering twelve hundred and forty-four repetitions, at length desisted from the endless account. The progress of an ulcer in his thigh might shorten, but it could not disturb this *celestial* life; and the patient Hermit expired without descending from his column.

The progress of Christianity had been marked by two glorious and decisive victories: over the learned and luxurious citizens of the Roman empire; and over the warlike barbarians of Scythia, who subverted the empire and embraced the religion of the Romans. The Goths were the foremost of these savage proselytes; the formidable Visigoths universally adopted the religion of the Romans, with whom they maintained a perpetual intercourse of war, of friendship, or of conquest. These barbarian proselytes displayed an ardent and successful zeal in the propagation of the faith. The Merovingian kings and their successors, Charlemagne and the Othos, extended by their laws and victories the dominion of the cross. England produced the apostle of Germany; and the evangelic light was gradually diffused from the neighborhood of the Rhine to the nations of the Elbe, the Vistula, and the Baltic.

CHAPTER THIRTY-EIGHT

Reign and Conversion of Clovis—His Victories over the Alemanni, Burgundians, and Visigoths—Establishment of the French Monarchy in Gaul—Laws of the Barbarians—State of the Romans—The Visigoths of Spain—Conquest of Britain by the Saxons

As soon as Odoacer had extinguished the Western empire, he resigned all the Roman conquests beyond the Alps, as far as the Rhine and the Ocean, to Euric, king of the Visigoths; upon the premature death of Euric his adversary Clovis succeeded, who, though he died in his forty-fifth year, had accomplished the establishment of the French monarchy in Gaul. After Clovis's successes against the Goths, the usurpation of Gaul was virtually recognized by the emperor Anastasius; twenty-five years after the death of Clovis the independence of the Merovingian throne was more formally declared in a treaty between Clovis's sons and the emperor Justinian. The Visigoths were compensated for their loss of Gaul by the easy conquest of Spain, which they continued to rule until the overthrow of their monarchy by the Saracens in the eighth century. Britain, the third great diocese of the præfecture of the West, was conquered by the Saxons.

I have now accomplished the laborious narrative of the

decline and fall of the Roman empire, from the fortunate age of Trajan and the Antonines to its total extinction in the West, about five centuries after the Christian era.

GENERAL OBSERVATIONS ON THE FALL OF THE ROMAN EMPIRE IN THE WEST

. . . The arms of the republic, sometimes vanquished in battle, always victorious in war, advanced with rapid steps to the Euphrates, the Danube, the Rhine, and the Ocean; and the images of gold, or silver, or brass, that might serve to represent the nations and their kings, were successively broken by the *iron* monarchy of Rome.

The rise of a city, which swelled into an empire, may deserve, as a singular prodigy, the reflection of a philosophic mind. But the decline of Rome was the natural and inevitable effect of immoderate greatness. Prosperity ripened the principle of decay; the causes of destruction multiplied with the extent of conquest; and as soon as time or accident had removed the artificial supports, the stupendous fabric yielded to the pressure of its own weight. The story of its ruin is simple and obvious; and instead of inquiring *why* the Roman empire was destroyed, we should rather be surprised that it had subsisted so long. . . . The foundation of Constantinople more essentially contributed to the preservation of the East than to the ruin of the West.

As the happiness of a *future* life is the great object of religion, we may hear without surprise or scandal that the introduction, or at least the abuse of Christianity, had some influence on the decline and fall of the Roman empire. . . . If the decline of the Roman empire was hastened by the conversion of Constantine, his victorious religion broke the violence of the fall and mollified the ferocious temper of the conquerors . . . we may therefore acquiesce in the pleasing conclusion that every age of the world has increased and still increases the real wealth, the happiness, the knowledge, and perhaps the virtue, of the human race.

CHAPTER THIRTY-NINE

Zeno and Anastasius, Emperors of the East—Birth, Education, and first Exploits of Theodoric the Ostrogoth—His Invasion and Conquest of Italy—The Gothic Kingdom of Italy—State of the West—Military and Civil Government—The Senator Boethius—Last Acts and Death of Theodoric

After the fall of the Roman empire in the West, an interval of fifty years, till the memorable reign of Justinian, is faintly marked by the obscure names and imperfect annals of Zeno, Anastasius, and Justin, who successively ascended the throne of Constantinople. During the same period, Italy revived and flourished under the government of a Gothic king who might have deserved a statue among the best and bravest of the ancient Romans.

Theodoric, the fourteenth in descent of a royal family of the Ostrogoths, made himself so feared and so useful to the Eastern emperor Zeno that he was raised to the rank of patrician and consul and given command of the Palatine troops. As long as Theodoric condescended to serve, he supported with courage and fidelity the cause of his benefactor; but Theodoric soon grew restive, and the Byzantine court joyfully accepted his proposal to march, with his national troops, against

Odoacer and restore Italy to the Roman empire. After three victories Theodoric first consented to share the rule with Odoacer, and then procured his assassination; Theodoric became master of Italy, with the ambiguous consent of the emperor of the East.

Among the barbarians of the West the victory of Theodoric had spread a general alarm. But as soon as it appeared that he was satisfied with conquest and desirous of peace, terror was changed into respect, and they submitted to a powerful mediation, which was uniformly employed for the best purposes of reconciling their quarrels and civilising their manners. The life of Theodoric represents the rare and meritorious example of a barbarian who sheathed his sword in the pride of victory and the vigour of his age. A reign of three and thirty years was consecrated to the duties of civil government, and the hostilities, in which he was sometimes involved, were speedily terminated by the conduct of his lieutenants, the discipline of his troops, the arms of his allies, and even by the terror of his name. The greatness of a servant, who was named perfidious because he was successful, awakened the jealousy of the emperor Anastasius, who promoted a war on the Dacian frontier. Theodoric repulsed a naval expedition from the East, but continued to address the Eastern throne in respectful if ambiguous terms.

The ministers of Theodoric, Cassiodorus and Boethius, have reflected on his reign the lustre of their genius and learning. The senator Boethius is the last of the Romans whom Cato or Tully could have acknowledged for their countryman. His authority restrained the pride and oppression of royal officers. When the senator Albinus was accused and already convicted on the presumption of *hoping,* as it was said, the liberty of Rome, Boethius spoke out. "If Albinus be criminal," he exclaimed, "the senate and myself are all guilty of the same crime. If we are innocent, Albinus is equally entitled to the protection of the laws." A devout and dutiful attachment to the senate was condemned as criminal by the trembling voices of the senators themselves. While Boethius, oppressed with fetters, expected each moment the stroke of death, he composed in the tower of Pavia the *Consolation of Philosophy*; a golden volume not unworthy of the leisure of Plato or Tully, but which claims incomparable merit from the barbarism of the times and the situation of the author.

After a life of virtue and glory, Theodoric was now descending with shame and guilt into the grave: his mind was humbled by the contrast of the past, and justly alarmed by the invisible terrors of futurity. One evening, as it is related, when the head of a large fish was served on the royal table, he suddenly exclaimed that he beheld the angry countenance of Symmachus, his eyes glaring fury and revenge, and his mouth armed with long sharp teeth, which threatened to devour him. The monarch instantly retired to his chamber, and, as he lay trembling with aguish cold under a weight of bed-clothes, he expressed in broken murmurs to his physician Elpidius his deep repentance for the murders of Boethius and Symmachus. His malady increased, and, after a dysentery which continued three days, he expired in the palace of Ravenna, in the thirty-third, or, if we compute from the invasion of Italy, in the thirty-seventh year of his reign.

CHAPTER FORTY

*Elevation of Justin the Elder—Reign of Justinian
—I. The Empress Theodora—II. Factions of the
Circus, and Sedition of Constantinople—III.
Trade and Manufacture of Silk—IV. Finances
and Taxes—V. Edifices of Justinian—Church of
St. Sophia—Fortifications and Frontiers of the
Eastern Empire—Abolition of the Schools of Athens
and the Consulship of Rome*

The emperor Justinian was born near the ruins of Sardica (the
modern Sophia), of an obscure race of barbarians, the inhabitants of a wild and desolate country, to which the names of
Dardania, of Dacia, and of Bulgaria have been successively
applied. His elevation was prepared by the adventurous spirit
of his uncle Justin, who, with two other peasants of the same
village, deserted for the profession of arms the more useful
employment of husbandmen or shepherds. On foot, with a
scanty provision of biscuit in their knapsacks, the three youths
followed the high road of Constantinople, and were soon
enrolled, for their strength and stature, among the guards of
the emperor Leo. Under the two succeding reigns, the fortunate peasant emerged to wealth and honours; and on the death
of Anastasius the Dacian peasant was invested with the purple
by the unanimous consent of the soldiers. The elder Justin, as

he is distinguished from another emperor of the same family
and name, ascended the Byzantine throne at the age of sixty-
eight years. The aged emperor adopted the talents and ambition of his nephew Justinian, an aspiring youth whom his
uncle had drawn from the rustic solitude of Dacia and educated at Constantinople. After Justin had ruled for nine years
he placed the diadem upon the head of his nephew. The life of
Justin was prolonged about four months; but from the instant
of this ceremony he was considered as dead to the empire,
which acknowledged Justinian, in the forty-fifth year of his
age, for the lawful sovereign of the East.

From his elevation to his death, Justinian governed the
Roman empire thirty-eight years, seven months, and thirteen
days. The events of his reign, which excite our curious attention by their number, variety, and importance, are diligently
related by the secretary of Belisarius, a rhetorician, whom
eloquence had promoted to the rank of senator and præfect of
Constantinople. According to the vicissitudes of courage or
servitude, of favour or disgrace, Procopius successively composed the *history,* the *panegyric,* and the *satire* of his own
times. The eight books of the Persian, Vandalic, and Gothic
wars, which are continued in the five books of Agathias, deserve our esteem as a laborious and successful imitation of the
Attic, or at least of the Asiatic, writers of ancient Greece. His
facts are collected from the personal experience and free conversation of a soldier, a statesman, and a traveller; his style
continually aspires, and often attains, to the merit of strength
and elegance; his reflections, more especially in the speeches,
which he too frequently inserts, contain a rich fund of political
knowledge; and the historian, excited by the generous ambition of pleasing and instructing posterity, appears to disdain
the prejudices of the people and the flattery of courts. From
Procopius's materials I shall now proceed to describe the reign
of Justinian.

In the exercise of supreme power, the first act of Justinian
was to divide it with the woman whom he loved, the famous
Theodora, whose strange elevation cannot be applauded as the
triumph of female virtue. From her early youth she had served
the public and private pleasures of the Byzantine people. Her

beauty was the subject of flattering praise, and the source of exquisite delight. But this beauty was degraded by the facility with which it was exposed to the public eye, and prostituted to licentious desire. Her venal charms were abandoned to a promiscuous crowd of citizens and strangers, of every rank and of every profession: the fortunate lover who had been promised a night of enjoyment was often driven from her bed by a stronger or more wealthy favourite; and when she passed through the streets, her presence was avoided by all who wished to escape either the scandal or the temptation. The satirical historian has not blushed to describe the naked scenes which Theodora was not ashamed to exhibit in the theatre. After exhausting the arts of sensual pleasure, she most ungratefully murmured against the parsimony of Nature; but her murmurs, her pleasures, and her arts, must be veiled in the obscurity of a learned language.

Theodora's beauty, assisted by art or accident, soon attracted, captivated, and fixed, the patrician Justinian, while he yet reigned, with absolute sway, under the name of his uncle. The laws of Rome expressly prohibited the marriage of a senator with any female who had been dishonoured by a servile origin or theatrical profession; but a law was promulgated, in the name of the emperor Justin, which abolished the rigid jurisprudence of antiquity. This indulgence was speedily followed by the solemn nuptials of Justinian and Theodora; her dignity was gradually exalted with that of her lover; and, as soon as Justin had invested his nephew with the purple, the patriarch of Constantinople placed the diadem on the heads of the emperor and empress of the East. The prostitute who, in the presence of innumerable spectators, had polluted the theatre of Constantinople, was adored as a queen in the same city, by grave magistrates, orthodox bishops, victorious generals, and captive monarchs. Her numerous spies observed and zealously reported every action, or word, or look, injurious to their royal mistress. Her chastity, from the moment of her union with Justinian, is founded on the silence of her implacable enemies. The affections of Justinian she preserved, by art or merit, until, in the twenty-fourth year of her marriage, and the twenty-second of her reign, she was consumed by a cancer.

A material difference may be observed in the games of antiquity: the most eminent of the Greeks were actors, the Romans were merely spectators. A senator, or even a citizen, conscious of his dignity, would have blushed to expose the person or his horses in the circus of Rome. But a passionate devotion came to be attached to the *factions*, distinguished by the colours *white*, *red*, *green*, and *blue*, which contested the races, and this devotion came to subsume differences in religion, politics, and even fashions of dress. Dissensions between the factions gave rise to bloody disorders. On one occasion Constantinople was abandoned to the factions for a space of five days; their watchword, NIKA, *vanquish!* has given a name to this memorable sedition. Only the firmness of Theodora prevented the emperor Justinian from disgraceful flight and abdication.

Justinian reigned over sixty-four provinces and nine hundred and thirty-five cities; his dominions were blessed by nature with the advantages of soil, situation, and climate, and the improvements of human art had been diffused by interchange. Society was enriched by the division of labour and the facility of exchange; and every Roman was lodged, clothed, and subsisted by the industry of a thousand hands. Silk, in particular, was in such great demand that the procurement of an adequate supply became a matter of high importance. Eventually the Romans learned the art of propagating the insects which produce silk, and their manufacture of silken fabrics was not inferior to that of the Chinese.

The subjects of Justinian were dissatisfied with the times and with the government. Europe was overrun by the barbarians and Asia by the monks: the poverty of the West discouraged the trade and manufactures of the East; the produce of labour was consumed by the unprofitable servants of the church, the state, and the army; and a rapid decrease was felt in the fixed and circulating capitals which constitute the national wealth. The riches of Justinian were speedily exhausted by alms and buildings, by ambitious wars and ignominious treaties. His revenues were found inadequate to his expenses.

Every art was tried to extort from the people the gold and silver which he scattered with a lavish hand from Persia to France: his reign was marked by the vicissitudes, or rather by the combat, of rapaciousness and avarice, of splendour and poverty; he lived with the reputation of hidden treasures, and bequeathed to his successor the payment of his debts. Taxation was oppressive, and offices and honours were sold, with the permission, or at least with the connivance, of Justinian and Theodora. Dishonour might be ultimately reflected on the character of Justinian; but much of the guilt, and still more of the profit, was intercepted by the ministers, who were seldom promoted for their virtues and not always selected for their talents.

The *edifices* of Justinian were cemented with the blood and treasure of his people; but those stately structures appeared to announce the prosperity of the empire, and actually displayed the skill of their architects. The principal church, which was dedicated by the founder of Constantinople to Saint Sophia, or the eternal wisdom, had been twice destroyed by fire; after the exile of John Chrysostom and during the *Nika* of the blue and green faction. The church was rebuilt, with great splendour, by the piety of Justinian, and remains, after twelve centuries, a stately monument of his fame. The architecture of St. Sophia, which is now converted into the principal mosque, has been imitated by the Turkish sultans, and that venerable pile continues to excite the fond admiration of the Greeks, and the more rational curiosity of European travellers. By the benefactions of Justinian almost every saint in the calendar acquired the honours of a temple—almost every city in the empire obtained the solid advantages of bridges, hospitals, and aqueducts.

The fortifications of Europe and Asia were multiplied by Justinian; the repetition of those timid and fruitless precautions exposes, to a philosophic eye, the debility of the empire. From Belgrade to the Euxine, from the conflux of the Save to the mouth of the Danube, a chain of above fourscore fortified places was extended along the banks of the great river. The eastern frontiers were gurded no less diligently, but as the sequel proved, less effectively.

Justinian suppressed the schools of Athens and the consulship of Rome, which had given so many sages and heroes to mankind. Both these institutions had long since degenerated from their primitive glory, yet some reproach may be justly inflicted on the avarice and jealousy of a prince by whose hand such venerable ruins were destroyed. The Gothic arms had been less fatal to the schools of Athens than the establishment of a new religion, whose ministers superseded the exercise of reason, resolved every question by an article of faith, and condemned the infidel or sceptic to eternal flame. Finally, the succession of consuls ceased in the thirteenth year of Justinian, whose despotic temper might be gratified by the silent extinction of a title which admonished the Romans of their ancient freedom.

CHAPTER FORTY-ONE

Conquests of Justinian in the West—Character and first Campaigns of Belisarius—He invades and subdues the Vandal Kingdom of Africa—His Triumph—The Gothic War—He recovers Sicily, Naples, and Rome—Siege of Rome by the Goths—Their Retreat and Losses—Surrender of Ravenna —Glory of Belisarius—His domestic Shame and Misfortunes

When Justinian ascended the throne, about fifty years after the fall of the Western Empire, the kingdoms of the Goths and Vandals had obtained a solid, and, as it might seem, a legal establishment both in Europe and Africa. After Rome herself had been stripped of the Imperial purple, the princes of Constantinople assumed the sole and sacred sceptre of the monarchy; demanded, as their rightful inheritance, the provinces which had been subdued by the consuls or possessed by the Cæsars; and feebly aspired to deliver their faithful subjects of the West from the usurpation of heretics and barbarians. When Justinian had purchased peace of the Persians after five years of war, he was able to employ his forces against the Vandals; and the internal state of Africa afforded an honourable motive, and promised a powerful support to the Roman arms. A magnificent armada was prepared for this enterprise, and entrusted to Belisarius, one of those heroic names which are familiar to every age and to every nation. Belisarius was able to inform the emperor that in the space of three months he had achieved the conquest of Africa. Belisarius was traduced by ambitious rivals, and prudently returned to Constantinople, where, however, he was allowed to celebrate a magnificent triumph over the captive Vandal king Gelimer.

The Goths, both of Italy and of Spain, insensible of their approaching danger, beheld with indifference and even with joy, the rapid downfall of the Vandals. In Spain the weaker of two candidates for the sceptre solicited the assistance of Justinian and so forfeited his country's independence. The error of the Goths who reigned in Italy was less excusable than that of their Spanish brethren, and their punishment was still more immediate and terrible. From a motive of private revenge, they enabled their most dangerous enemy to destroy their most valuable ally. Amalsontha, the regent of Italy, succumbed to domestic intrigue; Justinian beheld with joy the dissensions of the Goths, and the mediation of an ally concealed and promoted the ambitious views of the conqueror. Belisarius occupied Sicily, and made a rapid progress northward to Rome. Without reflecting that Italy must sink into a province of Constantinople, the clergy and senate fondly hailed the restoration of a Roman emperor as a new era of freedom and prosperity, and invited the lieutenant of Justinian to accept their voluntary allegiance. The following spring the Goths under their king Vitiges assembled a great army and marched upon Rome. Their seige, which continued above a year, is one of the most memorable in history. The Goths were finally defeated, with enormous slaughter. An effort of the Franks to assist the Goths miscarried, and without unsheathing his sword Justinian assumed the title of conqueror of the Franks.

As soon as Belisarius was delivered from his foreign and domestic enemies, he seriously applied his forces to the final reduction of Italy. The multitudes which still adhered to the standard of Vitiges far surpassed the number of the Roman troops; but when the Goths found their king vacillating, they offered their arms, treasures, and fortifications of Ravenna to Belisarius if he would disclaim the authority of a master, accept the choice of the Goths, and assume, as he had deserved, the kingdom of Italy. Belisarius was able to acquire the resources of the Goths without pledging his faith; his inflexible loyalty rejected, except as the substitute of Justinian, their oaths of allegiance, and he was not offended by the reproach of their deputies that he rather chose to be a slave than a king. After the second victory of Belisarius, envy again whispered, Justinian listened, and the hero was recalled. He had subdued Africa, Italy, and the adjacent islands; led away captives the successors of Genseric and Theodoric; filled Constantinople with the spoils of their palaces; and in the space of six years recovered half the provinces of the Western empire.

What has polluted the fame and even the virtue of Belisarius is the lust and cruelty of his wife Antonina, who was the favorite of the empress Theodora. Though Belisarius had repeated and ocular proof of her infidelity, he yielded to her domination, and was disgraced and impoverished through her agency. His friends and even the public were persuaded that his subservience was dissimulation, and that his wife, Theodora, and perhaps the emperor himself, would be sacrificed to the just revenge of a virtuous rebel. Their hopes were deceived; and the unconquerable patience and loyalty of Belisarius appeared either *below* or *above* the character of a MAN.

CHAPTER FORTY-TWO

State of the Barbaric World—Establishment of the Lombards on the Danube—Tribes and Inroads of the Sclavonians—Origin, Empire, and Embassies of the Turks—The Flight of the Avars—Chosroes I., or Nushirvan, King of Persia—His Prosperous Reign and Wars with the Romans—The Colchian or Lazic War—The Æthiopians.

CHAPTER FORTY-THREE

Rebellions of Africa—Restoration of the Gothic Kingdom by Totila—Loss and Recovery of Rome—Final Conquest of Italy by Narses—Extinction of the Ostrogoths—Defeat of the Franks and Alemanni—Last Victory, Disgrace, and Death of Belisarius—Death and Character of Justinian—Comet, Earthquakes, and Plague

The review of the nations from the Danube to the Nile has exposed, on every side, the weakness of the Romans; and our wonder is reasonably excited that they should presume to enlarge an empire whose ancient limits they were incapable of defending. But the wars, the conquests, and the triumphs of Justinian, are the feeble and pernicious efforts of old age, which exhaust the remains of strength and accelerate the decay of the powers of life. He exulted in the glorious act of restoring Africa and Italy to the republic; but the calamities which followed the departure of Belisarius betrayed the impotence of the conqueror, and accomplished the ruin of those unfortunate countries.

In Africa mismanagement of the Byzantine agents and an uprising of the Moors reduced the once flourishing province to a solitude. In Italy the courage of the Goths was revived by the enforced departure of Belisarius. Their new king Totila gained a series of rapid successes over the agents of Justinian and won many of his adversaries to his standard. Roman captives and deserters were tempted to enlist in his service, and slaves were attracted by the promise that they should never be delivered to their masters.

The return of Belisarius to save the country which he had subdued was pressed with equal vehemence by his friends and enemies, and the Gothic war was imposed as a trust or an exile on the veteran commander. But his efforts were hampered and his powers were still inadequate to the deliverance of Rome, which Totila held under close siege. Rome fell, after suffering extremes of deprivation, but Totila's design to destroy the city was suspended at the remonstrance of Belisarius. Upon Totila's departure Belisarius recovered Rome and fortified it, and then defeated Totila. But instead of being supported or recalled Belisarius was left to languish helplessly in Italy. Even before Belisarius's recall to Constantinople, Totila again besieged and took Rome, and extended his conquests to Corsica and Sardinia, and the mainland of Greece.

Justinian was awakened from his indolence to resume the conquest and deliverance of Italy. The eunuch Narses, who was placed in charge of an expeditionary force, moved with dispatch, defeated the Goths in a battle near Rome, in which Totila was killed, and recovered the city. The Gothic war was kept alive by Totila's successor Teias. Teias was killed and the Goths defeated in a battle near Naples. Now a new deluge of barbarians from the north overwhelmed Italy. These were suppressed by the diligence of Narses and the effects of a plague.

After a reign of sixty years the throne of the Gothic kings was filled by the exarchs of Ravenna, the representatives in peace and war of the emperor of the Romans. Their jurisdiction was soon reduced to the limits of a narrow province; but Narses himself, the first and most powerful of the exarchs, administered above fifteen years the entire kingdom of Italy. Like Belisarius, he had deserved the honours of envy, calumny, and disgrace: but the favourite eunuch still enjoyed the confidence of Justinian; or the leader of a victorious army awed and repressed the ingratitude of a timid court. The remains of the Gothic nation evacuated the country or mingled with the people; and the Franks abandoned their Italian conquests without a struggle. The civil state of Italy, after the agitation of a long tempest, was fixed by a pragmatic sanction, which the emperor promulgated at the request of the pope. While the war in Italy was still in progress the territory of Constantinople itself was threatened by an invasion of Bulgarians and Sclavonians. Justinian trembled with apprehension, but the veteran Belisarius, who was recalled for the purpose, succeeded in routing the invaders. Belisarius was then accused of fomenting conspiracy, placed under guard, then vindicated; eight months later he died. If the emperor could rejoice in the death of Belisarius, he enjoyed the base satisfaction only eight months, the last period of a reign of thirty-eight and a life of eighty-three years.

CHAPTER FORTY-FOUR

Idea of the Roman Jurisprudence—The Laws of the Kings—The Twelve Tables of the Decemvirs—The Laws of the People—The Decrees of the Senate—The Edicts of the Magistrates and Emperors—Authority of the Civilians—Code, Pandects, Novels, and Institutes of Justinian:—I. Rights of Persons—II. Rights of Things—III. Private Injuries and Actions—IV. Crimes and Punishments

The vain titles of the victories of Justinian are crumbled into dust, but the name of the legislator is inscribed on a fair and everlasting monument. Under his reign, and by his care, the civil jurisprudence was digested in the immortal works of the CODE, the PANDECTS, and the INSTITUTES: the public reason of the Romans had been silently or studiously transfused into the domestic institutions of Europe, and the laws of Justinian still command the respect or obedience of independent nations. Wise or fortunate is the prince who connects his own reputation with the honour and interest of a perpetual order of men.

(The remainder of this chapter is devoted to a full exposition of Roman law.)

CHAPTER FORTY-FIVE

Reign of the younger Justin—Embassy of the Avars—Their Settlement on the Danube—Conquest of Italy by the Lombards—Adoption and Reign of Tiberius—Of Maurice—State of Italy under the Lombards and the Exarchs—Of Ravenna—Distress of Rome—Character and Pontificate of Gregory the First

Justinian was succeeded by his nephew, the younger Justin. On the seventh day of his reign a delegation of Avars, a Tartar people which had been subsidized by Justinian, made exorbitant demands upon him, and when these were rejected, they retired to the Danube and eventually formed an alliance with Alboin, king of the Lombards, who had been thwarted in his ambition to conquer the Gepidae and marry their princess Rosamond. The alliance destroyed the kingdom of the Gepidae, and Alboin turned to the conquest of Italy. Narses had become disaffected with his Byzantine masters and Roman subjects and had himself invited the invaders; soon he became reconciled, but died before he could organize resistance to Alboin. Alboin swept through the northern portions of Italy, but was murdered by his wife Rosamond, who was ambitious to rule in the name of her lover. Clepho was elected by the Lombards to succeed Alboin, but was assassinated after eighteen months. The regal office was suspended above ten years during the minority of his son Autharis, and Italy was divided and oppressed by a ducal aristocracy of thirty tyrants.

When the nephew of Justinian ascended the throne, he proclaimed a new era of happiness and glory. The annals of the second Justin are marked with disgrace abroad and misery at home. In the West the Roman empire was afflicted by the loss of Italy, the desolation of Africa, and the conquests of the Persians. Injustice prevailed both in the capital and the provinces: the rich trembled for their property, the poor for their safety; the ordinary magistrates were ignorant or venal, the occasional remedies appear to have been arbitrary and violent, and the complaints of the people could no longer be silenced by the splendid names of a legislator and a conqueror. Justin determined to lay down the weight of the diadem, and at the suggestion of his wife Sophia appointed Tiberius to be his successor. The four last years of the emperor Justin were passed in tranquil obscurity.

After recording the vice or folly of so many Roman princes, it is pleasing to repose for a moment on a character conspicuous by the qualities of humanity, justice, temperance, and fortitude; but in less than four years after the death of Justin, his worthy successor sunk into a mortal disease, which left him only sufficient time to bestow the diadem upon the most deserving of his fellow-citizens. He selected Maurice— a judgment more precious than the purple itself. Maurice ascended the throne at the mature age of forty-three years; and he reigned above twenty years over the East and over himself. He enjoyed the glory of restoring the Persian monarch to his throne; his lieutenants waged a doubtful war against the Avars of the Danube, and he cast an eye of pity, of ineffectual pity, on the abject and distressful state of his Italian provinces.

The dukes of the Lombards had provoked by frequent inroads their powerful neighbours of Gaul. As soon as they were apprehensive of a just retaliation, they renounced their feeble and disorderly independence: the advantages of regal government, union, secrecy, and vigour, were unanimously confessed; and Autharis, the son of Clepho, had already attained the strength and reputation of a warrior. Under the standard of their new king the conquerors of Italy withstood three successive invasions, and the victorious Autharis asserted his claim to the dominion of Italy. For a period of two hundred years Italy was in fact divided, unequally, between the kingdom of the Lombards and the exarchate of Ravenna. The laws and usages of the Lombards were admirable. The succession of their kings is marked with virtue and ability; the troubled series of their annals is adorned with fair intervals of peace, order, and domestic happiness; and the Italians enjoyed a milder and more equitable government than any of the other kingdoms which had been founded on the ruins of the Western empire.

Rome, about the close of the sixth century, reached the lowest period of her depression. By the removal of the seat of empire and the successive loss of the provinces, the sources of public and private opulence were exhausted. The greater part of the Romans was condemned to hopeless indigence and celibacy. The edifices of Rome were exposed to ruin and decay. The writings of Gregory reveal an implacable aversion to the monuments of classic genius. The name of Rome might have been erased from the earth, if the city had not been animated by a vital principle, which again restored her to honour and dominion. The relics of St. Peter and St. Paul, genuine or fictitious, were adored as the Palladium of Christian Rome. The power, as well as the virtue, of the apostles resided with living energy in the breast of their successors; and the chair of St. Peter was filled under the reign of Maurice by the first and greatest of the name of Gregory. His pontificate, which lasted thirteen years, is one of the most edifying periods of the history of the church and at the same time illustrates the insensible rise of the temporal power of the popes.

CHAPTER FORTY-SIX

Revolutions of Persia after the Death of Chosroes or Nushirvan—His Son Hormouz, a Tyrant, is deposed—Usurpation of Bahram—Flight and Restoration of Chosroes II.—His Gratitude to the Romans—The Chagan of the Avars—Revolt of the Army against Maurice—His Death—Tyranny of Phocas—Elevation of Heraclius—The Persian War—Chosroes subdues Syria, Egypt, and Asia Minor—Siege of Constantinople by the Persians and Avars—Persian Expeditions—Victories and Triumph of Heraclius

The conflict of Rome and Persia was prolonged from the death of Crassus to the reign of Heraclius. The peace which had been concluded between the two empires four years before the death of Justinian was broken in the seventh year of Justin; and war continued during the reigns of Tiberius and Maurice, until Chosroes came to terms with the latter. Till the death of Maurice, the peace and alliance of the two empires was faithfully maintained.

While the majesty of the Roman was revived in the East, the prospect in Europe is less pleasing and less glorious. By the departure of the Lombards and the ruin of the Gepidae the balance of power was destroyed on the Danube; and the Avars spread their permanent dominion from the foot of the Alps to the sea-coast of the Euxine. From Belgrade to the walls of Constantinople a line may be measured of six hundred miles: that line was marked with flames and with blood; the horses of the Avars were alternately bathed in the Euxine and the Hadriatic; and the Roman pontiff, alarmed by the approach of a more savage enemy was reduced to cherish the Lombards as the protectors of Italy. The Persian alliance restored the troops of the East to the defence of Europe; and Maurice, who had supported ten years the insolence of the chagan, declared his resolution to march in person against the barbarians. Instead he sent Peter, his brother, and Priscus, an able general. The latter won sundry victories, but his success was transient and barren, and he was soon recalled by the apprehension that the chagan Baian, with dauntless spirit and recruited forces, was preparing to avenge his defeat under the walls of Constantinople.

The attempts of Maurice to reform their discipline had alienated the soldiers, who forced him to abdicate and made the repulsive Phocas their sovereign. One of his first acts was to cause the death of the five sons of Maurice in their father's sight, and then of Maurice himself. Ignorant of letters, of laws, and even of arms, Phocas indulged in the supreme rank a more ample privilege of lust and drunkenness, and his brutal pleasures were either injurious to his subjects or disgraceful to himself. His reign afflicted Europe with ignominious peace and Asia with desolating war.

The widow of Maurice, who had conspired against Phocas, was tortured and beheaded. The popularity of Phocas' son-in-law Crispus aroused his jealousy, and Crispus solicited Heraclius, the exarch of Africa, to save and govern the country. Heraclius, whose ambition was chilled by age, resigned the enterprise to his like-named son. Heraclius sailed to Constantinople, seized and beheaded the tyrant, and ascended the throne. His coronation was accompanied by that of his wife Eudoxia, and their posterity, till the fourth generation, continued to reign over the empire of the East.

Even after his death the republic was afflicted by the

crimes of Phocas, which armed with a pious cause the most formidable of her enemies. Chosroes declared himself the avenger of his benefactor Maurice, and rapidly overran the Roman dominions in Mesopotamia, Syria, Palestine, Egypt, and Asia Minor. The reign of the grandson of Nushirvan was suddenly extended to the Hellespont and the Nile, the ancient limits of the Persian monarchy. While the Persian monarch contemplated the wonders of his art and power, he received an epistle from an obscure citizen of Mecca, inviting him to acknowledge Mohammed as the apostle of God. He rejected the invitation, and tore the epistle. "It is thus," exclaimed the Arabian prophet, "that God will tear the kingdom and reject the supplication of Chosroes." Placed on the verge of the two great empires of the East, Mohammed observed with secret joy the progress of their mutual destruction; and in the midst of the Persian triumphs he ventured to foretell that, before many years should elapse, victory would again return to the banners of the Romans.

At the time when this prediction is said to have been delivered, no prophecy could be more distant from its accomplishment, since the first twelve years of Heraclius announced the approaching dissolution of the empire. Syria, Egypt, and the provinces of Asia were subdued by the Persian arms; while Europe, from the confines of Istria to the long wall of Thrace, was oppressed by the Avars, unsatiated by the blood and rapine of the Italian war. By these implacable enemies Heraclius, on either side, was insulted and besieged: and the Roman empire was reduced to the walls of Constantinople, with the remnant of Greece, Italy, and Africa, and some maritime cities, from Tyre to Trebizond, of the Asiatic coast. Yet the experience of six years at length persuaded the Persian monarch to renounce the conquest of Constantinople, and to specify the annual tribute or ransom of the Roman empire: a thousand talents of gold, a thousand talents of silver, a thousand silk robes, a thousand horses, and a thousand virgins. Heraclius subscribed these ignominious terms; but the time and space which he obtained to collect such treasures from the poverty of the East was industriously employed in the preparation of a bold and desperate attack.

With an energy that his antecedent lassitude makes astonishing, Heraclius gathered money and men, and in three separate campaigns so defeated Chosroes that he was disgraced among his own people and murdered by his son Siroes, who became his successor. A treaty of alliance, easily defined and faithfully executed, was subscribed to by the two empires. The victor was not ambitious of enlarging the weakness of the empire; the son of Chosroes abandoned without regret the conquests of his father; the Persians who evacuated the cities of Syria and Egypt were honourably conducted to the frontier; and a war which had wounded the vitals of the two monarchies produced no change in their external and relative situation.

In the popular estimation, the fame of Moses, Alexander, and Hercules was eclipsed by the superior merit and glory of the great Heraclius. Yet the deliverer of the East was indigent and feeble. Of the Persian spoils the most valuable portion had been expended in the war, distributed to the soldiers, or buried, by an unlucky tempest, in the waves of the Euxine. The conscience of the emperor was oppressed by the obligation of restoring the wealth of the clergy, which he had borrowed for their own defence: a perpetual fund was required to satisfy these inexorable creditors; the provinces, already wasted by the arms and avarice of the Persians, were compelled to a second payment of the same taxes; and the arrears of a simple citizen, the treasurer of Damascus, were commuted to a fine of one hundred thousand pieces of gold. The loss of two hundred thousand soldiers, who had fallen by the sword, was of less fatal importance than the decay of arts, agriculture, and population in this long and destructive war; and although a victorious army had been formed under the standard of Heraclius, the unnatural effort appears to have exhausted rather than exercised their strength. While the emperor triumphed at Constantinople or Jerusalem, an obscure town on the confines of Syria was pillaged by the Saracens, and they cut in pieces some troops who advanced to its relief; an ordinary and tri-

fling occurrence, had it not been the prelude of a mighty revolution. These robbers were the apostles of Mohammed; their
fanatic valour had emerged from the desert; and in the last
eight years of his reign Heraclius lost to the Arabs the same
provinces which he had rescued from the Persians.

CHAPTER FORTY-SEVEN

Theological History of the Doctrine of the Incarnation—The Human and Divine Nature of Christ —Enmity of the Patriarchs of Alexandria and Constantinople—St. Cyril and Nestorius—Third General Council of Ephesus—Heresy of Eutyches —Fourth General Council of Chalcedon—Civil and Ecclesiastical Discord—Intolerance of Justinian—The Three Chapters—The Monothelite Controversy—State of the Oriental Sects—I. The Nestorians—II. The Jacobites—III. The Maronites—IV. The Armenians—V. The Copts and Abyssinians

After the extinction of paganism, the Christians in peace and piety might have enjoyed their solitary triumph. But the principle of discord was alive in their bosom, and they were more solicitous to explore the nature, than to practise the laws, of their founder. I have already observed that the disputes of the TRINITY were succeeded by those of the INCARNATION; alike scandalous to the church, alike pernicious to the state, still more minute to their origin, still more durable in their effects. It is my design to comprise in the present chapter a religious war of two hundred and fifty years, to represent the ecclesias-

239

tical and political schism of the Oriental sects, and to introduce their clamorous or sanguinary contests by a modest inquiry into the doctrines of the primitive church.

(The lengthy theological disquisition which follows is of the nature of an appendix, summarizing the history of Christian doctrine during the entire period covered by the forty-six chapters preceding, which constitute the principal portion of the Decline and Fall. The remainder of the work, as is made plain in the opening of the chapter following, is different in scale and in approach.)

CHAPTER FORTY-EIGHT

Plan of the last two {quarto} Volumes —Succession and Characters of the Greek Emperors of Constantinople, from the Time of Heraclius to the Latin Conquest

I have now deduced from Trajan to Constantine, from Constantine to Heraclius, the regular series of the Roman emperors; and faithfully exposed the prosperous and adverse fortunes of their reigns. Five centuries of the decline and fall of the empire have already elapsed; but a period of more than eight hundred years still separates me from the term of my labours, the taking of Constantinople by the Turks. Should I persevere in the same course, should I observe the same measure, a prolix and slender thread would be spun through many a volume, nor would the patient reader find an adequate reward of instruction or amusement. At every step, as we sink deeper in the decline and fall of the Eastern empire, the annals of each succeeding reign would impose a more ungrateful and melancholy task. These annals must continue to repeat a tedious and uniform tale of weakness and misery; the natural connection of causes and events would be broken by frequent and hasty transitions, and a minute accumulation of circumstances must destroy the light and effect of those general pictures which compose the use and ornament of a remote

241

history. From the time of Heraclius the Byzantine theatre is contracted and darkened: the line of empire, which had been defined by the laws of Justinian and the arms of Belisarius, recedes on all sides from our view; the Roman name, the proper subject of our inquiries, is reduced to a narrow corner of Europe, to the lonely suburbs of Constantinople; and the fate of the Greek empire has been compared to that of the Rhine, which loses itself in the sands before its waters can mingle with the ocean. The scale of dominion is diminished to our view by the distance of time and place; nor is the loss of external splendour compensated by the nobler gifts of virtue and genius. In the last moments of her decay Constantinople was doubtless more opulent and populous than Athens at her most flourishing era; but the subjects of the Byzantine empire, who assume and dishonour the names both of Greeks and Romans, present a dead uniformity of abject vices, which are neither softened by the weakness of humanity nor animated by the vigour of memorable crimes. The absence, or loss, or imperfection of contemporary evidence, must be poorly supplied by the doubtful authority of more recent compilers.

From these considerations I should have abandoned without regret the Greek slaves and their servile historians, had I not reflected that the fate of the Byzantine monarchy is *passively* connected with the most splendid and important revolutions which have changed the state of the world. The space of the lost provinces was immediately replenished with new colonies and rising kingdoms: the active virtues of peace and war deserted from the vanquished to the victorious nations; and it is in their origin and conquests, in their religion and government, that we must explore the causes and effects of the decline and fall of the Eastern empire. Nor will this scope of narrative, with riches and variety of these materials, be incompatible with the unity of design and composition. As, in his daily prayers, the Musulman of Fez or Delhi still turns his face towards the temple of Mecca, the historian's eye shall be always fixed on the city of Constantinople. The excursive line may embrace the wilds of Arabia and Tartary, but the circle will be ultimately reduced to the decreasing limit of the Roman monarchy.

On this principle I shall now establish the plan of the last two volumes of the present work. The first chapter will contain, in a regular series, the emperors who reigned at Constantinople during a period of six hundred years, from the days of Heraclius to the Latin conquest: a rapid abstract, which may be supported by a *general* appeal to the order and text of the original historians. In this introduction I shall confine myself to the revolutions of the throne, the succession of families, the personal characters of the Greek princes, the mode of their life and death, the maxims and influence of their domestic government, and the tendency of their reign to accelerate or suspend the downfall of the Eastern empire. Such a chronological review will serve to illustrate the various argument of the subsequent chapters; and each circumstance of the eventful story of the barbarians will adapt itself in a proper place to the Byzantine annals. The internal state of the empire, and the dangerous heresy of the Paulicians, which shook the East and enlightened the West, will be the subject of two separate chapters; but these inquiries must be postponed till our farther progress shall have opened the view of the world in the ninth and tenth centuries of the Christian era. After this foundation of Byzantine history, the following nations will pass before our eyes, and each will occupy the space to which it may be entitled by greatness or merit, or the degree of connection with the Roman world and the present age. I. The FRANKS; a general appellation which includes all the barbarians of France, Italy, and Germany, who were united by the sword and sceptre of Charlemagne. The persecution of images and their votaries separated Rome and Italy from the Byzantine throne, and prepared the restoration of the Roman empire in the West. II. The ARABS or SARACENS. Three ample chapters will be devoted to this curious and interesting object. In the first, after a picture of the country and its inhabitants, I shall investigate the character of Mohammed; the character, religion, and success of the prophet. In the second I shall lead the Arabs to the conquest of Syria, Egypt, and Africa, the provinces of the Roman empire; nor can I check their victorious career till they have overthrown the monarchies of Persia and Spain. In the third I shall inquire how Constantinople and

Europe were saved by the luxury of arts, the division and decay, of the empire of the caliphs. A single chapter will include, III. The BULGARIANS, IV. HUNGARIANS, and V. RUSSIANS who assaulted by sea or by land the provinces and the capital; but the last of these, so important in their present greatness, will excite some curiosity in their origin and infancy. VI. The NORMANS; or rather the private adventurers of that warlike people, who founded a powerful kingdom in Apulia and Sicily, shook the throne of Constantinople, displayed the trophies of chivalry, and almost realised the wonders of romance. VII. The LATINS; the subjects of the pope, the nations of the West, who enlisted under the banner of the cross for the recovery or relief of the holy sepulchre. The Greek emperors were terrified and preserved by the myriads of pilgrims who marched to Jerusalem with Godfrey of Bouillon and the peers of Christendom. The second and third crusades trod in the footsteps of the first: Asia and Europe were mingled in a sacred war of two hundred years; and the Christian powers were bravely resisted and finally expelled by Saladin and the Mamalukes of Egypt. In these memorable crusades a fleet and army of French and Venetians were diverted from Syria to the Thracian Bosphorus: they assaulted the capital, they subverted the Greek monarchy: and a dynasty of Latin princes was seated near threescore years on the throne of Constantine. VIII. The GREEKS themselves, during this period of captivity and exile, must be considered as a foreign nation; the enemies, and again the sovereigns of Constantinople. Misfortune had rekindled a spark of national virtue; and the Imperial series may be continued with some dignity from their restoration to the Turkish conquest. IX. The MOGULS and TARTARS. By the arms of Zingis and his descendants the globe was shaken from China to Poland and Greece: the sultans were overthrown: the caliphs fell, and the Cæsars trembled on their throne. The victories of Timour suspended above fifty years the final ruin of the Byzantine empire. X. I have already noticed the first appearance of the TURKS; and the names of the fathers, of *Selijuk* and *Othman*, discriminate the two successive dynasties of the nation which emerged in the eleventh century from the Scythian wilderness.

The former established a potent and splendid kingdom from the banks of the Oxus to Antioch and Nice; and the first crusade was provoked by the violation of Jerusalem and the danger of Constantinople. From a humble origin the *Ottomans* arose the scourge of terror of Christendom. Constantinople was besieged and taken by Mohammed II., and his triumph annihilates the remnant, the image, the title, of the Roman empire in the East. The schism of the Greeks will be connected with their last calamities and the restoration of learning in the Western world. I shall return from the capacity of the new to the ruins of ancient ROME; and the venerable name, the interesting theme, will shed a ray of glory on the conclusion of my labours.

(The remainder of this chapter contains a dynastic history from Heraclius to the Latin conquest of Constantinople in 1204, which is intended to provide the political background for the chapters following. Its substance may conveniently be presented in tabular form.

Heraclian dynasty, 610–717: Following the death of Heraclius I in 641 two of his relatives occupied the throne for periods of weeks, and the third, Constans II, ruled 641–668. He was followed by Constantine IV Pogonatus, Justinian II Rhinotmetus, Leontius, Tiberius Absimarus, again Justinian II, Philippicus, Anastasius II, Theodosius III. The latter part of this dynasty marked a period of decline.

Isaurian dynasty, 717–820: Leo III Isaurus, Constantine V Copronymus, Leo IV Chazarus, Constantine VI, Irene, Nicephorus I, Michael I Rhangabe, Leo V Armenius. During this dynasty there were great disputes about the use of images in worship. The Iconoclasts were responsible for important civil, military, and legal reforms.

Phrygian dynasty, 820–867: Michael II Balbus, Theophilus, Michael III.

Macedonian dynasty, 867–1057: Basil I Macedo, Leo VI Sapiens, Constantine VII Porphyrogenitus, Romanus I Lecapenus, Romanus II, Nicephorus II Phocas, Joannes I Zimisces, Basil II, Constantine IX, Romanus III Argyrus, Michael IV Paphlago, Michael V Calaphates, Zoe and Theodora, Constantine X Monomachus, Michael VI Stratioticus. During this period the division between Emperor and Patriarch in the East and Emperor and Pope in the West was sharpened; the schism between the churches became final in 1054. The Slavs became more important to the Empire than the nations of the West. There was some recovery of power under Joannes Zimisces and Basil II, but this was transitory.

Comnenian dynasty, 1057–1204: Isaac I Comnenus, Constantine XI Ducas, Romanus IV Diogenes, Michael VII Parapinaces, Nicephorus III Botaniates, Alexis I Comnenus, Joannes II Comnenus, Manuel I Comnenus, Alexis II Comnenus, Andronicus I Comnenus, Isaac II Angelus, Alexis III Angelus, Alexis IV Angelus, Alexis V Ducas. The victory of the Seljuk Turks in 1071 was disastrous. Appeals were made to the West, and the First Crusade began in 1095. In 1204 the Fourth Crusade captured and sacked Constantinople and ended the Comnenian dynasty.)

CHAPTER FORTY-NINE

Introduction, Worship, and Persecution of Images
—Revolt of Italy and Rome—Temporal Dominion
of the Popes—Conquest of Italy by the Franks—
Establishment of Images—Character and Corona-
tion of Charlemagne—Restoration and Decay of
the Roman Empire in the West—Independence of
Italy—Constitution of the Germanic Body

In the connection of the church and state I have considered the former as subservient only, and relative, to the latter; a salutary maxim, if in fact as well as in narrative it had ever been held sacred. The oriental philosophy of the Gnostics, the dark abyss of predestination and grace, and the strange transformation of the Eucharist from the sign to the substance of Christ's body, I have purposely abandoned to the curiosity of speculative divines. But I have reviewed with diligence and pleasure the objects of ecclesiastical history by which the decline and fall of the Roman empire were materially affected, the propagation of Christianity, the constitution of the Catholic church, the ruin of Paganism, and the sects that arose from the mysterious controversies concerning the Trinity and incarnation. At the head of this class we may justly rank the worship of images, so fiercely disputed in the eighth and ninth centuries; since a question of popular superstition produced the revolt of

Italy, the temporal power of the popes, and the restoration of the Roman empire in the West.

Under the successors of Constantine, in the peace and luxury of the triumphant church, the more prudent bishops consented to indulge a visible superstition for the benefit of the multitude; and after the ruin of Paganism they were no longer restrained by the apprehension of an odious parallel. The worship of images had stolen into the church by insensible degrees, and each petty step was pleasing to the superstitious mind, as productive of comfort and innocent of sin. But in the beginning of the eighth century, in the full magnitude of the abuse, the more timorous Greeks were awakened by an apprehension that, under the mask of Christianity, they had restored the religion of their fathers: they heard, with grief and impatience, the name of idolators—the incessant charge of the Jews and Mohammedans, who derived from the Law and the Koran an immortal hatred to graven images and all relative worship.

Leo the Third, who ascended the throne of the East from the mountains of Isauria, was ignorant of sacred and profane letters but had been inspired with a hatred of images; and it was held to be the duty of a prince to impose on his subjects the dictates of his own conscience. The sect of the Iconoclasts (or image-breakers) was supported by the zeal and despotism of six emperors, and the issue involved the East and West in a conflict of one hundred and twenty years. The patient East abjured with reluctance her sacred images; they were fondly cherished, and vigorously defended, by the independent zeal of the Italians. The sovereignty of the Greek emperors was extinguished in Italy, and the authority of the popes confirmed.

The Lombards were irresistibly tempted by the disorders of Italy, the nakedness of Rome, and the unwarlike profession of her new chief. In his distress the first Gregory had implored the aid of the hero of the age, of Charles Martel, who governed the French monarchy, and who, by his signal victory over the Saracens, had saved his country, and perhaps Europe, from the Mohammedan yoke. The greatness of Charles's occupations, and the shortness of his life, prevented his interference in the affairs of Italy, except by a friendly and ineffectual mediation. His son Pepin, the heir of his power and virtues, assumed the office of champion of the Roman church. The mutual obligations of the popes and the Carlovingian family form the important link of ancient and modern, of civil and ecclesiastical history. The translation of the Western empire to Charlemagne consummated the separation of East and West.

After the recovery of Italy and Africa by the arms of Justinian, the importance and danger of those remote provinces required the presence of a supreme magistrate; he was indifferently styled the exarch or the patrician; and these governors of Ravenna, who fill their place in the chronology of princes, extended their jurisdiction over the Roman city. Since the revolt of Italy and the loss of the Exarchate, the distress of the Romans had exacted some sacrifice of their independence. Yet, even in this act, they exercised the right of disposing of themselves; and the decrees of the senate and people successively invested Charles Martel and his posterity with the honours of patrician of Rome. The leaders of a powerful nation would have disdained a servile title and subordinate office; but the reign of the Greek emperors was suspended; and, in the vacancy of the empire, they derived a more glorious commission from the pope and the republic. The Roman ambassadors presented these patricians with the keys of the shrine of St. Peter, as a pledge and symbol of sovereignty; with a holy banner which it was their right and duty to unfurl in the defence of the church and city. In the time of Charles Martel and of Pepin, the interposition of the Lombard kingdom covered the freedom, while it threatened the safety, of Rome; and the *patriciate* represented only the title, the service, the alliance, of these distant protectors. The power and policy of Charlemagne annihilated an enemy and imposed a master. In his first visit to the capital he was received with all the honours which had formerly been paid to the exarch, the representative of the emperor; and these honours obtained some new decorations from the joy and gratitude of Pope Adrian the First.

The Carlovingians are consecrated as the saviours and benefactors of the Roman church. Her ancient patrimony of farms and houses was transformed by their bounty into the temporal

dominion of cities and provinces; and the donation of the Exarchate was the first-fruits of the conquests of Pepin. The
splendid donation was granted in supreme and absolute dominion, and the world beheld for the first time a Christian
bishop invested with the prerogatives of a temporal prince—
the choice of magistrates, the exercise of justice, the imposi-
tion of taxes, and the wealth of the palace of Ravenna. Before
the end of the eighth century some apostolical scribe composed the decretals and the donation of Constantine, the two
magic pillars of the spiritual and temporal monarchy of the
popes. If Constantine had indeed resigned to the popes the
free and perpetual sovereignty of Rome, the Greek princes
were convinced of the guilt of usurpation; and the revolt of
Gregory was the claim of his lawful inheritance. The popes
were delivered from their debt of gratitude; and the nominal
gifts of the Carlovingians were no more than the just and
irrevocable restitution of a scanty portion of the ecclesiastical
state. The sovereignty of Rome no longer depended on the
choice of a fickle people; and the successors of St. Peter and
Constantine were invested with the purple and prerogatives of
the Cæsars.

While the Popes established in Italy their freedom and dominion, the images, the first cause of their revolt, were restored in the Eastern empire; nevertheless, the popes
consummated the separation of Rome and Italy, by the translation of the empire to the less orthodox Charlemagne. They
were compelled to choose between the rival nations: religion
was not the sole motive of their choice; the difference of language and manners had perpetuated the enmity of the two
capitals, and they were alienated from each other by the hostile opposition of seventy years. In that schism the Romans
had tasted of freedom, and the popes of sovereignty: their
submission would have exposed them to the revenge of a jealous tyrant; and the revolution of Italy had betrayed the impotence, as well as the tyranny, of the Byzantine court. On the
festival of Christmas, the last year of the eighth century,
Charlemagne appeared in the church of St. Peter; and, to gratify the vanity of Rome, he had exchanged the simple dress of
his country for the habit of a patrician. After the celebration of

the holy mysteries, Leo suddenly placed a precious crown on his head, and the dome resounded with the acclamations of the people, "Long life and victory to Charles, the most pious Augustus, crowned by God the great and pacific emperor of the Romans!" The head and body of Charlemagne were consecrated by the royal unction: after the example of the Cæsars, he was saluted or adored by the pontiff: his coronation oath represents a promise to maintain the faith and privileges of the church; and the first-fruits were paid in his rich offerings to the shrine of the apostle. In his familiar conversation the emperor protested his ignorance of the intentions of Leo, which he would have disappointed by his absence on that memorable day. But the preparations of the ceremony must have disclosed the secret; and the journey of Charlemagne reveals his knowledge and expectation: he had acknowledged that the Imperial title was the object of his ambition, and a Roman synod had pronounced that it was the only adequate reward of his merit and services.

CHAPTER FIFTY

*Description of Arabia and its Inhabitants —Birth,
Character, and Doctrine of Mohammed —He
preaches at Mecca —Flies to Medina —Propagates
his Religion by the Sword —Voluntary or reluctant
Submission of the Arabs —His Death and Successors —The Claims and Fortunes of Ali and his
Descendants*

After pursuing above six hundred years the fleeting Cæsars of
Constantinople and Germany, I now descend, in the reign of
Heraclius, on the eastern borders of the Greek monarchy.
While the state was exhausted by the Persian war, and the
church was distracted by the Nestorian and Monophysite
sects, Mohammed, with the sword in one hand and the Koran
in the other, erected his throne on the ruins of Christianity and
of Rome. The genius of the Arabian prophet, the manners of
his nation, and the spirit of his religion, involve the causes of
the decline and fall of the Eastern empire; and our eyes are
curiously intent on one of the most memorable revolutions
which have impressed a new and lasting character on the nations of the globe.

(The accounts of the origins of Islam and of the character
of its founder in Chapter L, of its conquests in Chapter LI, and
of its first conflicts with Constantinople in Chapter LII are

here omitted, except for the chapter headings, which indicate the scope of the treatment. Interesting and instructive as these chapters are, it is the consequences of the events they describe rather than the events themselves that are most relevant to the theme of the Decline and Fall.)

CHAPTER FIFTY-ONE

The Conquest of Persia, Syria, Egypt, Africa, and Spain, by the Arabs or Saracens—Empire of the Caliphs, or Successors of Mohammed—State of the Christians, etc., under their Government

CHAPTER FIFTY-TWO

*The Two Sieges of Constantinople by the Arabs—
Their Invasion of France, and Defeat by Charles
Martel—Civil War of the Ommiades and Abbas-
sides—Learning of the Arabs—Luxury of the Ca-
liphs—Naval Enterprises on Crete, Sicily, and
Rome—Decay and Division of the Empire of the
Caliphs—Defeats and Victories of the Greek Em-
perors*

CHAPTER FIFTY-THREE

*State of the Eastern Empire in the Tenth Century
—Extent and Division—Wealth and Revenue—
Palace of Constantinople—Titles and Offices
Pride and Power of the Emperors—Tactics of the
Greeks, Arabs, and Franks—Loss of the Latin
Tongue—Studies and Solitude of the Greeks*

A ray of historic light seems to beam from the darkness of the tenth century from the volumes of Constantine Porphyrogenitus. In the first of his works he minutely describes the pompous ceremonies of the church and palace of Constantinople; in the second he attempts an accurate survey of the provinces, the *themes*, as they were then denominated, both of Europe and Asia; the third deals with military organization; and the fourth with administration and policy. Yet despite these and lesser treasures, we may still deplore our poverty and ignorance. From such scanty materials I shall investigate the form and substance of the Byzantine empire; the provinces and wealth, the civil government and military force, the character and literature, of the Greeks in a period of six hundred years, from the reign of Heraclius to the successful invasion of the Franks or Latins.

After the final division between the sons of Theodosius, the swarms of barbarians from Scythia and Germany overspread the provinces and extinguished the empire of ancient Rome. The weakness of Constantinople was concealed by extent of dominion; her limits were inviolate, or at least entire; and the kingdom of Justinian was enlarged by the splendid acquisition of Africa and Italy. But the possession of these new conquests was transient and precarious, and almost a moiety of the Eastern empire was torn away by the arms of the Saracens. Syria and Egypt were oppressed by the Arabian caliphs, and, after the reduction of Africa, their lieutenants invaded and subdued the Roman province which had been changed into the Gothic monarchy of Spain. The islands of the Mediterranean were not inaccessible to their naval powers; and it was from their extreme stations, the harbours of Crete an the fortresses of Cilicia, that the faithful or rebel emirs insulted the majesty of the throne and capital. The remaining provinces, under the obedience of the emperors, were cast into a new mould; and the jurisdiction of the presidents, the consulars, and the courts was superseded by the institution of the *themes*, or military governments, which prevailed under the successors of Heraclius, and are described by the pen of the royal author. Of the twenty-nine themes, twelve in Europe and seventeen in Asia, the origin is obscure, the etymology doubtful or capricious, the limits were arbitrary and fluctuating. In the eleventh century the prospect was again clouded by new enemies and new misfortunes; the relics of Italy were swept away by the Norman adventurers, and almost all the Asiatic branches were dissevered from the Roman trunk by the Turkish conquerors. After these losses the emperors of the Comnenian family continued to reign from the Danube to Pelopponnesus, and from Belgrade to Nice, Trebizond, and the winding stream, of the Meander. The spacious provinces of Thrace, Macedonia, and Greece were obedient to their sceptre; the possession of Cyprus, Rhodes, and Crete was accompanied by the fifty islands of the Ægean or Holy Sea, and the remnant of their empire transcends the measure of the largest of the European kingdoms.

The same princes might assert, with dignity and truth, that of all the monarchs of Christendom they possessed the greatest city, the most ample revenue, the most flourishing and populous state. With the decline and fall of the empire the cities of the West had decayed and fallen; nor could the ruins of Rome, or the mud walls, wooden hovels, and narrow precincts of Paris and London, prepare the Latin stranger to contemplate the situation and extent of Constantinople, her stately palaces and churches, and the arts and luxury of an innumerable people. Her treasures might attract, but her virgin strength had repelled, and still promised to repel, the audacious invasion of the Persian and Bulgarian, the Arab and the Russian. The provinces were less fortunate and impregnable, and few districts, few cities, could be discovered which had not been violated by some fierce barbarian, impatient to despoil, because he was hopeless to possess. From the age of Justinian the Eastern empire was sinking below its former level; the powers of destruction were more active than those of improvement; and the calamities of war were embittered by the more permanent evils of civil and ecclesiastical tyranny. The captive who had escaped from the barbarians was often stripped and imprisoned by the ministers of his sovereign; the Greek superstition relaxed the mind by prayer, and emaciated the body by fasting; and the multitude of convents and festivals diverted many hands and many days from the temporal service of mankind. Yet the subjects of the Byzantine empire were still the most dexterous and diligent of nations; their country was blessed by nature with every advantage of soil, climate, and situation; and, in the support and restoration of the arts, their patient and peaceful temper was more useful than the warlike spirit and feudal anarchy of Europe. The provinces that still adhered to the empire were repeopled and enriched by the misfortunes of those which were irrecoverably lost. From the yoke of the caliphs, the Catholics of Syria, Egypt, and Africa retired to the allegiance of their prince, to the society of their brethren; the movable wealth, which eludes the search of oppression, accompanied and alleviated their exile, and Constantinople received into her bosom the fugitive trade of Alexandria and Tyre.

In the Byzantine palace the emperor was the first slave of the ceremonies which he imposed, of the rigid forms which regulated each word and gesture, besieged him in the palace, and violated the leisure of his rural solitude. But the lives and fortunes of millions hung on his arbitrary will; and the firmest minds, superior to the allurements of pomp and luxury, may be seduced by the more active pleasure of commanding their equals. The legislative and executive powers were centred in the person of the monarch, and the last remains of the authority of the senate were finally eradicated by Leo the Philosopher. A lethargy of servitude had benumbed the minds of the Greeks: in the wildest tumults of rebellion they never aspired to the idea of a free constitution; and the private character of the prince was the only source and measure of their public happiness. Superstition riveted their chains; in the church of St. Sophia he was solemnly crowned by the patriarch; at the foot of the altar they pledged their passive and unconditional obedience to his government and family.

The wealth of the Greeks enabled them to purchase the service of the poorer nations, and to maintain a naval power for the protection of their coasts and the annoyance of their enemies. A commerce of mutual benefit exchanged the gold of Constantinople for the blood of the Sclavonians and Turks, the Bulgarians and Russians: their valour contributed to the victories of Nicephorus and Zimisces; and if a hostile people pressed too closely on the frontier, they were recalled to the defence of their country, and the desire of peace, by the well-managed attack of a more distant tribe. The command of the Mediterranean, from the mouth of the Tanais to the Columns of Hercules, was always claimed, and often possessed, by the successors of Constantine. Their capital was filled with naval stores and dexterous artificers: the situation of Greece and Asia, the long coasts, deep gulfs, and numerous islands, accustomed their subjects to the exercise of navigation; and the trade of Venice and Amalfi supplied a nursery of seamen to the Imperial fleet.

In the lowest periods of degeneracy and decay, the name of ROMANS adhered to the last fragments of the empire of Constantinople, and while ruins of the Latin speech were darkly preserved, Greek was the language of literature and philosophy. After the fall of paganism and the extinction of the schools of Alexandria and Athens, the studies of the Greeks insensibly retired to some regular monasteries, and, above all, to the royal college of Constantinople. But the seventh and eighth centuries were a period of discord and darkness; the library was burned, the college was abolished, the Iconoclasts are represented as the foes of antiquity, and a savage ignorance and contempt of letters has disgraced the princes of the Heraclean and Isaurian dynasties. In the ninth century we traced the first dawnings of the restoration of science. After the fanaticism of the Arabs had subsided, the caliphs aspired to conquer the arts, rather than the provinces, of the empire: their liberal curiosity rekindled the emulation of the Greeks, brushed away the dust from their ancient libraries, and taught them to know and reward the philosophers.

The Greeks of Constantinople acquired the free use of their ancient language, the most happy composition of human art, and a familiar knowledge of the sublime masters who had pleased or instructed the first of nations. But these advantages only tend to aggravate the reproach and shame of a degenerate people. They held in their lifeless hands the riches of their fathers, without inheriting the spirit which had created and improved that sacred patrimony: they read, they praised, they compiled, but their languid souls seemed alike incapable of thought and action. In the revolution of ten centuries, not a single discovery was made to exalt the dignity or promote the happiness of mankind. Not a single idea has been added to the speculative systems of antiquity, and a succession of patient disciples became in their turn the dogmatic teachers of the next servile generation. Not a single composition of history, philosophy, or literature, has been saved from oblivion by the intrinsic beauties of style or sentiment, or original fancy, or even of successful imitation.

CHAPTER FIFTY-FOUR

*Origin and Doctrine of the Paulicians—Their
Persecution by the Greek Emperors—Revolt in Armenia, etc.—Transplantation into Thrace—Propagation in the West—The Seeds, Character, and
Consequences of the Reformation*

(The Paulicians, whose rise and persecution are described
in this chapter, were a gnostic sect; Gibbon suggests that some
of their notions foreshadowed those of the Reformation.)

CHAPTER FIFTY-FIVE

The Bulgarians—Origin, Migrations, and Settlement of the Hungarians—Their Inroads in the East and West—The Monarchy of Russia—Geography and Trade—Wars of the Russians against the Greek Empire—Conversion of the Barbarians

(This chapter describes the establishment of Bulgarians, Croats, and Hungarians in the old provinces of the Danube, the origin of the Russian monarchy, and the conversion of the Russians and other northerly peoples to Christianity.)

CHAPTER FIFTY-SIX

The Saracens, Franks, and Greeks, in Italy—
First Adventures and Settlement of the Normans—
Character and Conquests of Robert Guiscard, Duke
of Apulia—Deliverance of Sicily by his Brother
Roger—Victories of Robert over the Emperors of the
East and West—Roger, King of Sicily, invades
Africa and Greece—The Emperor Manuel Com-
nenus—Wars of Greeks and Normans—Extinc-
tion of the Normans

The three great nations of the world, the Greeks, the Saracens, and the Franks, encountered each other on the theatre of Italy. The establishment of the Normans in the kingdoms of Naples and Sicily is an event most romantic in its origin, and in its consequences most important both to Italy and the Eastern empire. The broken provinces of the Greeks, Lombards, and Saracens were exposed to every invader, and every sea and land were invaded by the adventurous spirit of the Scandinavian pirates. After a long indulgence of rapine and slaughter, a fair and ample territory was accepted, occupied, and named, by the Normans of France: they renounced their gods for the God of the Christians; and the dukes of Normandy acknowledged themselves the vassals of the successors of Charlemagne and Capet. The savage fierceness which they had brought from the snowy mountains of Norway was refined, without being corrupted, in a warmer climate; the companions of Rollo insensibly mingled with the natives; they imbibed the manners, language, gallantry, of the French nation; and, in a martial age, the Normans might claim the palm of valour and glorious achievements. Of the fashionable superstitions, they embraced with ardour the pilgrimages of Rome, Italy, and the Holy Land.

In the rivalries between Capua, Beneventum, Salerno, and Naples, the superior spirit and discipline of the Normans gave victory to the side which they espoused; and their cautious policy observed the balance of power, lest the preponderance of any rival state should render their aid less important and their service less profitable. Their domination of Apulia placed the Normans on the verge of the two empires, and, according to the policy of the hour, they accepted the investiture of their lands from the sovereigns of Germany or Constantinople. The Normans under Count Roger took possession of Sicily, and the ambitious Robert Guiscard laid seige to Durazzo in Epirus and took it, after an extended struggle, despite the intervention of the emperor Alexius. The younger Guiscard evacuated the conquests he could not defend, and Alexius returned to Constantinople with the advantages, rather than the honour, of victory.

Of the Latin princes, the allies of Alexius and enemies of Robert, the most prompt and powerful was Henry the Third or Fourth, king of Germany and Italy, and future emperor of the West. Henry was the sincere adversary of the Normans, the allies and vassals of Gregory the Seventh, his implacable foe. But when Henry besieged Rome he was driven off by Robert, who again invaded Greece. After his death attacks upon Greece were prosecuted by Roger, who had made conquests in Africa. Roger liberated Louis the Seventh, who had been taken captive by the Greeks on his return from his unfortunate crusade, and made a descent upon Constantinople itself. The Normans were driven off by the emperor Manuel, who proceeded to reduce Apulia and Calabria. His designs to acquire Italy and the Western empire failed, but when peace was made the Normans acknowledged the authority of the Roman empire. Manuel's inhuman successor Isaac Angelus renewed bloody but indecisive hostilities. Before the expiration of twenty years the rival nations were lost or degraded in foreign servitude; and the successors of Constantine did not long survive the fall of the Sicilian monarchy.

CHAPTER FIFTY-SEVEN

The Turks of the House of Seljuk—Their Revolt against Mahmud, Conqueror of Hindostan—Togrul subdues Persia, and protects the Caliphs—Defeat and Captivity of the Emperor Romanus Diogenes by Alp Arslan—Power and Magnificence of Malek Shah—Conquest of Asia Minor and Syria—State and Oppression of Jerusalem—Pilgrimages to the Holy Sepulchre

From the isle of Sicily the reader must transport himself beyond the Caspian Sea to the original seat of the Turks or Turkmans, against whom the first crusade was principally directed. Their Scythian empire of the sixth century was long since dissolved, but the name was still famous among the Greeks and Orientals, and the fragments of the nation, each a powerful and independent people, were scattered over the desert from China to the Oxus and the Danube: the colony of Hungarians was admitted into the republic of Europe, and the thrones of Asia were occupied by slaves and soldiers of Turkish extraction. While Apulia and Sicily were subdued by the Norman lance, a swarm of these northern shepherds overspread the kingdoms of Persia; their princes of the race of Seljuk erected a splendid and solid empire from Samarcand to the confines of Greece and Egypt, and the Turks have maintained their dominion in Asia Minor till the victorious crescent has been planted on the dome of St. Sophia.

Since the fall of the caliphs, the discord and degeneracy of the Saracens respected the Asiatic provinces of Rome; which, by the victories of Nicephorus, Zimisces, and Basil, had been extended as far as Antioch and the eastern boundaries of Armenia. Twenty-five years after the death of Basil, his successors were suddenly assaulted by an unknown race of barbarians, who united the Scythian valour with the fanaticism of new proselytes, and the art and riches of a powerful monarchy.

The leader who initiated the Seljuk career of conquest was Togrul; his more spectacularly successful nephew Alp Arslan carried his attacks to the very heart of the empire. His alarming progress compelled the empress Eudocia to give herself and her sceptre into the hands of a soldier, Romanus Diogenes. In three laborious campaigns Romanus drove the Turks beyond the Euphrates, but when he undertook the deliverance of Armenia he suffered defeat and capture, and his authority was disclaimed in Constantinople. Alp Arslan was succeeded by his eldest son Malek Shah, who enlarged Seljuk power to the East. His merit and the extent of his empire made him the greatest prince of his age; with him the greatness and unity of the Turkish empire expired.

Since the first conquests of the caliphs, the establishment of the Turks in Anatolia or Asia Minor was the most deplorable loss which the church and empire had sustained. But the most interesting conquest of the Seljukian Turks was that of Jerusalem, which soon became the theatre of nations. Pilgrims from the East and West continued to visit the holy sepulchre and the adjacent sanctuaries until the ambitious and intolerant Fatimite Hakem demolished the structures. The succeeding caliphs resumed the policy of toleration, and the pilgrims returned with an increase of appetite to the spiritual feast. Among the Franks the zeal of pilgrimage prevailed beyond the example of former times, and the roads were covered with multitudes of either sex and of every rank, who professed their contempt of life so soon as they should have kissed the tomb of their Redeemer. Princes and prelates abandoned the care of their dominions, and the number of these pious caravans were a prelude to the armies which marched in the ensuing age under the banner of the cross. About thirty years before the first crusade, the archbishop of Mentz, with the bishops of Utrecht, Bamberg, and Ratisbon, undertook this laborious journey from the Rhine to the Jordan, and the multitude of their followers amounted to seven thousand persons.

CHAPTER FIFTY-EIGHT

Origin and Numbers of the First Crusade—Characters of the Latin Princes—Their March to Constantinople—Policy of the Greek Emperor Alexius —Conquest of Nice, Antioch, and Jerusalem, by the Franks—Deliverance of the Holy Sepulchre —Godfrey of Bouillon, First King of Jerusalem —Institutions of the French or Latin Kingdom

About twenty years after the conquest of Jerusalem by the Turks, the holy sepulchre was visited by a hermit of the name of Peter, a native of Amiens, in the province of Picardy in France. His resentment and sympathy were excited by his own injuries and the oppression of the Christian name; he mingled his tears with those of the patriarch, and earnestly inquired if no hopes of relief could be entertained from the Greek emperors of the East. The patriarch exposed the vices and weakness of the successors of Constantine. "I will rouse," exclaimed the hermit, "the martial nations of Europe in your cause;" and Europe was obedient to the call of the hermit. When he painted the sufferings of the natives and pilgrims of Palestine, every heart was melted to compassion; every breast glowed with indignation when he challenged the warriors of the age to defend their brethren, and rescue their Saviour: his ignorance of art and language was compensated by sighs, and tears, and ejaculations; and Peter supplied the deficiency of reason by loud and frequent appeals to Christ and his mother, to the saints and angels of paradise, with whom he had personally conversed. The most perfect orator of Athens might have envied the success of his eloquence: the rustic enthusiast inspired the passions which he felt, and Christendom expected with impatience the counsels and decrees of the supreme pontiff.

The glory or reproach of executing, though not in person, this holy enterprise, was reserved for Urban the Second, who convoked a council, first at Placentia and then at Clermont in France. The *holy war* against the infidels was proposed and adopted with enthusiasm. The pope proclaimed a *plenary indulgence* to those who should enlist under the banner of the cross; the absolution of *all* their sins, and a full receipt for *all* that might be due of canonical penance. The cold philosophy of modern times is incapable of feeling the impression that was made on a sinful and fanatic world. At the voice of their pastor, the robber, the incendiary, the homicide, arose by thousands to redeem their souls by repeating on the infidels the same deeds which they had exercised against their Christian brethren; and the terms of atonement were eagerly embraced by offenders of every rank and determination. None were pure; none were exempt from the guilt and penalty of sin; and those who were the least amenable to the justice of God and the church were the best entitled to the temporal and eternal recompense of their pious courage. If they fell, the spirit of the Latin clergy did not hesitate to adorn their tomb with the crown of martyrdom; and should they survive, they could expect without impatience the delay and increase of their heavenly reward. They offered their blood to the Son of God, who had laid down his life for their salvation: they took up the cross, and entered with confidence into the way of the Lord. His providence would watch over their safety; perhaps his visible and miraculous power would smooth the difficulties of their holy enterprise. The cloud and pillar of Jehovah had marched before the Israelites into the promised land. Might not the Christians more reasonably hope that the rivers would open for their passage; that the walls of the strongest cities would fall at the sound of their trumpets; and that the sun would be arrested in his mid-career to allow them time for the destruction of the infidels?

Of the chiefs and soldiers who marched to the holy sepulchre, I will dare to affirm that *all* were prompted by the spirit of enthusiasm, the belief of merit, the hope of reward, and the assurance of divine aid. But I am equally persuaded that in *many* it was not the sole, that in *some* it was not the leading, principle of action. The use and abuse of religion are feeble to stem, they are strong and irresistible to impel, the stream of national manners. Against the private wars of the barbarians, their bloody tournaments, licentious loves, and judicial duels, the popes and synods might ineffectually thunder. It is a more easy task to provoke the metaphysical disputes of the Greeks, to drive into the cloister the victims of anarchy or despotism, to sanctify the patience of slaves and cowards, or to assume the merit of the humanity and benevolence of modern Christians. War and exercise were the reigning passions of the Franks or Latins; they were enjoined, as a penance, to gratify those passions, to visit distant lands, and to draw their swords against the nations of the East. Their victory, or even their attempt, would immortalise the names of the intrepid heroes of the cross; and the purest piety could not be insensible to the most splendid prospect of military glory. In the petty quarrels of Europe they shed the blood of their friends and countrymen for the acquisition, perhaps, of a castle or a village. They could march with alacrity against the distant and hostile nations who were devoted to their arms; their fancy already grasped the golden sceptres of Asia; and the conquest of Apulia and Sicily by the Normans might exalt to royalty the hopes of the most private adventurer. Christendom, in her rudest state, must have yielded to the climate and cultivation of the Mohammedan countries; and their natural and artificial wealth had been magnified by the tales of pilgrims and the gifts of an imperfect commerce. The vulgar, both the great and small, were taught to believe every wonder, of lands flowing with milk and honey, of mines and treasures, of gold and diamonds, of palaces of marble and jasper, and of odoriferous groves of cinnamon and frankincense. In this earthly paradise each warrior depended on his sword to carve a plenteous and honourable establishment, which he measured only by the extent of his wishes. Their vassals and soldiers trusted their fortunes to God and their master: the spoils of a Turkish emir might enrich the meanest follower of the camp; and the flavour of the wines, the beauty of the Grecian women, were temptations more adapted to the nature, than to the profession, of the champions of the cross. The love of freedom was a powerful incitement to the multitudes who were oppressed by feudal or ecclesiastical tyranny. Under this holy sign, the peasants and burghers, who were attached to the servitude of the glebe, might escape from a haughty lord, and transplant themselves and their families to a land of liberty. The monk might release himself from the discipline of his convent, the debtor might suspend the accumulation of usury and the pursuit of his creditors, and outlaws and malefactors of every cast might continue to brave the laws and elude the punishment of their crimes.

These motives were potent and numerous: when we have singly computed their weight on the mind of each individual, we must add the infinite series, the multiplying powers of example and fashion. The first proselytes became the warmest and most effectual missionaries of the cross: among their friends and countrymen they preached the duty, the merit, and the recompense of their holy vow, and the most reluctant hearers were insensibly drawn within the whirlpool of persuasion and authority. The martial youths were fired by the reproach or suspicion of cowardice; the opportunity of visiting with an army the sepulchre of Christ was embraced by the old and infirm, by women and children, who consulted rather their zeal than their strength; and those who in the evening had derided the folly of their companions were the most eager, the ensuing day, to tread in their footsteps. The ignorance which magnified the hopes, diminished the perils, of the enterprise. Since the Turkish conquest, the paths of pilgrimage were obliterated; the chiefs themselves had an imperfect notion of the length of the way and the state of their enemies; and such was the stupidity of the people, that, at the sight of the first city or castle beyond the limits of their knowledge, they were ready to ask whether that was not the Jerusalem, the term and object of their labours. Yet the more prudent of the crusaders, who were not sure that they should be fed from heaven with a shower of quails or manna, provided themselves with those precious metals which, in every country, are the representatives of every commodity. To defray, according to their rank, the expenses of the road, princes alienated their provinces, nobles their lands and castles, peasants their cattle and the instruments of husbandry. The value of property was depreciated by the eager competition of multitudes; while the price of arms and horses was raised to an exorbitant height by the wants and impatience of the buyers. Those who remained at home, with sense and money, were enriched by the epidemical disease: the sovereigns acquired at a cheap rate the domains of their vassals, and the ecclesiastical purchasers completed the payment by the assurance of their prayers.

The day fixed for departure by the leaders was anticipated by the thoughtless and needy crowd of plebeians, which, because of their numbers, were divided into two hosts, one under Peter himself and the other under Walter the Penniless. The Bulgarians retaliated upon them severely for the Balkan cities they had sacked. Only scattered bands reached Constantinople, and these were speedily transported by the emperor Alexius to Asia Minor, where they were defeated by the Turks. Later in the year the leaders and their organized forces arrived, swore fealty (with the exception of Tancred and Raymond) to Alexius, and eventually took Jerusalem. The election of Godfrey of Bouillon as Defender of the Holy Sepulchre marked the beginning of the Latin Kingdom of Jerusalem.

CHAPTER FIFTY-NINE

Preservation of the Greek Empire—Numbers, Passage, and Event of the Second and Third Crusades—St. Bernard—Reign of Saladin in Egypt and Syria—His Conquest of Jerusalem—Naval Crusades—Richard the First of England—Pope Innocent the Third; and the Fourth and Fifth Crusades—The Emperor Frederic the Second—Louis the Ninth of France and the two last Crusades—Expulsion of the Latins or Franks by the Mamalukes

(The first was the only crusade that achieved more than ephemeral results; the Latin Kingdom of Jerusalem subsisted until Saladin conquered Jerusalem in 1187. The crusades after the first, which are described in Chapter LIX, were for the most part only expeditions to support the earlier crusades already in Palestine. The emperors in Constantinople grew increasingly uneasy in the face of the overt ambitions of the Latin chieftains. Open hostility broke out in the course of the Fourth Crusade, which therefore has a more direct bearing on the fate of the Roman Empire. The final schism between the Greeks and Latins is dealt with in Chapter LX).

CHAPTER SIXTY

Schism of the Greeks and Latins—State of Con-
stantinople—Revolt of the Bulgarians—Isaac An-
gelus dethroned by his Brother Alexius—Origin of
the Fourth Crusade—Alliance of the French and
Venetians with the Son of Isaac—Their Naval
Expedition to Constantinople—The two Sieges and
Final Conquest of the City by the Latins

The restoration of the Western empire by Charlemagne was
speedily followed by the separation of the Greek and Latin
churches. A religious and national animosity still divides the
two largest communions of the Christian world; and the
schism of Constantinople, by alienating her most useful allies,
and provoking her most dangerous enemies, has precipitated
the decline and fall of the Roman empire in the East.

The difference in creed between the Greek and Latin
churches turns on the question whether the Holy Spirit *pro-*
ceeded from the Father alone, perhaps *by* the Son, or from the
Father *and* the Son. The first of these opinions was asserted
by the Greeks, the second by the Latins; and the addition to
the Nicene creed of the word *filioque* kindled the flame of
discord between the Oriental and the Gallic churches. Rules of
discipline also varied. The craft or superstition of Rome has
imposed on her priests and deacons the rigid obligation of

275

celibacy; among the Greeks it is confined to the bishops, and the parochial clergy, the papas, enjoy the conjugal society of the wives whom they have married before their entrance into holy orders. Bigotry and national aversion are powerful magnifiers of every object of dispute; but the immediate cause of the schism of the Greeks may be traced in the emulation of the leading prelates, who maintained the supremacy of the old metropolis, superior to all, and of the reigning capital, inferior to none, in the Christian world. Friction eventually reached the point that the pope's legates deposited on the altar of St. Sophia a direful anathema which enumerates the seven mortal heresies of the Greeks, and devotes the guilty teachers, and their unhappy sectaries, to the eternal society of the devil and his angels. According to the emergencies of the church and state, a friendly correspondence was sometimes resumed; the language of charity and concord was sometimes affected; but the Greeks have never recanted their errors, the popes have never repealed their sentence; and from this thunderbolt we may date the consummation of the schism. It was enlarged by each ambitious step of the Roman pontiffs: the emperors blushed and trembled at the ignominious fate of their royal brethren of Germany; and the people was scandalised by the temporal power and military life of the Latin clergy.

The aversion of the Greeks and Latins was nourished and manifested in the three first expeditions to the Holy Land. About ten or twelve years after the loss of Jerusalem the nobles of France were again summoned to the holy war, and their enterprise was supported by the powerful Venetians, who had large commercial interests in the East. The young Alexius, whose father Isaac Angelus had been deposed by his uncle Alexius Angelus and who had family ties with the rulers of the West, allied himself with the crusaders with a view to recovering his throne. The Latins took Constantinople, and Isaac and his son were restored. Renewed friction with their allies and their own people resulted in their deposition and death, and the Latins again besieged and finally stormed Constantinople. Not content with the untold wealth which the pillage of the ancient metropolis yielded, the Latin victors wantonly committed atrocities upon its people, desecrated its sanctuaries, destroyed its works of art, and burnt its books. The literature of the Greeks had almost centred in the metropolis; and without computing the extent of our loss, we may drop a tear over the libraries that have perished in the triple fire of Constantinople.

CHAPTER SIXTY-ONE

Partition of the Empire by the French and Vene-
tians—Five Latin Emperors of the Houses of
Flanders and Courtenay—Their Wars against the
Bulgarians and Greeks—Weakness and Poverty of
the Latin Empire—Recovery of Constantinople by
the Greeks—General Consequences of the Crusades

(After its capture by the Latins in 1204 Constantinople was
ruled by a series of Latin emperors, Baldwin I and his four
successors. Meanwhile Theodore Lascaris established a Greek
government in exile at Nicaea, and there was another claimant
in Trebizond. The rule of the Latin emperors was incompetent
and disastrous, and in 1261 the Greeks recovered Constantinople and made Michael Palæologus emperor.)

After this narrative of the expeditions of the Latins to Palestine and Constantinople, I cannot dismiss the subject without revolving the general consequences on the countries that
were the scene, and on the nations that were the actors, of
these memorable crusades. As soon as the arms of the Franks
were withdrawn, the impression, though not the memory, was
erased in the Mohammedan realms of Egypt and Syria. The
faithful disciples of the prophet were never tempted by a profane desire to study the laws or language of the idolaters; nor
did the simplicity of their primitive manners receive the

slightest alteration from their intercourse in peace and war with the unknown strangers of the West. The Greeks, who thought themselves proud, but who were only vain, showed a disposition somewhat less inflexible. In the efforts for the recovery of their empire they emulated the valour, discipline, and tactics of their antagonists. The modern literature of the West they might justly despise; but its free spirit would instruct them in the rights of man; and some institutions of public and private life were adopted from the French. The correspondence of Constantinople and Italy diffused the knowledge of the Latin tongue; and several of the fathers and classics were at length honoured with a Greek version. But the national and religious prejudices of the Orientals were inflamed by persecution; and the reign of the Latins confirmed the separation of the two churches.

If we compare the era of the crusades, the Latins of Europe and the Greeks and Arabians, their respective degrees of knowledge, industry, and art, our rude ancestors must be content with the third rank in the scale of nations. The Latins learned little from their experiences in the East; the principle of the crusades was a savage fanaticism, and the most important effects were analogous to the cause. The belief of the Catholics was corrupted by new legends, their practice by new superstitions; and the establishment of the inquisition, the mendicant orders of monks and friars, the last abuse of indulgences, and the final progress of idolatry, flowed from the baleful fountain of the holy war. The active spirit of the Latins preyed on the vitals of their reason and religion; and if the ninth and tenth centuries were the time of darkness, the thirteenth and fourteenth were the age of absurdity and fable.

In one respect I can indeed perceive the accidental operation of the crusades, not so much in producing a benefit as in removing an evil. The larger portion of the inhabitants of Europe was chained to the soil, without freedom, or property, or knowledge; and the two orders of ecclesiastics and nobles, whose numbers were comparatively small, alone deserved the name of citizens and men. This oppressive system was supported by the arts of the clergy and the swords of the barons. The authority of the priests operated in the darker ages as a salutary antidote: they prevented the total extinction of letters, mitigated the fierceness of the times, sheltered the poor and defenceless, and preserved or revived the peace and order of civil society. But the independence, rapine and discord of the feudal lords were unmixed with any semblance of good; and every hope of industry and improvement was crushed by the iron weight of the martial aristocracy. Among the causes that undermined the Gothic edifice, a conspicuous place must be allowed to the crusades. The estates of the barrons were dissipated, and their race was often extinguished in these costly and perilous expeditions. Their poverty extorted from their pride those charters of freedom which unlocked the fetters of the slave, secured the farm of the peasant and the shop of the artificer, and gradually restored a substance and a soul to the most numerous and useful part of the community.

CHAPTER SIXTY-TWO

The Greek Emperors of Nice and Constantinople—
Elevation and Reign of Michael Palæologus—His
false Union with the Pope and the Latin Church
—Hostile Designs of Charles of Anjou—Revolt of
Sicily—War of the Catalans in Asia and Greece
—Revolutions and present State of Athens

The loss of Constantinople restored a momentary vigour to the Greeks. From their palaces the princes and nobles were driven into the field; and the fragments of the falling monarchy were grasped by the hands of the most vigorous or the most skilful candidates. In the long and barren pages of the Byzantine annals it would not be an easy task to equal the two characters of Theodore Lascaris and John Ducas Vataces, who replanted and upheld the Roman standard at Nice in Bithynia. But the son of John Vataces, also named Theodore Lascaris, was inferior to his father, and after his death a conspiracy transferred authority to Michael Palæologus. Michael made his triumphal entry into Constantinople only twenty days after the expulsion of the Latins. Michael entered into and then abjured a union with the Latins, instigated John of Procida to raise a rebellion against Charles of Anjou in Sicily; it was the presence of John which probably aroused the peasants to the widespread massacre of the French, which has obtained the name of the SICIL-

IAN VESPERS. It was by involving the kingdoms of the West in rebellion and blood that the first Palæologus saved his empire.

CHAPTER SIXTY-THREE

Civil Wars, and Ruin of the Greek Empire—
Reigns of Andronicus the Elder and Younger, and
John Palæologus—Regency, Revolt, Reign, and
Abdication of John Cantacuzene—Establishment of
a Genoese Colony at Pera or Galata—Their Wars
with the Empire and City of Constantinople

The long reign of Andronicus the Elder is chiefly memorable
by the disputes of the Greek church, the invasion of the Catalans, and the rise of the Ottoman power. Andronicus was succeeded, after three civil wars, by his like-named grandson,
who was no more glorious and fortunate than his grandfather.
John Cantacuzene, who was regent for the infant John
Palæologus, presently assumed the purple and defended his
position in a civil war; but a noble Genoese, attached to the
cause of John Palæologus, obtained admission for his small
fleet under pretence of distress and forced the abdication of
Cantacuzene and the restoration of John Palæologus. Cantacuzene joined arms with the Venetians, the principal commercial
rivals of the Genoese, but a Genoese victory over the Greeks
and Venetians gave them a monopoly of trade and almost a
right of dominion. The Roman empire (I smile in transcribing
the name) might soon have sunk into a province of Genoa if
the ambition of the republic had not been checked by the ruin

of her freedom and naval power. A long contest of one hundred and thirty years was determined by the triumph of Venice; and the factions of the Genoese compelled them to seek for domestic peace under the protection of a foreign lord, the duke of Milan, or the French king. Yet the spirit of commerce survived that of conquest; and the colony of Pera still awed the capital and navigated the Euxine, till it was involved by the Turks in the final servitude of Constantinople itself.

CHAPTER SIXTY-FOUR

*Conquests of Zingis Khan and the Moguls from
China to Poland—Escape of Constantinople and
the Greeks—Origin of the Ottoman Turks in Bithynia—Reigns and Victories of Othman, Orchan,
Amurath the First, and Bajazet the First—Foundation and Progress of the Turkish Monarch in
Asia and Europe—Danger of Constantinople and
the Greek Empire*

From the petty quarrels of a city and her suburbs, from the
cowardice and discord of the falling Greeks, I shall now
ascend to the victorious Turks; whose domestic slavery was
ennobled by martial discipline, religious enthusiasm, and the
energy of the national character. The rise and progress of the
Ottomans, the present sovereigns of Constantinople, are connected with the most important scenes of modern history; but
they are founded on a previous knowledge of the great erup-
tion of the Moguls and Tartars, whose rapid conquests may be
compared with the primitive convulsions of nature, which
have agitated and altered the surface of the globe. I have long
since asserted my claim to introduce the nations, the immediate or remote authors of the fall of the Roman empire; nor can
I refuse myself to those events which, from their uncommon

magnitude, will interest a philosophic mind in the history of blood.

From the spacious highlands between China, Siberia, and the Caspian Sea the tide of emigration and war has repeatedly been poured. These ancient seats of the Huns and Turks were occupied in the twelfth century by many pastoral tribes, of the same descent and similar manners, which were united and led to conquest by the formidable Zingis. The conquests of Zingis and his successors extended from China to Poland, but Constantinople escaped the fate of Pekin, Samarcand, and Bagdad. The decline of the Moguls gave a free scope to the rise and progress of the OTTOMAN EMPIRE.

The Ottoman Turks established themselves in Asia Minor and gained a foothold in Europe. The Greeks were now surrounded, both in Asia and Europe, by the arms of the same hostile monarchy; but the Ottoman prince Amurath satisfied his pride with the frequent and humble attendance of the emperor John Palæologus and his four sons. Thousands of European captives were selected to be educated by the Ottomans in religion and arms and formed into a militia called Janizaries. They possessed a decisive superiority in war; since a regular body of infantry, in constant exercise and pay, was not maintained by any of the princes of Christendom. The Janizaries fought with the zeal of proselytes against their *idolatrous* countrymen. The conquests of Amurath's son and successor Bajazet extended from the Euphrates to the Danube. In the battle of Nicopolis, in his Hungarian campaign, Bajazet defeated a confederate army of a hundred thousand Christians, who had proudly boasted that if the sky should fall they could uphold it on their lances.

After his enfranchisement from an oppressive guardian, John Palæologus remained thirty-six years the helpless, and, as it should seem, the careless, spectator of the public ruin. Ottoman pressure and dissensions among the Greeks had contracted the Roman world to a corner of Thrace, between the Propontis and the Black Sea, about fifty miles in length and thirty in breadth. Apprehending that the conquest of Constantinople might unite the powers of Christendom in a second and more formidable crusade, Bajazet granted the metropolis a ten-years truce at the price of an enormous indemnity, and enjoyed the glory of establishing a Turkish cadhi, and founding a royal mosque, in the metropolis of the Eastern church. But the restless sultan soon claimed the city as his own; and, on the refusal of the emperor John, Constantinople was more closely pressed by the calamities of war and famine. Against such an enemy prayers and resistance were alike unavailing; and the savage would have devoured his prey if, in the fatal moment, he had not been overthrown by another savage stronger then himself. By the victory of Timour or Tamerlane the fall of Constantinople was delayed about fifty years; and this important though accidental service may justly introduce the life and character of the Mogul conqueror.

CHAPTER SIXTY-FIVE

Elevation of Timour or Tamerlane to the Throne of Samarcand—His Conquests in Persia, Georgia, Tartary, Russia, India, Syria, and Anatolia—His Turkish War—Defeat and Captivity of Bajazet—Death of Timour—Civil War of the Sons of Bajazet—Restoration of the Turkish Monarchy by Mohammed the First—Siege of Constantinople by Amurath the Second

The conquest and monarchy of the world was the first object of the ambition of TIMOUR. To live in the memory and esteem of future ages was the second wish of his magnanimous spirit. All the civil and military transactions of his reign were diligently recorded in the journals of his secretaries; the authentic narrative was revised by the persons best informed of each particular transaction; and it is believed in the empire and family of Timour that the monarch himself composed the *commentaries* of his life and the *institutions* of his government. But these cares were ineffectual for the preservation of his fame, and these precious memorials in the Mogul or Persian language were concealed from the world, or, at least, from the knowledge of Europe. The nations which he vanquished exercised a base and impotent revenge; and ignorance has long repeated the tale of calumny which had disfigured the birth and character, the person, and even the name, of *Tamerlane*. Yet his real merit would be enhanced rather than debased by the elevation of a peasant to the throne of Asia; nor can his lameness be a theme of reproach, unless he had the weakness to blush at a natural, or perhaps an honourable, infirmity.

Timour's irresistible sweep through the East culminated in his defeat and capture of Bajazet at Angora. The *iron cage* in which Bajazet was imprisoned by Tamerlane, so long and so often repeated as a moral lesson, is now rejected as a fable. his premature death might, without injustice, be ascribed to the severity of Timour. He warred not with the dead: a tear and a sepulchre were all that he could bestow on a captive who was delivered from his power; and if Mousa, the son of Bajazet, was permitted to reign over the ruins of Boursa, the greatest part of the province of Anatolia had been restored by the conqueror to their lawful sovereigns.

From the Irtish and Volga to the Persian Gulf, and from the Ganges to Damascus and the Archipelago, Asia was in the hand of Timour: his armies were invincible, his ambition was boundless, and his zeal might aspire to conquer and convert the Christian kingdoms of the West, which already trembled at his name. He touched the utmost verge of the land; but an insuperable, though narrow sea, rolled between the two continents of Europe and Asia, and the lord of so many *tomans* or myriads of horse was not master of a single galley.

The massy trunk of the Ottoman monarchy was bent to the ground, but no sooner did the hurricane pass away than it again rose with fresh vigour and more lively vegetation. For a decade after Timour's evacuation of Anatolia the five sons of Bajazet contested the rule, until Mahomet was acknowledged. After a peaceful rule of eight years Mahomet bequeathed an undisputed succession to his son Amurath, who reunited the Ottoman empire and give it new strength. Amurath was able to bring two hundred thousand Turks to attack Constantinople, but after a siege of two months was recalled by domestic revolt, which had been kindled by Greek treachery. While he led his Janizaries to new conquests in Europe and Asia, the Byzantine empire was indulged in a servile and precarious respite

of thirty years. Manuel sank into the grave; and John
Palæologus was permitted to reign, for an annual tribute of
three hundred thousand aspers, and the dereliction of almost
all that he held beyond the suburbs of Constantinople.

The only hope of salvation for the Greek empire and the
adjacent kingdoms would have been some more powerful
weapon, some discovery in the art of war, that should give
them a decisive superiority over their Turkish foes. Such a
weapon was in their hands; such a discovery had been made in
the critical moment of their fate. The chemists of China or
Europe had found, by casual or elaborate experiments, that a
mixture of saltpetre, sulphur, and charcoal produces, with a
spark of fire, a tremendous explosion. It was soon observed
that, if the expansive force were compressed in a strong tube,
a ball of stone or iron might be expelled with irresistible and
destructive velocity. The precise era of the invention and application of gunpowder is involved in doubtful traditions and
equivocal language; yet we may clearly discern that it was
known before the middle of the fourteenth century, and that
before the end of the same the use of artillery in battles and
sieges by sea and land was familiar to the states of Germany,
Italy, Spain, France, and England. The priority of nations is of
small account; none could derive any exclusive benefit from
their previous or superior knowledge; and in the common improvement they stood on the same level of relative power and
military science. Nor was it possible to circumscribe the secret
within the pale of the church; it was disclosed to the Turks by
the treachery of apostates and the selfish policy of rivals; and
the sultans had sense to adopt, and wealth to reward, the talents of a Christian engineer. The Genoese, who transported
Amurath into Europe, must be accused as his preceptors; and
it was probably by their hands that his cannon was cast and
directed at the siege of Constantinople. The first attempt was
indeed unsuccessful; but in the general warfare of the age the
advantage was on *their* side who were most commonly the
assailants; for a while the proportion of the attack and defence
was suspended, and this thundering artillery was pointed
against the walls and towers which had been erected only to
resist the less potent engines of antiquity. By the Venetians the

use of gunpowder was communicated without reproach to the sultans of Egypt and Persia, their allies against the Ottoman power; the secret was soon propagated to the extremities of Asia; and the advantage of the European was confined to his easy victories over the savages of the new world. If we contrast the rapid progress of this mischievous discovery with the slow and laborious advances of reason, science, and the arts of peace, a philosopher, according to his temper, will laugh or weep at the folly of mankind.

CHAPTER SIXTY-SIX

Applications of the Eastern Emperors to the Popes —Visits to the West of John the First, Manuel, and John the Second, Palæologus—Union of the Greek and Latin Churches promoted by the Council of Basil, and concluded at Ferrara and Florence— State of Literature at Constantinople—Its Revival in Italy by the Greek Fugitives—Curiosity and Emulation of the Latins

In the four last centuries of the Greek emperors their friendly or hostile aspects towards the pope and the Latins may be observed as the thermometer of their prosperity or distress— as the scale of the rise and fall of the barbarian dynasties. Manuel himself visited the countries of the West and made large efforts to engage their assistance. Manuel's son and successor, John Palæologus the Second, showed greater zeal, and his efforts to unite the churches of East and West were promoted by rivalries within the Latin church. After long negotiation representatives of the two nations assembled in the Cathedral of Florence; Cardinal Julian, and Bessarion, Archbishop of Nice, appeared in the pulpit, and after reading in their respective tongues the act of union, they mutually embraced in the name and presence of their applauding brethren. Though the union was but transitory, the interchange was productive of a beneficial consequence—the revival of the Greek learning in Italy, from whence it was propagated to the last nations of the West and North. Petrarch and Boccace, the Greek professors who taught in Italy, Cosmo and Lorenzo of Medicis, all helped promote the revival of learning.

Before the arrival of classic literature the barbarians in Europe were immersed in ignorance; and their vulgar tongues were marked with the rudeness and poverty of their manners. The students of the more perfect idioms of Rome and Greece were introduced to a new world of light and science; to the society of the free and polished nations of antiquity; and to a familiar converse with those immortal men who spoke the sublime language of eloquence and reason. Such an intercourse must tend to refine the taste and to elevate the genius of the moderns; and yet, from the first experiment, it might appear that the study of the ancients had given fetters, rather than wings, to the human mind. However laudable, the spirit of imitation is of a servile cast; and the first disciples of the Greeks and Romans were a colony of strangers in the midst of their age and country. The minute and laborious diligence which explored the antiquities of remote times might have improved or adorned the present state of society; the critic and metaphysician were the slaves of Aristotle; the poets, historians, and orators were proud to repeat the thoughts and words of the Augustan age: the works of nature were observed with the eyes of Pliny and Theophrastus; and some Pagan votaries professed a secret devotion to the gods of Homer and Plato. The Italians were oppressed by the strength and number of their ancient auxiliaries: the century after the deaths of Petrarch and Boccace was filled with a crowd of Latin imitators, who decently repose on our shelves; but in that era of learning, it will not be easy to discern a real discovery of science, a work of invention or eloquence, in the popular language of the country. But as soon as it had been deeply saturated with the celestial dew, the soil was quickened into vegetation and life; the modern idioms were refined; the classics of Athens and Rome inspired a pure taste and a generous emulation; and in Italy, as afterwards in France and England, the pleasing reign of poetry and fiction was succeeded by the light of speculative and experimental philosophy. Genius may anticipate the season of maturity; but in the education of a people, as in that of an individual, memory must be exercised before the powers of reason and fancy can be expanded; nor may the artist hope to equal or surpass, till he has learned to imitate, the works of his predecessors.

CHAPTER SIXTY-SEVEN

Schism of the Greeks and Latins—Reign and Character of Amurath the Second—Crusade of Ladislaus, King of Hungary—His Defeat and Death—John Huniades—Scanderbeg—Constantine Palæologus, last Emperor of the East

The last hope of the falling city and empire was placed in the harmony of the mother and daughter, in the maternal tenderness of Rome, and the filial obedience of Constantinople. In the Synod of Florence, the Greeks and Latins had embraced and subscribed and promised; but these signs of friendship were perfidious or fruitless, and the baseless fabric of the union vanished like a dream. Ladislaus, king of Poland and Hungary, undertook a holy war against the Turks at the instance of the pope, and John Huniades and Scanderbeg, prince of Albania, revolted against the Turk; their efforts hampered the Turk but could not prevent the final issue. About four years after the Hungarian crusade John Palæologus was succeeded by his oldest brother Constantine, who proved to be the last Roman emperor in Constantinople.

CHAPTER SIXTY-EIGHT

Reign and Character of Mohammed the Second—Siege, Assault, and Final Conquest of Constantinople by the Turks—Death of Constantine Palæologus—Servitude of the Greeks—Extinction of the Roman Empire in the East—Consternation of Europe—Conquests and Death of Mohammed the Second

The siege of Constantinople by the Turks attracts our first attention to the person and character of the great destroyer. Mohammed the Second was the son of the second Amurath; and though his mother has been decorated with the titles of Christian and princess, she is more probably confounded with the numerous concubines who peopled from every climate the harem of the sultan. His first education and sentiments were those of a devout Musulman; and as often as he conversed with an infidel he purified his hands and face by the legal rites of ablution. Age and empire appear to have relaxed this narrow bigotry: his aspiring genius disdained to acknowledge a power above his own; and in his looser hours he presumed (it is said) to brand the prophet of Mecca as a robber and impostor. Yet the sultan persevered in a decent reverence for the doctrine and discipline of the Koran: his private indiscretion must have been sacred from the vulgar ear; and we should suspect the credulity of strangers and sectaries, so prone to believe that a mind which is hardened against truth must be armed with superior contempt for absurdity and error. Under the tuition of the most skilful masters Mohammed advanced with an early and rapid progress in the paths of knowledge; and besides his native tongue it is affirmed that he spoke or understood five languages, the Arabic, the Persian, the Chaldæan or Hebrew, the Latin, and the Greek.

In preparation for the siege of Constantinople Mohammed built a strong fortress at Asomaton on the Bosphorus and engaged a Dane or Hungarian, who had been almost starved in the Greek service, to cast a cannon of tremendous power. To counter a hostile fleet Mohammed tansported his own vessels overland from the Bosphorus into the harbour. After a siege of fifty-three days a general assault was launched against the city, against which the heroism of the defenders was vain. Constantine himself was killed. The city was pillaged and its monasteries and churches profaned.

From the first hour of the memorable twenty-ninth of May, disorder and rapine prevailed in Constantinople till the eighth hour of the same day, when the sultan himself passed in triumph through the gate of St. Romanus. He was attended by his viziers, bashaws, and guards, each of whom (says a Byzantine historian) was robust as Hercules, dexterous as Apollo, and equal in battle to any ten of the race of ordinary mortals. The conqueror gazed with satisfaction and wonder on the strange though splendid appearance of the domes and palaces, so dissimilar from the style of Oriental architecture. In the hippodrome, or *atmeidan*, his eye was attracted by the twisted column of the three serpents; and, as a trial of his strength, he shattered with his iron mace or battle-axe the under jaw of one of these monsters, which in the eyes of the Turks were the idols or talismans of the city. At the principal door of St. Sophia he alighted from his horse and entered the dome; and such was his jealous regard for that monument of his glory, that, on observing a zealous Musulman in the act of breaking the marble pavement, he admonished him with his scimitar that, if the spoil and captives were granted to the soldiers, the public and private buildings had been reserved for the prince.

By his command the metropolis of the Eastern church was transformed into a mosque: the rich and portable instruments of superstition had been removed; the crosses were thrown down; and the walls, which were covered with images and mosaics, were washed and purified, and restored to a state of naked simplicity. On the same day, or on the ensuing Friday, the *muezin*, or crier, ascended the most lofty turret, and proclaimed the *ezan*, or public invitation, in the name of God and his prophet; the imam preached; and Mohammed the Second performed the *namaz* of prayer and thanksgiving on the great altar, where the Christian mysteries had so lately been celebrated before the last of the Cæsars. From St. Sophia he proceeded to the august but desolate mansion of a hundred successors of the great Constantine, but which in a few hours had been stripped of the pomp of royalty. A melancholy reflection on the vicissitudes of human greatness forced itself on his mind, and he repeated an elegant distich of Persian poetry: "The spider has wove his web in the Imperial palace, and the owl hath sung her watchsong on the towers of Afrasiab."

Constantinople had been left naked and desolate, without a prince or a people. But she could not be despoiled of the incomparable situation which marks her for the metropolis of a great empire; and the genius of the place will ever triumph over the accidents of time and fortune. Boursa and Adrianople, the ancient seats of the Ottomans, sunk into provincial towns; and Mohammed the Second established his own residence and that of his successors on the same commanding spot which had been chosen by Constantine. The fortifications of Galata, which might afford a shelter to the Latins, were prudently destroyed; but the damage of the Turkish cannon was soon repaired, and before the month of August great quantities of lime had been burnt for the restoration of the walls of the capital. As the entire property of the soil and buildings, whether public or private or profane or sacred, was now transferred to the conqueror, he first separated a space of eight furlongs from the point of the triangle for the establishment of his seraglio or palace. It is here, in the bosom of luxury, that the *Grand Signor* (as he has been emphatically named by the Italians) appears to reign over Europe and Asia; but his person on the shores of the Bosphorus may not always be secure from the insults of a hostile navy. In the new character of a mosque, the cathedral of St. Sophia was endowed with an ample revenue, crowned with lofty minarets, and surrounded with groves and fountains for the devotion and refreshment of the Moslems. The same model was imitated in the *jami*, or royal mosques; and the first of these was built by Mohammed himself, on the ruins of the church of the holy apostles and the tombs of the Greek emperors.

The importance of Constantinople was felt and magnified in its loss. The pontificate of Nicholas the Fifth, however peaceful and prosperous, was dishonoured by the fall of the Eastern empire; and the grief and terror of the Latins revived, or seemed to revive, the old enthusiasm of the crusades. Aeneas Sylvius, when he was raised to the papal throne, under the name of Pius the Second, devoted his life to the prosecution of the Turkish war. In the council of Mantua he excited some sparks of a false or feeble enthusiasm; but when the pontiff appeared at Ancona, to embark in person with the troops, engagements vanished in excuses; a precise day was adjourned to an indefinite term; and his effective army consisted of some German pilgrims, whom he was obliged to disband with indulgences and alms. Regardless of futurity, his successors and the powers of Italy were involved in the schemes of present and domestic ambition; and the distance or proximity of each object determined in their eyes its apparent magnitude. A more enlarged view of their interest would have taught them to maintain a defensive and naval war against the common enemy; and the support of Scanderbeg and his brave Albanians might have prevented the subsequent invasion of the kingdom of Naples. The siege and sack of Otranto by the Turks diffused a general consternation; and Pope Sixtus was preparing to fly beyond the Alps, when the storm was instantly dispelled by the death of Mohammed the Second, in the fifty-first year of his age. His lofty genius aspired to the conquest of Italy: he was possessed of a strong city and a capacious harbour; and the same reign might have been decorated with the trophies of the NEW and the ANCIENT ROME.

CHAPTER SIXTY-NINE

State of Rome from the Twelfth Century—Temporal Dominion of the Popes—Seditions of the City—Political Heresy of Arnold of Brescia—Restoration of the Republic—The Senators—Pride of the Romans—Their Wars—They are deprived of the Election and Presence of the Popes, who retire to Avignon—The Jubilee—Noble Families of Rome—Feud of the Colonna and Ursini

CHAPTER SEVENTY

Character and Coronation of Petrarch—Restoration of the Freedom and Government of Rome by the Tribune Rienzi—His Virtues and Vices, his Expulsion and Death—Return of the Popes from Avignon—Great Schism of the West—Reunion of the Latin Church—Last Struggles of Roman Liberty—Statutes of Rome—Final Settlement of the Ecclesiastical State

(The fall of Constantinople and the extinction of the office of emperor, narrated in Chapter LXVIII, mark the final fall of the Roman Empire. The remainder of the Decline and Fall is really in the nature of an appendix on the subsequent fortunes of the heirs of the Western empire until the dawn of the Renaissance.)

CHAPTER SEVENTY-ONE

Prospect of the Ruins of Rome in the Fifteenth Century—Four Causes of Decay and Destruction—Example of the Coliseum—Renovation of the City—Conclusion of the whole Work

In the last days of Pope Eugenius the Fourth, two of his servants, the learned Poggius and a friend, ascended the Capitoline hill, reposed themselves among the ruins of columns and temples, and viewed from that commanding spot the wide and various prospect of desolation. The place and the object gave ample scope for moralising on the vicissitudes of fortune, which spares neither man nor the proudest of his works, which buries empires and cities in a common grave; and it was agreed that, in proportion to her former greatness, the fall of Rome was the more awful and deplorable.

After a diligent inquiry I can discern four principal causes of the ruin of Rome, which continued to operate in a period of more than a thousand years. I. The injuries of time and nature. II. The hostile attacks of the barbarians and Christians. III. The use and abuse of the materials. And, IV. The domestic quarrels of the Romans.

I. Hurricanes, earthquakes, fires and inundations have demonstrably been responsible for much damage.

II. The crowd of writers of every nation, who impute the destruction of the Roman monuments to the Goths and the

Christians, have neglected to inquire how far they were animated by a hostile principle, and how far they possessed the means and the leisure to satiate their enmity. In the preceding volumes of this History I have described the triumph of barbarism and religion; and I can only resume, in a few words, their real or imaginary connection with the ruin of ancient Rome. In simple truth, the northern conquerors were neither sufficiently savage, nor sufficiently refined, to entertain such aspiring ideas of destruction and revenge. The shepherds of Scythia and Germany had been educated in the armies of the empire, whose discipline they acquired, and whose weakness they invaded; with the familiar use of the Latin tongue they had learned to reverence the name and titles of Rome; and, though incapable of emulating, they were more inclined to admire than to abolish the arts and studies of a brighter period. From these innocent barbarians the reproach may be transferred to the Catholics of Rome. The statues, altars, and houses of the demons were an abomination in their eyes; and in the absolute command of the city, they might labour with zeal and perseverance to erase the idolatry of their ancestors.

III. The barbarian conquerors of Rome usurped in a moment the toil and treasure of successive ages; but, except the luxuries of immediate consumption, they must view without desire all that could not be removed from the city in the Gothic wagons or the fleet of the Vandals. The edifices of Rome might be considered as a vast and various mine; the first labour of extracting the materials, was already performed; the metals were purified and cast; the marbles were hewn and polished; and after foreign and domestic rapine had been satiated, the remains of the city, could a purchaser have been found, were still venal. The fairest columns of the Ionic and Corinthian orders, the richest marbles of Paros and Numidia, were degraded, perhaps to the support of a convent or a stable.

IV. I have reserved for the last the most potent and forcible cause of destruction, the domestic hostilities of the Romans themselves. In a dark period of five hundred years Rome was perpetually afflicted by the sanguinary quarrels of the nobles and the people, the Guelphs and Ghibelines, the Colonna and

Ursini. With some slight alterations, a theatre, an amphitheatre, a mausoleum, was transformed into a strong and spacious citadel. Even the churches were encompassed with arms and bulwarks, and the military engines on the roof of St. Peter's were the terror of the Vatican and the scandal of the Christian world. Whatever is fortified will be attacked; and whatever is attacked may be destroyed. These general observations may be separately applied to the amphitheatre of Titus, which has obtained the name of the COLISEUM, either from its magnitude, or from Nero's colossal statue: an edifice, had it been left to time and nature, which might perhaps have claimed an eternal duration. The abolition at Rome of the ancient games must be understood with some latitude; and the carnival sports, of the Testacean mount and the Circus Agonalis, were regulated by the law or custom of the city. This use of the amphitheatre was a rare, perhaps a singular, festival: the demand for the materials was a daily and continual want, which the citizens could gratify without restraint or remorse.

But the clouds of barbarism were gradually dispelled; and the peaceful authority of Martin the Fifth and his successors restored the ornaments of the city as well as the order of the ecclesiastical state. The map, the description, the monuments of ancient Rome, have been elucidated by the diligence of the antiquarian and the student; and the footsteps of heroes, the relics, not of superstition, but of empire, are devoutly visited by a new race of pilgrims from the remote and once savage countries of the North.

Of these pilgrims, and of every reader, the attention will be excited by a History of the Decline and Fall of the Roman Empire; the greatest, perhaps, and most awful scene in the history of mankind. The various causes and progressive effects are connected with many of the events most interesting in human annals: the artful policy of the Cæsars, who long maintained the name and image of a free republic; the disorders of military despotism; the rise, establishment, and sects of Christianity; the foundation of Constantinople; the division of the monarchy; the invasion and settlements of the barbarians of Germany and Scythia; the institutions of the civil law; the character and religion of Mohammed; the temporal sovereignty of the popes; the restoration and decay of the Western empire of Charlemagne; the crusades of the Latins in the East; the conquests of the Saracens and Turks; the ruin of the Greek empire; the state and revolutions of Rome in the middle ages. The historian may applaud the importance and variety of his subject; but, while he is conscious of his own imperfections, he must often accuse the deficiency of his materials. It was among the ruins of the Capitol that I first conceived the idea of a work which has amused and exercised near twenty years of my life, and which, however inadequate to my own wishes, I finally deliver to the curiosity and candour of the public.

LAUSANNE,

June 27, 1787

INDEXED CHRONOLOGY

ABOUT THE AUTHOR

The name Edward Gibbon has become synonymous with the title of his immortal masterwork. Certainly no historian of any age has enjoyed greater or more enduring popularity. THE DECLINE AND FALL OF THE ROMAN EMPIRE will stand forever as the noble monument of a man and an age.

"Here is history written with majesty and grace, a subtlety and power unmatched except in the greatest poetry. And even if we are indifferent to the significant experience of the past and deaf to the magic of magnificent utterance, Gibbon remains continuously relevant for his insights into the permanent patterns of human response to recurrent military and political challenges. He is a classic because he is concerned with the universal as well as the particular, because he is philosopher as well as chronicler."
—MOSES HADAS

The Editor

MOSES HADAS received his master's degree and his Ph.D. from Columbia University, where he taught for many years and where he occupied the chair of Jay Professor of Greek. He was the author of *A History of Latin Literature; Ancilla to Classical Reading; Humanism; Old Wine, New Bottles;* and was the editor of such volumes as *The Complete Works of Tacitus, The Basic Works of Cicero, The Greek Poets, Greek Drama, Essential Works of Stoicism,* and *The History of Rome.* He also translated W. E. Otto's *The Homeric Gods,* J. Burckhardt's *Age of Constantine the Great,* and Joseph ben Meir Zabara's *The Book of Delight,* in addition to *Three Greek Romances,* and Caesar's *Gallic War & Other Writings.* He died on August 18, 1966.